THE AMERICAN FAR RIGHT

THE AMERICAN FAR RIGHT

A CASE STUDY OF
BILLY JAMES HARGIS
AND CHRISTIAN CRUSADE

JOHN HAROLD REDEKOP
Professor of Political Science
Pacific College
Fresno, California

WILLIAM B. EERDMANS PUBLISHING COMPANY
GRAND RAPIDS, MICHIGAN

To
the Memory
of My Parents

JACOB F. REDEKOP   AGNES J. REDEKOP

FOREWORD

In my keynote speech before the Republican National Convention in 1964, I denounced extremist groups "including the Communist Party, the Ku Klux Klan, and the John Birch Society" and counseled that such elements in the Republican Party "must be overcome."

I had anticipated a strong reaction to my keynote remarks but was frankly shocked at the intensely emotional and irrational tone of much of the correspondence.

This type of political extremism feeds on fear and frustration. The massive domestic problems and international crises that we fear we cannot cope with — as individuals, and even as a society — have left many people desperate to return to a simpler time.

The political extremists have reacted to this frustration with determination to purify the American dream, to remold our institutions and way of life according to their prescription for a perfect society. The Far Right has been relatively successful and has gained considerable political force because of its unity and well-focused thrusts.

It is important to understand how this unity has been achieved. Many of us share the Far Right's suspicion of the ability of a massive governmental bureaucracy to solve all our problems, and we share its dismay with the rapid impersonalization of society. But our frustrations have not always been joined into a sustained political force. The Far Right has been successfully united by a well-designed, well-financed, and persistent campaign of fear. The fear of Communism is both the fire and fuel of the Far Right movement. And the continual fanning of this fear by the Billy James Hargises and other "crusaders" has created such a distortion in the perceptions of some adherents of the Far Right that they can no longer distinguish between fantasy and reality, or between cause and effect.

As Far Righters continually repeat their suspicions, these

suspicions are transformed, in their mind, into fact. Thus, Far Righters can — with sincere conviction if not logic — insist that federal projects and welfare programs are socialistic; that socialism is essentially the same as Communism; and, therefore, most people in government in the past 30 years have been agents of Communism.

If the Far Righters were to present a picture of the world, their medium would be block-printing. They could thus represent the world in sharp blacks and whites, in Communist and anti-Communist divisions. The validity of their judgments rests on the logic of "either/or" and they have little tolerance or even comprehension of a middle ground between these two extremes. They would deny that gray is often the color of the complex truth.

"The logical fallacy of the excluded middle," as it has been termed, makes extremism — either Right or Left — a liability to our political system. The democratic process must be founded on a correct assessment of the nature of problems and guided by rational political discussion. The Far Right often denies both of these necessary elements.

The "Communist conspiracy" is seen by the Far Righters as the cause of everything from ghetto riots to fluoridated water. In so distorting the nature of the problems we face, they propose solutions that are irrelevant, and they often effectively detour efforts to find the appropriate answer. They further retard the workings of our political processes through their inability to discuss issues *rationally*. Their outlook and appeals are often purely emotional, and it becomes very difficult to establish a rational political dialogue. Instead of participating in an exchange of ideas, one finds himself listening to a monologue of conditioned responses to emotional slogans.

Extremism is not a new blemish on the American political body. Periodically Far Right or Far Left movements fester and poison the bloodstream of responsible political action and discussion. What distinguishes the current Far Right from most previous extremist movements are its *twin* foundations of political philosophy and religious conviction.

I have no objection to personal religious convictions forming the basis for an individual's political outlook, but I strongly object to the reverse of this situation. Political philosophies should not mold religious convictions.

Far Right crusaders would deny that a man is Christian if he does not share their political beliefs. Their "either/or" philosophy extends into the realm of religion, and they counsel that you can accept either the welfare state or Christ — but not both. Far Righters often equate Communism with the devil and America with God. And God, to the Far Righters, is a personification of a white, Protestant, anti-Communist American. They have turned the scriptural tables and created God in *their* image.

This unholy marriage of religion and politics has produced a perverted Christianity based not on love but hate, not on charity but persecution. The Far Righters are definitely not practicing religious fundamentalism, as they claim, but are actually practicing a form of paganism. They worship at the idol of "country" and have substituted the gospel of anti-Communism for the gospel of Christ.

In almost all aspects, political extremism is a negative force in our society; it is a force that should be understood and its power properly respected. Professor Redekop's very scholarly study of the American Far Right should do a great deal to increase understanding of this movement.

But it is vital that equal effort and scholarship be devoted to an analysis of the political power this group wields. I, like many other political figures, am aware of the potential power of the Far Right but too little research has been conducted concerning the real extent of its influence. All we can be sure of is that the Far Right will continue to be a major force at all levels of our political system. If the momentum of the Far Right, as of this date, is sustained, it is likely that this group will help form a third political party during 1968 to nominate a candidate for the Presidency. The long-term consequences of political extremism must be anticipated, and responsible Americans must be determined that political discussion and action be conducted on a rational, informed basis.

— MARK O. HATFIELD
United States Senator

December 1, 1967

PREFACE

SURELY ONE OF THE MOST INTERESTING AND SIGNIFICANT DEVELOP-
ments in contemporary American politics is the dramatic burgeoning of the Far Right. Although much has been written about it
and some writers have purportedly produced definitive works,[1] much
remains to be done. There is an abundance of free-swinging condemnation, not to mention ridicule, some informative description,
but very little serious analysis. One of the most important shortcomings is the widespread failure to evaluate the significance of
Christian fundamentalism, or even orthodox Christianity, as a contributing factor, especially in conjunction with traditional Americanism. Another is the general tendency to view the contemporary
Far Right as something totally outside of the American tradition,
to see it as an isolated phenomenon. This monograph is an attempt
to fill some of the gaps and to review some of the evidence.

It has become customary to dismiss all Rightists from serious
analysis by describing them as seditionists, native fascists, hate-
mongers, paranoiacs, and schizophrenics. Such an approach is
inadequate. It is too frequently forgotten that agitators and dema-

---

[1] See, for example, Arnold Forster and Benjamin Epstein, *Danger on the
Right* (New York: Random House, 1964). In the "Foreword" Dore Schary
states that the authors "have attempted to write a definitive book on
the attitudes, personnel, and influence of the Radical Right and the Ex-
treme Conservatives on the American scene." Other important accounts are:
Daniel Bell, ed., *The Radical Right* (Garden City, New York: Doubleday,
1963; Anchor Paperback, 1964). Roger Burlingame, *The Sixth Column*
(Philadelphia: Lippincott, 1962). Edward Cain, *They'd Rather Be Right:
Youth and the Conservative Movement* (New York: Macmillan, 1963).
Richard Dudman, *Men of the Far Right* (New York: Pyramid Books, 1962).
Ralph E. Ellsworth and Sarah M. Harris, *The American Right Wing* (Wash-
ington, D.C.: Public Affairs Press, 1962). Donald Janson and Bernard
Eismann, *The Far Right* (New York: McGraw-Hill, 1963). Pete Martin,
"I Call on Billy James Hargis," *The Christian Herald*, Vol. 90 (February,
1967); the second installment appears in the March issue. Harry Overstreet
and Bonaro Overstreet, *The Strange Tactics of Extremism* (New York: Nor-
ton, 1964). Harold M. Proshansky and Richard I. Evans, "American Political
Extremism in the 1960's" in *The Journal of Social Issues*, Vol. 19 (April,
1963). *The Reformed Journal*, Vol. 15, No. 1 (January, 1965): Three articles
relevant to this study are: "Fundamentalism and Political Rightism" by Henry
Stob, "Extremism, A Style of Life" by J. Marion Snapper, "Fight for the
Right" by Dirk W. Jellema. Ralph Lord Roy, *Apostles of Discord* (Boston:
Beacon, 1953). Mark Sherwin, *The Extremists* (New York: St. Martin's,
1963). Brooks R. Walker, *The Christian Fright Peddlers* (Garden City, New
York: Doubleday, 1964).

gogues, crusaders and extremists, may also be intelligent, honest people. Thus, at least from an academic point of view, the need is not for more ridicule and discrediting, but for understanding and dispassionate study.

Although much of the description and evaluation presented in the various chapters applies to the Far Right as a whole, my aim is to present an in-depth analysis of a major spokesman for the Far Right rather than a cursory overview of the entire phenomenon. There are several reasons why the Reverend Billy James Hargis, founder-director of Christian Crusade, was selected as the main subject of this case study. Not only is Hargis already widely known, but he is also a truly representative figure. Furthermore, he has written extensively on a great variety of subjects, and has stated his views in a straightforward, understandable manner. This writer concurs with the recent observation of several critics that, "Of all American evangelists propagandizing for the Radical Right, Hargis is the most zealous and energetic and perhaps leaves the greatest impact."[2]

As already suggested, my main thesis is that Hargis, a prominent spokesman for a significant phenomenon in contemporary American politics, has not been explained adequately. My aim is to present his political views, to analyze these views, to ascertain why he holds these views, to place Hargis in the American scene, past and present, and to outline some conclusions and judgments. While the emphasis throughout is on Hargis, the broader aim is to facilitate a better understanding of the Far Right in general.

Part One, chapters one through eight, includes a brief introduction to the man and his organization, a survey of his views on those areas of politics about which he has written extensively, a description of his view of government, and an evaluation of his political thought. Chapters two through six are presented without critical comment; criticisms are stated in chapters seven and eight.

Part Two, chapters nine, ten, and eleven, deals with the question, "Why does Hargis hold the views described and evaluated in Part One?" It attempts to present the sources of "Hargisism" and to view Hargis in his own frame of reference.

---

2 Forster and Epstein, *op. cit.*, p. 68. Cf. the description of Hargis by John Adams in *Nation*, September 30, 1961, p. 192: "a half-sophisticated, determined young spellbinder. ..." The Overstreets, *op. cit.*, p. 191, state that "Hargis has probably done more, in fact, than any other one person to make an effective whole out of the multiple organizations that exist on the Right extreme."

After analyzing Hargis's political views and asking why he holds these views, we deal in the third major section with the question, "How does Hargis fit into the American scene, past and present?" Chapters twelve, thirteen, and fourteen discuss the relation of Hargis's so-called conservative, Christian, extremist political-religious beliefs to the American tradition. Chapter fifteen is a study of contemporary religious Far Rightism and Hargis's place in that movement. Part Four, chapters sixteen and seventeen, includes a final evaluation of Hargis and some concluding observations on him and the Far Right in general.

It should be emphasized that this monograph does not purport to evaluate the adequacy of Hargis's theological doctrines and principles.[3] Within very broad limits — and Hargis appears to be within those limits — every person is entitled to subscribe to the religious creed of his choice. But the question of whether Hargis is true to the tenets of Protestant Christianity is quite another matter. Some of the present writer's criticisms on this count are given in chapter eight.

Terminology is a major problem when writing on right-wing politics. What terms should one use and what do they mean? A variety of labels is currently in use. Thus one reads of "The Rampageous Right," "The Radical Right," "The Reactionary Right," "The Religious Right," "The Far Right," "Right-Wing Extremists," "The Fanatical Right," "The Dangerous Right," and "The Un-American Right." I shall avoid these as much as possible, except for the term "Far Right," by which I mean that segment of the right half of the political spectrum which attributes evil motives to recent and contemporary political leaders, which sees liberalism and Communism as being basically identical, and which opposes the United Nations and what it terms "one-world internationalism." The Far Right is also characterized by opposition to most types of social reform, by admiration for the late Senator Joseph McCarthy (and the late General Douglas MacArthur), by a tendency to see "the Red conspiracy" at work virtually everywhere, and by a nostalgic desire to return to a state of "traditional Americanism." Rightists long for the "good old days" in which "Christian patriotism" was presumably revered by all and in which the income tax and civil rights marches were unknown.

---

[3] Hargis has written extensively on his fundamentalist evangelical beliefs. Four significant pamphlets are: *This I Believe;* *"Unto God's Glory";* *Jesus Christ, God Wrapped in Human Flesh;* and *Short Course in Bible Knowledge.* They are published in Tulsa, Oklahoma, by *Christian Crusade.*

Troublesome terms such as "conservative" and "liberal" will be defined later, although it should be stated here that the writer is aware of the shift of meaning each has undergone since the eighteenth century. Clearly, traditional liberalism opposed centralization of political power and the promotion of the welfare state, especially if at the expense of individual initiative and responsibility. And traditional conservatism has little in common with its modern proponents who believe government to be inherently evil.

Several methodological difficulties are present in a study of Hargis's political thought. Perhaps the most important, but also the least surprising, is the fact that Hargis nowhere presents a comprehensive and systematic account of his political beliefs. The components must be collected from an array of source material, and even then gaps remain. Another problem is that on some points Hargis is vague and even contradictory. I have sought to present this situation in proper perspective and to avoid both of the extremes to which Hargis refers — with considerable justification — when he says that he "is either loyally supported or bitterly attacked by all."[4] Also, the fact that Hargis is still active and still developing his thought means that any definitive treatment is not yet possible. This work is an attempt to catch his image, to describe his orientation, to present his political views, to ascertain his political significance, and to give a balanced assessment. Any conclusions or judgments presented claim to be nothing more than tentative, but considered, responses by a detached but concerned observer.

I have made extensive use of direct quotations, especially in Part One, since the statements made by the man under scrutiny deserve to be studied in their original form.

My debt for assistance in this work is great. I am deeply grateful for the encouragement and the helpful suggestions given me by Professor Hugh Bone, Professor William Harbold, and especially Professor Linden Mander. I wish also to acknowledge the helpful cooperation given me by the library staff at the University of Washington, and the secretarial and library staff at Pacific College in Fresno, California. My indebtedness to the many authors cited in the bibliography is obvious. Apart from their work a case study of this nature would be impossible. Finally, I should like to thank the Reverend Mr. Hargis and his staff for the interviews granted me and for their overall cooperation in this venture.

---

[4] Billy James Hargis, *The Facts About Communism and Our Churches* (Tulsa: Christian Crusade, 1962), back cover.

CONTENTS

PART ONE

THE POLITICAL VIEWS OF BILLY JAMES HARGIS

"There is no need to fear. God is guiding us. . . . I am convinced that this is the time for God's conservatives across the nation to step up their attacks against liberalism and/or communism. . . . We accept the challenge of God. We are conscious of His leadership."
Billy James Hargis, Christian Crusade (*January, 1963*), *p. 13.*

"Most of the devil's brew, mixed by the Moscow clinic to slide us painlessly into the mental coma which is communism, has two basic ingredients, (1) the progressive income tax and (2) foreign aid."
Billy James Hargis, Weekly Crusader (*March 30, 1962*), *p. 8.*

"America is one of the greatest gifts that God has ever given man, outside of the gift of His only begotten Son and His divinely-inspired Bible."
Billy James Hargis, The Far Left, *p. 5.*

1. BILLY JAMES HARGIS AND CHRISTIAN CRUSADE

BILLY JAMES HARGIS, SON OF A TRUCK DRIVER, WAS BORN ON AUGUST 3, 1925, in Texarkana, Texas. There appears to be nothing particularly striking in his background. Raised in a fundamentalist, typically Southern home, he grew up during the Depression in an area which knew hard times at their worst.

On May 30, 1943, at the age of 17, Hargis was ordained a minister of the Gospel by the Rose Hill Christian Church (Disciples of Christ) of Texarkana. In 1964 his membership was still there.[1]

After graduating from high school as a superior student, Billy James enrolled at Ozark Bible College in Bentonville, Arkansas, a small school which then had only 20 to 30 students. Reminiscing in 1962, Hargis said that the one and one-half years he spent there constitute all the formal college education he ever had.[2] In 1954 Hargis received his first honorary doctorate (Doctor of Divinity) — one which he uses constantly — from The Defender Seminary in Puerto Rico. In 1956 Hargis completed the requirements for a Bachelor of Arts and was awarded that degree from Burton College and Seminary of Manitou Springs, Colorado, from which he also received a Bachelor of Theology two years later. It is perhaps noteworthy that Burton College was on the official list of "degree

---

[1] Billy James Hargis, *The Far Left* (Tulsa: Christian Crusade, 1964), p. 2. For additional biographical material on Hargis see the following: Forster and Epstein, *op. cit.*, pp. 77f.; Janson and Eismann, *op. cit.*, pp. 70f.; *Dr. Billy James Hargis, His Christian Crusade, His Christian Echoes National Ministry, and Connections with Other Groups* (Washington: Group Research, Inc., 1962), p. 22; *Sowing Dissention in the Churches* (New York: Episcopal Church Center, n.d.), pp. 11f.

[2] Hargis, *Weekly Crusader*, Vol. 2 (March 9, 1962), p. 7.

mills" issued by the United States Department of Health, Education, and Welfare in April, 1960.

A second honorary doctorate (Doctor of Laws) was conferred on Hargis in the spring of 1957 by Belin Memorial University, then located at Chillicothe, Missouri. This institution, too, was listed as a degree mill by the United States government. Recently a controversy has developed concerning the integrity of its founder-president. One account states, "Dr. Clyde Belin, president of the University, was indicted by a Federal grand jury in Kansas City on June 25, 1959, on six counts of using the mails to defraud, offered no defense, and was sentenced to a year in prison."[3] When queried by this writer concerning the Belin doctorate, Hargis insisted that he had nothing to do with the awarding of the degree and did not attend any convocation. Nevertheless, the July, 1957 issue of *Christian Crusade* announced that "Dr. Hargis has been awarded an honorary Doctor of Laws degree from Belin Memorial University, Chillicothe, Missouri." A third honorary doctorate was received in 1961 from Bob Jones University of Greenville, South Carolina.[4]

During the early years of his ministry Hargis was pastor of several churches: First Christian Church, Sallisaw, Oklahoma; First Christian Church, Granby, Missouri; and First Christian Church, Sapulpa, Oklahoma. He says that it was in 1947, during his pastorate in Sapulpa, that he first realized the dimensions of the leftist-Communist threat and set about organizing Christian Crusade to fight "Communism and its godless allies."

So much for our thumbnail biographical sketch. How does Hargis view himself, his motives? How does he view Christian Crusade? What is his orientation toward his work? We will let him state in his own words why he is in "the fight" and how "the fight" relates to his ministerial calling.

Hargis speaks rather frequently about himself. Basically, he sees himself as a "dedicated man, [one] who wants only to save his country and serve his God."[5] He insists that he is still only "a minister of the Gospel,"[6] and that his "messages are not for political purposes but are my religious convictions."[7] In answer to the question of why he organized Christian Crusade, he replies,

3 Forster and Epstein, *op. cit.*, p. 78.
4 *Christian Crusade*, Vol. 15 (January, 1963), p. 13.
5 Hargis, *Christian Crusade*, Vol. 15 (January, 1963), p. 13.
6 Hargis, *Weekly Crusader*, Vol. 3 (September 20, 1963), p. 1.
7 Hargis, *The Far Left* (*op. cit.*), p. 208.

"I began Christian Crusade because I had no other choice."[8] On the issue of motives he states categorically, "I fight Communism... because it is part of my ordination vows, of my creed."[9] The significance of this statement will become increasingly evident as this analysis progresses, especially as we come to see the extent to which Hargis conceives of Americanism, Christian fundamentalism, free enterprise, and anti-Communism as forming a single, tightly knit creed.

The notion that anti-Communism is central to the Christian Gospel is basic; it is the unifying concept in all that Hargis says and of the entire segment of the Right Wing which he represents. It is the driving force behind years of hard work and perseverance in the face of stinging attacks, and the explanation of much of his fanaticism. The "fight," as he sees it, "... is essentially a religious battle. It's Christ versus anti-Christ, God versus Satan, light versus darkness, and every day that we live, we are coming more and more to realize this."[10] That he personally and Christian Crusade in general have been commissioned to lead in "the battle" ought to be as self-evident to others as it is to him. "Christian Crusade is proud to be in the forefront of the eternal battle against Godless Communism and its fellow-travellers, accepting the un-equal odds and facing the tremendous financial resources of the liberal forces."[11] Despite these "tremendous resources," however,

> There is no need to fear. God is guiding us.... I am convinced that this is the time for God's conservatives across the nation to step up their attacks against liberalism and/or communism.... We accept the challenge of God. We are conscious of His leadership.[12]

When the going gets tough, as it sometimes does, Hargis does not despair easily. With the unqualified conviction and assurance of the "true believer," he carries on. After all,

> Christian Crusade's fight against Communism is Christ's fight. Christ is using this Movement. The very fact that Christian Crusade has existed through fourteen years of opposition from powerful forces in high and low circles, is proof that it is of God.

---

[8] Hargis, on KAIL-TV, Fresno, October 25, 1964.
[9] *Ibid.*
[10] Hargis, *Christian Crusade*, Vol. 15 (August, 1963), p. 35.
[11] Hargis, *Christian Crusade*, Vol. 16 (April, 1964), p. 4.
[12] Hargis, *Christian Crusade*, Vol. 14 (June, 1962), p. 11. Cf. Hargis's statement in Sherwin, *op. cit.*, p. 102, "We are not trying to capture both political parties. The goal of such a coalition would be to help conservative legislation and candidates."

> Destroy the structure of Christian Crusade and tomorrow God will raise up another to take its place.... I know we are on the right track, getting the job done for Jesus. ...[13]

Much of Hargis's self-image is indicated by his many references to supposedly analogous biblical situations. Thus, for example, Hargis frequently casts himself in the role of a Moses trying to lead a rebellious and disobedient modern Israel. This image was invoked during the "Midnight Ride" tour with General Edwin Walker. Reporting to the faithful, Hargis wrote, "God's Spirit goes before us and with us like a pillar of fire by night and a cloud by day. We are both conscious of His will being done in our lives."[14]

Hargis does not equivocate on the central purpose of Christian Crusade. "From the beginning we have set goals and objectives, and worked toward them. We feel our mission to be God-given; to awaken our fellow citizens to the twin dangers of Communism and/or socialism and religious apostasy."[15] With unrestrained enthusiasm, Hargis insists,

> For fifteen years, Christian Crusade has been aware of the hand of God upon this movement. He has led us thus far. We are conscious of the fact that God Almighty inspired this Christian Crusade and has sustained it for these·fifteen glorious years of service to God and country.[16]

When questioned on a 26-hour TV telethon about the nature of the Christian Crusade organization, Hargis again forcefully asserted, "I know beyond the shadow of a doubt that God is behind Christian Crusade."[17]

This conviction is "a source of strength and courage" for Hargis when criticized by those whom he terms "unwitting dupes," the "uninformed anti-anti-Communists." "Let there be no doubt that this satanic hatred which we see today aimed at the anti-Communist conservative ranks is directed in reality against the Church of Jesus Christ."[18] Accordingly, Hargis responds to criticism and denunciation not by justifying his own views, but by being alert to identify his critics, to label them "correctly," and then to expose them fully.

---

[13] Hargis, *Christian Crusade,* Vol. 14 (January-February, 1962), p. 3.

[14] Hargis, *Christian Crusade,* Vol. 15 (March, 1963), p. 3.

[15] Hargis, *Christian Crusade,* Vol. 14 (December, 1962), p. 1. In the *Weekly Crusader,* Vol. 2 (May 4, 1962), Hargis states that Christian Crusade is "a non-profit educational group" whose basic aim is "to save the church and America from Communist overthrow" (p. 7).

[16] Hargis, *Christian Crusade,* Vol. 14 (June, 1962), p. 11.

[17] Hargis, on KAIL-TV, Fresno, October 25, 1964.

[18] Hargis, *The Far Left (op. cit.),* p. 17.

Hargis is not perturbed when accused of being naive and un-sophisticated. Following the presumed logic of the biblical statement that "the wisdom of this world is foolishness with God," he simply replies, "I have never claimed educational attainments, but I do claim to know the mind of God...."[19] Not only is a university education generally unnecessary, but it may even be a hindrance in that it tends to produce "sophistication," for which he has only contempt. He observes, "I think it is ignorant people who are going to save this country."[20]

All of this alleged reliance on God and the deprecation of learning and human attainment does not mean, however, that Hargis minimizes his own person. Note his reference to himself and his speeches as "famous,"[21] and his comment about "the splendid broadcasts of Dr. Billy James Hargis...."[22] In his various publications he constantly refers to himself. His picture is everywhere, on the front page of every issue of the *Weekly Crusader* and throughout the pages of his monthly magazine. A spot check revealed that

---

[19] I Corinthians 3:19; Hargis, *Weekly Crusader*, Vol. 2 (March 9, 1962), p. 7. Various translations of this and other similar verses are cited frequently by Far Rightists. Favorite excerpts are: I Corinthians 1:18-21: "The preaching of the cross is, I know, nonsense to those who are involved in this dying world, but to us who are being saved from that death it is nothing less than the power of God. It is written: I will destroy the wisdom of the wise, and the prudence of the prudent will I reject. For consider, what have the philosopher, the writer and the critic of this world to show for all their wisdom? Has not God made the wisdom of this world look foolish? For it was after the world in its wisdom had failed to know God, that he in his wisdom chose to save all who would believe by the 'simplemindedness' of the gospel message." I Corinthians 1:26-29: "For look at your own calling as Christians, my brothers. You don't see among you many of the wise (according to this world's judgment) nor many of the ruling class, nor many from the noblest families. But God has chosen what the world calls foolish to shame the wise; he has chosen what the world calls weak to shame the strong. He has chosen things of little strength and small repute, yes and even things which have no real existence to explode the pretensions of the things that are, that no man may boast in the presence of God." I Corinthians 3:18-20: "Let no one be under any illusion over this. If any man among you thinks himself one of the world's clever ones, let him discard his cleverness that he may learn to be truly wise. For this world's cleverness is stupidity to God. It is written: He taketh the wise in their craftiness. And again: The Lord knoweth the reasonings of the wise, that they are vain."

[20] Hargis, *Weekly Crusader*, Vol. 2 (March 9, 1962), p. 7. See also Adams, *op. cit.*, p. 195.

[21] Hargis, *Christian Crusade*, Vol. 14 (June, 1962), p. 3. See also *Weekly Crusader*, Vol. 3 (July 26, 1963), pp. 6-7.

[22] Hargis, *Weekly Crusader*, Vol. 2 (August 31, 1962), p. 8.

in the May, 1962 issue of *Christian Crusade* (Vol. 14, No. 4) his
picture appeared seven times and his name, usually with the prefix
"Dr.," 47 times. The figures for the September, 1962 issue (Vol. 14,
No. 6) were 15 pictures and 45 references by name. A further
indication of Hargis's self-image is his statement that, "More and
more I thank God for the book that our Research Director, Julian
Williams, and I are now writing. . . ."[23]

Of Christian Crusade as a separate corporation we are given
a "no punches pulled" description:

> Christian Crusade is the popular name for Christian Echoes
> National Ministry, Inc., incorporated in 1947 under the laws
> of the State of Oklahoma as a non-profit, Christian educational
> ministry. Its purpose is to safeguard and preserve the Conserva-
> tive Christian ideals upon which America was founded, to
> protect our cherished freedoms, the heritage of every American,
> to oppose, militantly and aggressively, any person or organization
> whose words or actions endorse or parallel the philosophies of
> leftists, socialists or communists, intentionally or otherwise; to
> expose publicly the infiltration of such influences into American
> life, and to defend the Gospel of Jesus Christ. To these aims
> Christian Crusade is dedicated.[24]

This is Hargis's own conception. What about the views of out-
siders? What is the actual situation?

A casual observer visiting the Christian Crusade building in
Tulsa would rightly get the impression that, whatever else the
organization might be, it is first and foremost anti-Communist.
Hargis asserts that it is not "anti-racial, anti-Jew, anti-anything but
anti-Communist."[25] The general emphasis is two-fold, to give people

---

[23] Hargis, *Christian Crusade*, Vol. 15 (March, 1963), p. 2.

[24] Hargis, *American Socialism . . . Moving America Downhill* (Christian
Crusade Pamphlet, n.d.), inside cover.

[25] Hargis, *Weekly Crusader*, Vol. 2 (March 9, 1962), p. 2. Cf. his statements in *Christian Crusade*, Vol. 16 (July, 1964). "We thank God for every
man and movement fighting communism. We may not always agree with
their official pronouncements, but for their anti-communist efforts we are
eternally grateful. We will not publicly criticize anybody on our side in the
fight against communism" (p. 24). When accused of cooperating closely
with the John Birch Society, his response is, "I do not agree with everything
Robert Welch says. In fact, I do not agree with everything my wife says.
However, I feel the John Birch Society is one of the most effective anti-
Communist movements in the United States . . ." (p. 25). See also the
succeeding paragraphs. A survey of some of the "1964 Christian Crusade
Awards" is informative (*Christian Crusade*, Vol. 16 [October, 1964], pp.
7-8): Commentator of the Year — Dan Smoot; Author of the Year — John
Stormer for his *None Dare Call It Treason;* Real Man of the Year — Barry
Goldwater; Christian Patriot of the Year — Governor George C. Wallace of
Alabama.

"the facts" and to motivate people to action. "In our nation," writes Hargis, "there is a deep and perilous ignorance of the strength of the communist conspiracy inside our country and without, of the nature of Communism and of its methods and objectives."[26] To the complacent and the apathetic, the challenge is hurled forth in clear-cut terms. "Boiled down the question is this. . . . 'Do I want to serve God and save America?' If you sincerely answer yes, then you have NO CHOICE but to go and sell . . . and give. . . ."[27]

The growth of Christian Crusade has been impressive. From an inconsequential local effort in 1947, it has expanded into an important national organization, largely through the personal, seemingly inexhaustible dynamism of Hargis. Its diversified enterprises include a radio network, television releases, lecture tours, pamphlet production, pamphlet sales, book publication, book sales, anti-Communist "leadership training," a youth organization (The Torchbearers), an annual convention, a summer school, a monthly magazine, a weekly magazine, sale of patriotic paraphernalia, membership promotion, and a host of minor miscellanea. The five dominant themes in this gamut of enterprises are: Hargis, Christ, the United States (flag, constitution, etc.), anti-Communism, and conservatism. Key villains in addition to Communism are: liberalism, socialism, the National Council of Churches, the Reuther brothers, the Kennedys, President Lyndon Johnson, "Hubert Horatio," U Thant and the United Nations, most of the press, and Martin Luther King.

One reason for Christian Crusade's rapid expansion is that it is increasingly becoming a peak agency, to use group-therapy terminology. Hargis's zeal and determination have rallied a host of groups and individuals to his cause. One of the largest of these consists of military officers, mostly retired. Included are Brig. Gen. Richard Moran, Gen. Edwin Walker, Maj. George Racey Jordan, Capt. Eddie Rickenbacker, Maj. Gen. Charles Willoughby, Gen. W. P. Campbell, Col. Victor Fox, Col. Laurence Bunker, and Capt. Kenneth Ryker. Willoughby, Gen. MacArthur's former Chief of Intelligence, is an associate of Hargis and writes a Foreign Intelligence Digest in both the weekly and monthly magazines. Walker, for

---

[26] Hargis, *Weekly Crusader*, Vol. 4 (May 8, 1964), p. 1. That Hargis intends to denounce Communism per se, and not evil generally, is evident from his statement that Christian Crusade is not "anti anything else but anti-Communist." *Weekly Crusader*, Vol. 3 (January 18, 1963), p. 6.

[27] Hargis, *Communist America . . . Must It Be?* (Tulsa: Christian Crusade, 1960), p. 180.

whom Hargis shows virtually boundless admiration, has accompanied Hargis on several extensive tours. Both Moran and Willoughby are members of Christian Crusade's Advisory Board.

Other individuals and groups which frequently speak under Christian Crusade sponsorship are: Kent Courtney (The Conservative Society of America), Tom Anderson (Farm and Ranch Magazine), Dr. Bob Jones, Sr. and Dr. Bob Jones, Jr. (Bob Jones University), Robert Welch (John Birch Society), and radio commentators Hurst Amyx and Fulton Lewis, Jr. Tape-recorded lectures by each of these are regularly offered for sale.

How big is Christian Crusade in financial terms? An audited and published financial statement for the calendar year 1963 reveals a total income of $677,152.80 and a total expense of $685,904.31.[28] Some earlier years, prior to the mass media's widespread attacks on the organization, had brought in even larger contributions. Hargis is quoted as saying that in at least one year income surpassed the million mark.[29] Major expense items for 1963 included: Salaries & Wages (78 employees), $128,197.82; Radio & Television, $213,-793.52; and Printing & Publications, $119,883.41. Hargis himself draws a salary of $12,000 plus an expense account for official activities.[30] Financially, Christian Crusade appears to be on the upswing once again. Hargis said in a personal conversation with this writer on October 25, 1964, that this is "the greatest year we ever had."

Sometimes accused of being a mouthpiece for a few oil barons, Hargis has vigorously denied the charge. He insists, "Christian Crusade receives few large offerings annually. The average contribution that we get in the mail is around $4.00 and we will average about $1.25 per person in the offering during our public rallies."[31] Hargis has employed a wide array of fund-raising gimmicks, ranging from Holy Land mementos to subtle "personal" letters from his attractive wife Betty Jean, but generally there is only a straight, albeit passionate, appeal. "When people criticize my fund-raising," says Hargis, "I confess it hurts me a great deal. If I knew of ways to finance Christian Crusade other than those we

---

28 For a full financial report see *Christian Crusade*, Vol. 16 (April, 1964), pp. 13f. See the Appendix to this book for 1964 and 1965 financial statements.
29 Adams, *op. cit.*, p. 194.
30 Sherwin, *op. cit.*, p. 107.
31 Hargis, *Christian Crusade*, Vol. 16 (August, 1964), p. 6. See the December, 1962 issue of *Christian Crusade* for a survey of the work.

have used these seventeen years, God bear me witness, I would do it. . . . I die a little each time I ask for money."[32]

The core of Hargis's activity continues to be the radio appeal with daily and weekly broadcasts saturating the nation. (There is a fairly rapid turnover of stations — all stations that do not carry themselves financially after three months are summarily dropped.) The stated goal at one time was "One Thousand Radio Stations by December 1, 1964."[33] This figure was not reached. The actual count fluctuates between 400 and 450. The two giants, XEG (Monterrey, Mexico), and XERB (San Diego, California), each heard in some 40 states, continue to be the mainstays. Television has been tried, but has not become a major undertaking. Only about a dozen privately owned stations, mainly in the South and West, carry taped releases. A new technique is the 24-hour telethon in which distribution of mass-produced paperbacks is pushed to the limit. Thus the purpose of a telethon in Fresno, California, in April, 1964, was to distribute 25,000 copies of Hargis's book, *The Far Left*.[34] The occasion revealed Hargis's almost indefatigable energy. Without a minute's sleep, "the Doctor," as his associates call him, sang, preached, prayed, lectured, and small-talked his way through a full night and day on live television, all the while urging "you folks" to "keep the phones ringing." They rang. The use of patriotic and anti-Communist films added variety to the telethon and allowed for at least momentary relaxation.

A second major enterprise is publications. The organization's monthly magazine, *Christian Crusade*, which describes itself as "The National Christian American Monthly," has a circulation of about 120,000 with a total readership of a half million.[35] There is also the *Weekly Crusader*, at $10 a year, which puts less emphasis on fund-raising and more on what one reader called, "the inside track to truth." Pamphlets and booklets pour forth in a never-ending stream. Some of the titles written by Hargis include: "Should We Surrender to Castro or Smash Him?"; "Mental Health"; "Racial Strife"; "America — Let's Get Back to God"; "American Socialism . . . Moving America Downhill"; "How the Communists Influence American Elections"; "We Have Been Betrayed"; "The Ugly Truth About Drew Pearson"; and, "The Truth About UNESCO." Four "full-length" books by Hargis have been published by Christian

32 Hargis, *Christian Crusade*, Vol. 16 (August, 1964), p. 1.
33 Hargis, *Christian Crusade*, Vol. 16 (July, 1964), p. 20.
34 Hargis, *Christian Crusade*, Vol. 16 (April, 1964), pp. 10f.
35 *Christian Crusade*, Vol. 16 (July, 1964), p. 9.

Crusade. They are: *Communist America ... Must It Be?; Communism, The Total Lie!; The Facts About Communism and Our Churches;* and, *The Far Left.* The total circulation of these books runs into many hundreds of thousands. The first-mentioned alone reached 150,000 in the first five printings. Some of its chapter headings are: A Bird's Eye View of Treason; America Marked for Conquest; Patriotism — Once Revered, Now Smeared; Communism and Labor Unions; Communism and Racial Tension; Fantastic Foreign Aid; and United Nations — The Greatest Hoax Perpetrated on the American Public.

The sale of an endless variety of paraphernalia also brings in considerable sums. A number of record albums are listed. Among the best-sellers are: "The President's Assassin Speaks," a recorded debate between Oswald and a Cuban refugee in New Orleans 93 days before President John F. Kennedy's assassination; "The United Nations Hoax," a free-swinging lecture by Hargis; and "Songs and Sayings of Billy James Hargis," $4.00 high-fidelity, $5.00 stereo. "An Autographed Portrait" of "BJH" which shows him surrounded by the United States flag, a crusader sculpture, and a huge picture of Christ, is offered at the bargain price of $2.50 ("were $5.00"). An American flag complete with pole sells for $4.95. "Authentic reproductions on Antiqued Parchment" of the Monroe Doctrine "in the handwriting of President James Monroe" sell for $1.00 each. "Quality reproductions" of four documents (the Declaration of Independence, the United States Constitution, the Bill of Rights, and Lincoln's Gettysburg Address) sell for a price of $5.00. This package is listed as "the Patriotic Buy of the Year."[36]

Tape recordings of Hargis's major speeches, many delivered at the Annual Anti-Communist Leadership Schools and anniversary rallies, sell for $5.00 to $10.00 each, depending on supply and date delivered. Titles listed include: Betrayed By Political Liberals; Survival USA; The Red Peril of the Sixties; How the Communists are Winning; What's Wrong With America; and, The Red Army Within.

One of the recent innovations is the much publicized Anti-Communist Youth University. This designation is actually a misnomer, since the whole "undergraduate" program consists of a two-week session, of which six were offered in the summer of 1964, for which high school students and virtually any "Christian Conservative" are eligible. A letter of recommendation from a known

---

[36] *Weekly Crusader,* Vol. 3 (February 15, 1963).

"Christian Conservative" or pastor is mandatory. "Post Graduate sessions," another two-week course, is open to those students "who graduated last year" or "can offer evidence of advanced understanding in the Scriptures, Government, and anti-Communism."[37] The "faculty" consists of Hargis as "president," The Reverend David Nobel, his youthful assistant, as "dean," and the military notables and conservative spokesmen mentioned earlier as lecturers.[38] The curriculum, as described in glossy promotional literature, consists of "the Bible, the free enterprise system, Constitutional government, how to fight communism, and how to organize anti-communist youth chapters. . . ."[39] Classes for the several hundred summer session students (there are no winter classes) are conducted in what was formerly the Grand View Hotel, an old-fashioned but still functional 68-room edifice located near Manitou Springs, Colorado, at the foot of Pike's Peak. The hotel has been renamed "The Summit." Graduates of the "university" are expected to organize "Torchbearer" chapters in high schools and universities and to promote the new youth publication, *The Torch*. During the first year of activity following the initiation of the program at the first "university sessions" some 50 to 60 Torchbearer chapters were organized.[40]

Hargis gives the following rationale for this venture. "We are losing our young people. They are being brainwashed in our high schools and colleges with warmed-over Marxism (and worse)."[41] The "university," designed to counteract the above, is specifically intended for young people who "feel depleted and near exhaustion after nine months of liberal and socialistic gobbledegook," who need "a re-orientation" from their "mundane habitat."[42]

The most recent venture is the promotion of annual or lifetime memberships in Christian Crusade. Dues are $10 per year or $1000 for lifetime.[43] The latter figure seems rather odd, since it allows for a lifetime of 100 years and is thus hardly a bargain price. The purpose of the venture, aside from the monetary factor, is to organize "our more than a half-million crusaders"[44] into closely knit local study and action groups. In this attempt Hargis has, of course, taken

[37] *Christian Crusade*, Vol. 16 (May, 1964), p. 19.
[38] *Christian Crusade*, Vol. 16 (January, 1964), pp. 20f.
[39] Hargis, *Christian Crusade*, Vol. 14 (September, 1962), p. 22.
[40] *Christian Crusade*, Vol. 16 (April, 1964), p. 2.
[41] Hargis, *Weekly Crusader*, Vol. 4 (June 5, 1964), p. 8.
[42] Hargis, *Christian Crusade*, Vol. 16 (May, 1964), p. 18.
[43] *Weekly Crusader*, Vol. 3 (January 4, 1963), p. 8.
[44] Hargis, *Christian Crusade*, Vol. 14 (January-February, 1962), p. 3.

a page from the highly successful method employed by the founders
of the John Birch Society, of which group he is a great admirer and
supporter.[45] Here, as elsewhere, Hargis reveals an eager readiness to
try new techniques and to learn from the experience of others. This
trait accounts, in part, for the evolution of Christian Crusade to the
significant national organization which it is today.

---

[45] See, for example, the statement in *Christian Crusade,* Vol. 16 (July,
1964), pp. 24f.

2. VIEW OF AMERICA

THROUGHOUT HARGIS'S WRITINGS MUCH EMPHASIS IS PLACED ON the alleged uniqueness of America's political and religious origins. Perhaps the most basic assertion in this regard is that "America is and always has been a Christian nation."[1] Hargis believes that "America began as a Christian country, led by the Spirit of the Living God."[2] He frequently cites the Mayflower Compact of November 11, 1620, which announced to the world that the entire expedition to America was undertaken for "the glory of God and the advancement of the Christian faith."[3] Reviewing the numerous pro-Christian statements in colonial constitutions and colonial laws,[4] he concludes that "the Founders of America had no hesitation, and no shame in acknowledging the Bible as the Word of God and as the guide for their nation and their nation's rulers."[5]

As evidence for the contention that "the men and women who braved an uncharted wilderness to carve out this Republic were rich in faith," he states that "with a Bible under one arm, and a musket under the other, they were willing to fight for their faith and their freedom. . . ."[6]

Assuming the validity of the continuity argument, namely, that institutions remain basically what they once were, Hargis attempts to strengthen his case by citing the 1643 New England Articles of Confederation, which stated, "we all came into these parts of America with one and the same end and aim, namely to advance the

---

1 Hargis, *The Facts About Communism and Our Churches* (*op. cit.*), back cover.

2 Hargis, *Christian Crusade*, Vol. 15 (August, 1963), p. 15.

3 Hargis, *Communist America . . . Must It Be?* (*op. cit.*), p. 22.

4 *Ibid.*, pp. 34f.

5 *Ibid.*, p. 35.

6 *Ibid.*, p. 31.

Kingdom of our Lord Jesus Christ and to enjoy the liberties of the Gospel in purity with peace. . . ."[7]

The logic is that the United States was initially a Christian nation, and is now Christian, because the first American settlers described themselves individually as Christians and established small "pro-Christian" communities. The Christian-origins argument is also advanced as the explanation for all economic and material progress. "This country was built by strong religious people who came here seeking God rather than gold. The marvelous accomplishments of the United States are due to her faith in an Almighty God and Jesus Christ."[8] The implication is not only that virtue and prosperity are perfectly compatible but also that the latter is evidence of the former.

Hargis is full of praise when talking about things American, especially the American Revolution. Adulation of it has become part of his religious creed. In an article entitled "Promote the Spirit of 1776," he endorses all of the following pursuits as "excellent":

PROMOTE THE SPIRIT OF 1776 — Display the flag, sing the songs, read the Declaration of Independence, travel the trails, relive the past scenes, recapture the spirit, uphold Americanism.

Stores — "Ring up $17.76." Give flags, books, copies of documents of country, pictures. BUY AMERICAN.

Towns — "Drawing of 1776." Give gifts promoting the spirit of pure AMERICANISM. (1776 winners.)

Groups — Fourth [sic] picnics, speeches, poems, display flags, give copies of documents of AMERICANISM.

Congress — "Declare July 1st Week as AMERICANISM WEEK, FLAG WEEK, SPIRIT OF 1776 WEEK, RING THE BELLS WEEK." Sing, celebrate, proclaim AMERICANISM.

Press — "Review 1776." Review the documents, review the events, review the spirit of the founding fathers, promote Freedom, promote Liberty, promote AMERICANISM.

Schools — "Teach 1776." Teach its meaning, teach its documents. Uphold its principles, uphold its founding fathers, uphold, establish AMERICANISM.

Churches — "Preach 1776." Remember — ". . . endowed by their creator," "Freedom of religion," "One nation, under God," "In God We Trust," "God save this honorable court."

---

[7] Hargis, *Communist America . . . Must It Be?* (*op. cit.*), p. 35.
[8] Hargis, *Christian Crusade*, Vol. 15 (January, 1963), p. 14.

Families — "Honor 1776," by education, participation, dedication, voting, attending, proclaiming, upholding, in speaking, writing, teaching, living, praying at schools, churches, organizations, businesses, in city, country, nation, world. HONOR AMERICAN- ISM.[9]

Proof that the cause of the 1776 rebels was also the cause of God is in the fact that "on September 11, 1777, the Continental Congress voted an expenditure of $300,000 to buy copies of the Bible to be distributed throughout the colonies of these United States."[10] Further "proofs" cited are the ultimate victory of the colonists, the nature of the constitution which they drew up, and the institutions which they created.

The Constitution is praised and quoted in virtually all of Hargis's political writings, for he regards it as basic to all else in the American experience. For him it has a divine and therefore changeless quality. One gets the impression that the principles of Christianity and those of America's "sacred, God-given constitution"[11] are, if not identical, at least of the same general order. "Whether generally realized or not," says Hargis, "the principles of freedom set forth in the Declaration of Independence and codified in the constitution are inherent in the Christian faith. . . ."[12] We are informed that the "inherent rights of human beings" which are the "central foundation of this Constitutional Republic," "stem from God."[13] Hargis is explicit in asserting God's direct role in the formulation of the Constitution at the Philadelphia Convention.

> According to American history, that convention adjourned for three days, thereby providing the delegates assembled time aplenty to call on God for his help and guidance. After re-assembling, these delegates fresh from three days in the presence of God, began to form the constitution, known among all wise men as the greatest masterpiece of the ages, outside of the Holy Bible.[14]

At times it seems as if Hargis is casting the founders in the role of

---

[9] *Christian Crusade*, Vol. 16 (July, 1964), p. 23.

[10] Hargis, *Christian Crusade*, Vol. 15 (August, 1963), p. 15. But the evidence is not all on one side. "In 1796 a treaty was signed between the United States and Tripoli, in which one article opened with the words, 'As the government of the United States is not in any sense founded on the Christian religion'; and this treaty was ratified by the Senate without objection." Hans Kohn, *American Nationalism: An Interpretative Essay* (New York: Collier, 1957), p. 149.

[11] *Christian Crusade*, Vol. 14 (June, 1962), p. 11.

[12] Hargis, *Christian Crusade*, Vol. 14 (September, 1962), p. 7.

[13] *Loc. cit.*

[14] Hargis, *Christian Crusade*, Vol. 15 (August, 1963), p. 35.

Moses, with Philadelphia, more particularly Convention Hall, serving as Mount Sinai. He writes that the principles of the Constitution were "granted to mankind by the Lord,"[15] and that "the American system is as intimately based on the Bible as the Ten Commandments are."[16] Since these Commandments constitute a vital part of the inspired biblical canon itself, the latter is indeed a formidable claim.

On the question of separation of church and state, Hargis is very critical of "current trends." He asserts that the United States Supreme Court has misinterpreted the intentions of the founders. Harking back to the Mayflower Compact — "for the glory of God and the advancement of the Christian faith" — he states,

> Therefore, let it be remembered that separation of church and state simply means that there will be no official church in the United States but that all may be free to worship God, according to dictates of their conscience. Our founding fathers did not intend to establish a government that did not recognize God and Jesus Christ, but instead, their vision was to establish a government that did not recognize a church or an ecclesiastical body.[17]

He argues that "left-wingers and liberals" — the reference is obviously to the Supreme Court — who interpret the doctrine as meaning separation of state and God, are advocating "the opposite of the original meaning of this great principle and doctrine."[18] "Liberals," he claims, are wrong and only reveal their ignorance when they insist that the elimination of school prayers and of official references to God will advance the cause of liberty. His interpretation of American history is that present freedoms are derived directly from earlier Christian practices and principles. He outrightly rejects the notion that in the United States basic freedoms

---

[15] Hargis, *Christian Crusade,* Vol. 15 (February, 1963), p. 5. In Herbert J. Muller, *Religion and Freedom in the Modern World* (Chicago: University of Chicago Press, 1963), p. 129, is this quote from John Adams: "It will never be pretended that the men who set up the American governments had interviews with the gods, or were in any degree under the inspiration of Heaven."

[16] Hargis, *Christian Crusade,* Vol. 15 (October, 1963), p. 10.

[17] Hargis, *Christian Crusade,* Vol. 15 (June-July, 1963), p. 12. J. Marcellus Kik, in *Church and State: The Story of Two Kingdoms* (New York: Nelson, 1963), rejects the view of the United States as a secular state. The Reverend Kik states that the wall of separation is legal, not moral or spiritual, and he stresses the distinction between a Christian-State, the United States as he sees it, and a church-dominated state. See also James Hastings Nichols, "Separation of Church and State," *Christian Century,* Vol. 65 (March 3, 1948).

[18] *Loc. cit.*

had to be won in the face of bitter opposition on the part of the established churches.

As might be expected, Hargis believes that the constitution perfected in Philadelphia in no way authorized "big government" or any "interference" with personal freedoms. The federal government, in his view, was established as a creature of the individual states and should remain that.[19] He says, "all thinking Americans should remember that our government was not designed to run the affairs of the people but to administer justice among our independent people who run their own affairs."[20] What does he mean by the term "justice"? The repeated implication is that he means virtually unlimited property rights.

Hargis believes that just as the slightest addition to, or deletion from, the Holy Bible is gross sin, so also there must be no tampering with the Constitution. The values of this nation were given once and for all at the time of its founding, and were incorporated in the Constitution. Changes or modifications are not merely unwise or unnecessary, but evil. He obviously agrees with the view that "our nation in the beginning was actually founded on an adequate and sufficiently explicit theory revealed at one time [and that] later theorists can have only the minor tasks of exegesis, of explaining the sacred texts."[21]

On the related question of judicial review, Hargis's stand is that the entire doctrine is wrong and unconstitutional. He has no quarrel with decisions which are to his liking, such as Church of the Holy Trinity v. United States (1892) and the numerous other decisions which seem to endorse the notion of Christian-Americanism; and he praised the 1965 Supreme Court decision which upheld the legality of the military chaplaincy. But whenever court rulings appear contrary to his assumptions, he denounces them. For him the whole issue of constitutional interpretation is no problem at all. He applies the fundamentalist doctrine of personal revelation and the notion of "the living Word." Hargis believes that it is the actual "Word" which speaks and exudes power. There is only one possible interpretation of "the living Word" — all else is heresy. "The Word was made flesh and dwelt among men"; thereafter the issue is not one of ascertaining it but of accepting it. In this view, there is little or no place for reinterpretation or reapplication in the light of

---

19 Hargis, *Weekly Crusader*, Vol. 3 (July 26, 1963), p. 6.
20 Hargis, *Weekly Crusader*, Vol. 3 (July 5, 1963), p. 4.
21 Daniel J. Boorstin, *The Genius of American Politics* (Chicago: University of Chicago Press, 1953), Phoenix Books edition, pp. 17-18.

changed circumstances or altered public opinion. Meanings are self-
evident and merely need to be stated honestly and courageously. Applying this type of reasoning, Hargis concludes: "It does not make the
slightest difference what nine political experts who are called Supreme Court Justices say, anyone who can read English knows that
under the Constitution, education is a matter left strictly to the
states."[22] In keeping with his conviction that Congress is more
representative of the virtuous common people than is the Court, he
urges that "Congress should set up a committee to reconsider every
decision made by the Supreme Court from 1954 until the present
to test their constitutionality."[23] As the ultimate touchstone on constitutionality he again invokes the Mayflower Compact, which he
believes is the source of "the basic law and philosophy of America."[24]

A passionate belief in Christian-Americanism constitutes the
third general facet of Hargis's perception of things American. Although Americanism always remains a fuzzy concept — objects of
faith and adulation need to be somewhat obscure — support of
Americanism, no matter what the cost, is mandatory for all the
faithful. They must support the cause because pro-Americanism is
the corollary of anti-Communism, the unifying catalyst. The fact that
resistance to Communism is presumably needed more now than
ever before is taken as proof that pro-Americanism has not been
promoted with sufficient vigor — an error which must be corrected
with haste.

From Hargis's viewpoint a Crusade for Americanism, Christian-
Americanism, is always in season. But when Americanism is actually
being eroded away and replaced by the gospel of the Antichrist, as
Hargis believes is presently happening, the situation is critical. Something must be done, and done soon, to stem the tide. "Little by
little, decree by decree," says Hargis, "socialism is replacing Americanism — and socialism is nothing less than communism."[25] The
frustrating fact of the matter is that good Americans, "God's people,"

---

22 Hargis, *Christian Crusade*, Vol. 14 (December, 1962), p. 4. See also
Hargis, *Weekly Crusader*, Vol. 4 (October 9, 1964), p. 4: "Another mistaken concept of our constitution which has invaded American thinking is
the idea that the Supreme Court is the final authority on the Constitution
and that the Constitution means whatever the Supreme Court of any given
time chooses to say it means."

23 Hargis, *Christian Crusade*, Vol. 14 (September, 1962), p. 19.

24 Hargis, *Communist America . . . Must It Be?* (*op. cit.*), p. 32.

25 Hargis, *Communism, The Total Lie!* (Tulsa: Christian Crusade, 1963),
p. 68.

on whom everything depends, "lack the fanaticism"[26] which is essential if victory is to be achieved.

In an attempt to do something about this situation, Hargis undertook a much-publicized "Christ-centered Americanism" campaign. In addition to an extensive literature and radio emphasis, it consisted of a lecture tour featuring both Hargis and General Edwin Walker, who has been a major Hargis supporter since retiring from the military service. Hargis's role was to present the seriousness of the domestic crises; General Walker's assignment was to discredit the United Nations and the United States Department of Defense. Walker's major point was that both agencies either consciously or unconsciously facilitate the expansion of the Communist conspiracy in the United States: the former by serving as a base of Communist operations, and the latter by "bridling patriotism."[27] The symbol of this two-year venture, from January 1, 1963 to December 31, 1964, was an image of Christ superimposed on an outline map of the United States. Hopefully, from Hargis's point of view, one result of this effort would be that more people would realize that "Americans, whether they know it or not, are a religious people."[28] The Christian emphasis in Hargis's appeal to Americans to redeem their country rested on the assumption that no "person can help save America unless they [sic] are led by the Holy Spirit."[29] The appeal directed to young people, stated in numerous articles, reveals the same logic: "serve God and save America."[30] God and country become virtually synonymous for Hargis. To serve one is to aid the other, and to sacrifice oneself and one's possessions for the advancement of this double cause is the highest form of altruism.

American society is seen as one in which spiritual and temporal authorities, both of them divinely commissioned, are to cooperate in ushering in a modern "City of God" here and now. Explaining this view, Hargis quotes James Russell Lowell: "Our country hath

---

[26] Hargis, *Communist America . . . Must It Be?* (*op. cit.*), p. 6. The whole concept of "Un-Americanism" comes in here. Boorstin, *op. cit.*, pp. 14f. has well observed that American Alien and Sedition Acts and many Congressional investigations, etc., are directed not only against acts of espionage but against acts of irreverence toward the orthodox American creed.

[27] The present writer heard both men deliver their lectures to a large audience in Seattle. Hargis lived up to his reputation as an emotional spellbinder. Walker, it quickly became evident, would not have been promoted to the rank of general if the weapons of war were logic and rhetoric.

[28] Hargis, *Christian Crusade*, Vol. 15 (August, 1963), p. 4.

[29] Hargis, *Christian Crusade*, Vol. 15 (September, 1963), p. 28.

[30] See, for example, Hargis, *Christian Crusade*, Vol. 14 (April, 1962), p. 3.

a gospel of her own to practice before all the world, the freedom and divinity of man, the glorious claims of human brotherhood, and the soul's loyalty to none but God."[31]

Despite his frequent denunciation of Supreme Court rulings, Hargis takes great delight in quoting Justice Brewster's statement in the 1892 Trinity Church decision when he said, "No purpose of action against religion can be imputed to any legislation, state or national, because this is a religious people."[32] A similar judgment by Justice Sutherland in 1930 is said to be equally "correct."[33] Hargis states that it should surely be clear to everyone that Americans are "by profession, a Christian people. We recognize the great principles of Christianity in devotional services in our legislatures, in our courts of justice, and in the use of oaths in every department of public administration."[34]

Various kinds of arguments are advanced to "prove" the Christian quality of America. In addition to the above — judicial decision and official formality — there is, as suggested earlier, the argument from origins. "America is and always has been a Christian nation," says Hargis.[35] Stated another way, America is Christian because God is its architect: "America is one of the greatest gifts that God has ever given man, outside of the gift of His only begotten Son and His divinely-inspired Bible."[36] There is also the alleged identity of the contemporary American way of life with the Bible: "Most Americans realize that our American way of life is right but they are not familiar with the Scriptures that teach the American way";[37] "they need to be taught that the American system is as intimately based

---

[31] Hargis, *Communist America... Must It Be?* (*op. cit.*), p. 39.

[32] Cited in *Christian Crusade*, Vol. 14 (September, 1962), p. 7. See Hargis, *Christian Crusade*, Vol. 15 (June-July, 1963), p. 24.

[33] United States v. Macintosh, 283 U. S. Reports, 605-635, cited in Evarts B. Green, *Religion and the State* (Ithaca, New York: Cornell University Press, 1941, 1959), pp. 143f. Note the comment of Boorstin, *op. cit.*, p. 175. "Aspects of experience which are elsewhere sharply distinguished here seem to merge into each other; the private and the public, the religious and the political, even — as I have suggested — the 'is' and the 'ought,' the world of fact and the world of fancy, of science and of morals."

[34] Hargis, *Christian Crusade*, Vol. 15 (August, 1963), p. 26.

[35] Hargis, *Communist America... Must It Be?* (*op. cit.*), pp. 33f.

[36] Hargis, *The Far Left* (*op. cit.*), p. 5. Cf. Boorstin, *op. cit.*, p. 1, "The genius of American democracy comes not from any special virtue of the American people but from the unprecedented opportunities of this continent and from a peculiar and unrepeatable combination of historical circumstances."

[37] Hargis, *Weekly Crusader*, Vol. 3 (October 4, 1963), p. 7.

on the Bible as the Ten Commandments are."[38] Another argument
which Hargis sometimes uses is that America is Christian because
most individual Americans are Christians. The figure of 70 percent
is cited, but no justification for it is advanced.[39]

On the other hand, if the concept of Christian-Americanism
is accepted as a religious doctrine, then arguments are superfluous
and rational evidence unnecessary. One can state simply that the
United States is "the greatest Christian nation in the history of the
world."[40] The validity of a tenet of faith, such as belief in Christian-
Americanism, is not affected by its popularity or logic. As one of
Hargis's colleagues phrased it, "Ours is a Christian Republic regardless of how many people are confessing Christians or how sincere
and understanding they may be in their confession."[41] It is to be
hoped, nonetheless, that the unbelievers will duly be convicted of
their willful unbelief. Belief must surely come, truth will win in
the end, and the doctrine of Christian-Americanism will then be
warmly and widely embraced. "Jesus said it: 'Ye shall know the
truth, and the truth shall make you free.' We know that to be the
gospel. We also know that the average American IS fiercely patriotic
and that he DOES love his country and its cherished freedoms —
once he is AWARE of the truth and is aroused to the danger which
surrounds him."[42] Choose America, says Hargis, for it is "the freest
of the free nations, the loveliest of all homelands, and the most
wonderful country in world history."[43] And then comes the final
withering challenge and dogmatic claim: "Choose Christ, for Christ
loves America."[44]

On occasion, the veneration of Christian-Americanism posits
America as a modern Israel — God's chosen nation in our own time.
Old Testament Scripture pertaining to the tribes of Israel is applied
to the United States. The following argument appears frequently.
"Our hope as a nation," says Hargis, "is found in II Chronicles 7:14:
'If my people, which are called by my name, shall humble themselves, and pray, and seek my face, and turn from their wicked
ways; then will I hear from heaven, and will forgive their sin, and
will heal their land.' "[45] As Hargis sees it, God always tends to deal

---

[38] Hargis, Christian Crusade, Vol. 15 (October, 1963), p. 10.
[39] Hargis, Communist America . . . Must It Be? (op. cit.), pp. 33f.
[40] Hargis, Communism, The Total Lie! (op. cit.), p. 87.
[41] In Weekly Crusader, Vol. 4 (March 20, 1962), p. 2.
[42] Hargis, Christian Crusade, Vol. 16 (April, 1962), p. 10.
[43] Hargis, Communism, The Total Lie! (op. cit.), p. 74.
[44] Hargis, Communist America . . . Must It Be? (op. cit.), p. 176.
[45] Hargis, Weekly Crusader, Vol. 4 (December 13, 1963), p. 6.

with some nation in a special way. "God always has an elect people," he states; at first it was Israel, then other peoples, eventually Great Britain, and "now the United States. I think God put his hand on the United States." Hargis is convinced that if this nation as God's "chosen vessel" is not faithful to its calling, God will withdraw himself from it. "Then the United States candle will be removed from the candlestick" and "it will be too late."[46]

In keeping with the notion that Americans are today's chosen people, Hargis loves to repeat the phrase, "Let none but Americans be on guard tonight."[47] The idea is applied not only to internal affairs and defense, but to all aspects of the United Nations and international involvement which concern the United States. As one of his writers puts it, "In other words, just as the Israelites were to be ruled by Israelites, so Americans are to be ruled by Americans. How else can any nation protect itself from alien ideas and influences."[48] The United Nations and various forms of international cooperation are therefore to be denounced. What is foreign is evil! The duty of the American nation in this respect is to justify and protect its superior status in God's sight by maintaining itself "pure and unspotted from the world."

Assuming this closeness of God to the United States, Hargis embarked in 1959 on a national crusade to "Save America — For God and Our Children."[49] God, it appears, needs the United States; He cannot get along without it.

At this point it should be stated that it is the belief in the United States as a modern Israel, rather than bigotry, naiveté, and racial prejudice per se, which generates fervent and emotional support for the House Un-American Activities Committee and similar state and local committees. A modern Israel must constantly be alert to the wiles and infiltrations of a modern Philistia; and aliens, perhaps even the colored race, threaten the concept of national-

---

46 Hargis, in an interview with this writer, October 25, 1964.

47 Hargis, *Christian Crusade*, Vol. 15 (February, 1963), p. 7. The full statement reads, "Let one and all know that 'none but Americans shall be on guard,' and that you are sick and tired of filth, perversion, subversion, espionage, cooperation with communists, coexistence with communists, negotiations with communists, and treason."

48 Claude Bunzel, *Weekly Crusader*, Vol. 3 (May 31, 1963), p. 5. Hargis indicates approval.

49 Hargis, *Communist America . . . Must It Be?* (*op. cit.*), p. viii.

racial peculiarity. Presumably, God's call to America and Americans does not extend to the Negro slaves or to their descendants.[50]

As God's right-hand nation the United States has a duty to those not so favored. It must further the cause of righteousness, i.e., Christian-Americanism. "America must do battle in the name of the Lord Jesus Christ."[51] The unmistakable reference here is to both peaceful and military activity. America's record in this regard, at least in the non-military realm, is presumed to be outstanding. "What civilization there is now in the world is due to the missionaries sent out from America."[52] (It should be noted here that the members of the Far Right, and the many other Americans who share this view, do not see themselves so much as masters of mankind but as divinely commissioned tutors.) In the twentieth century the world is the American vineyard and it shall not be spoiled by little or big Red foxes.

Rarely does Hargis have words of praise for the government currently in power. His basic complaint is that "the totalitarian-inclined welfare-state-type government which we have in America today is something far different from what our founding fathers intended."[53] Generally his criticisms are much less restrained. Charges fly thick and fast. "The American government is becoming a deadly force against its patriotic Christian-American people," we are informed.[54] "America is being sold out by treasonous, traitorous leaders."[55] A strong charge, indeed, but hardly more so than the assertion that "the people of the United States have ceased to be their own rulers, — and the government now ruling them is heavily pro-

---

[50] In his early years Hargis wrote what might be termed a racist pamphlet but he later repudiated it. But see his *Unmasking the Deceiver, Martin Luther King, Jr.* (Christian Crusade Pamphlet, n.d.).

[51] Hargis, *Communism, The Total Lie!* (*op. cit.*), p. 88.

[52] Hargis, quoted in Adams, *op. cit.*, p. 194. For an impassioned treatment of this theme, see Manojlo Ratkovich, *The World Mission of the United States* (New York: Greenwich, 1959). Note also Charles W. Lowry, *Communism and Christ* (New York: Morehouse-Gorham, 1953), p. 101, "The opportunity of our great country, which God has so wonderfully led and so richly blessed, is to lead faltering mankind beyond the twilight and the hovering darkness into the sunshine of a larger and happier day. It is to use our vast resources and inspiring inheritance under God to usher the whole earth into a period of abundance, freedom, and brotherhood. It is to be a strategic agent in continuing God's recreative work in Christ."

[53] Hargis, *Weekly Crusader*, Vol. 4 (May 15, 1964), p. 8.

[54] Hargis, *Communism, The Total Lie!* (*op. cit.*), p. 64.

[55] Hargis, *Communist America . . . Must It Be?* (*op. cit.*), p. 40.

Communist."[56] How the "most perfect" of all possible constitutional systems operating in a "Christian" country can produce such leaders is not explained.

Communist infiltration is probably the most frequent charge. With a flourish of finality, Hargis cites the testimony of J. Edgar Hoover before the House Appropriations Sub-Committee in March, 1961, in which the long-time FBI Director warned that Communists "have infiltrated every conceivable sphere of activity: Youth groups; radio, television and motion picture industries; church, school, educational and cultural groups; the press; national minority groups and civil and political units."[57] More specifically, Hargis claims that,

> Within the United States Department of Health, Education and Welfare, according to Herbert A. Philbrick, who spent nine years in the Communist party as a counterspy for the FBI, will be found fully one-third of the top echelon of the Communist conspirators in this country. It is estimated that from 75 to 80 percent of the responsible officers in the department are conspirators.[58]

The situation is grave — "Communists are very close to grasping total control of America."[59] What is more, "Faced with the most fanatical enemy human freedom has ever encountered, the American people are soft, pliable, lazy, and shiftless. This applies to our leaders as well as to the rank and file — even more so."[60] But hope is not altogether lost. Hargis is happy to note that the American public is at last waking up. "The softening, putrefying Liberalism of Washington is being seen for what it really is — a broad, slick runway straight into Communism."[61]

In the course of his argumentation, Hargis claims even more influence for American Communists than they have ever claimed

---

[56] *Ibid.*, p. 110.

[57] Hargis, *The Far Left (op. cit.)*, pp. 116f.

[58] Hargis, *Communist America... Must It Be? (op. cit.)*, p. 59. See also the statement on page 135, which begins as follows, "The Communists now control from 30 to 50 percent of our foreign and internal policies...", and that found on page 20, "Within the past 25 years, Communists have been unusually successful in hiding their key men in the American Army, Navy, diplomatic corps, treasury, Congress, and other control points of government." One of Hargis's strongest charges on this point is found in *Communism, The Total Lie! (op. cit.)*, p. 38: "the depth and degree of the Communist conspiracy within America has grown so great that mass opinion is controlled. Blackouts are called whenever necessary to save the Soviet Union embarrassment." See also Herbert Philbrick, *I Led 3 Lives* (New York: Grosset and Dunlap, 1952).

[59] Hargis, *Communism, The Total Lie! (op. cit.)*, p. 43.

[60] Hargis, *Weekly Crusader*, Vol. 2 (March 23, 1962), p. 2.

[61] *Ibid.*, p. 8.

for themselves. To the Reds and their fulminations he attributes nearly all of America's social crises. "America has had no social crisis in two generations which has not been created and 'solved' by the enemies of our country." And who is this enemy? "Communism is the agitator of every social crisis in America."[62] Racial crises[63] and educational crises;[64] election manipulation[65] and labor problems[66] — all are traceable to the Red menace. The sad fact of the matter, says Hargis, is that, "in every phase of the American way of life, Communists maneuver the multitudes of American people as they will."[67] A case in point: "Today in America there is growing hatred among employees for their employers because disciples of Marx had stirred up such hatred in America in obedience to the unholy spirit."[68]

Hargis appears to be so obsessed with Communist penetration and influence that he is apparently not inclined to accept any other possible cause of social action. This tendency is evident when he says, "Not all of the 'social reforms' already adopted by America have been bad, for the Communists have been willing to advocate a few good things just to gain practice and power...."[69] The logic

---

[62] Hargis, *Communism, The Total Lie!* (*op. cit.*), p. 70. In *Communist America... Must It Be?* (*op. cit.*), p. 24, he states that the United States "has faced no social crisis which was not created by the Communists in a quarter of a century...." Again, in *Communism, The Total Lie!*, p. 16, he insists that "the communist Manifesto... is the doctrine which is at the base of every 'social crisis' today in America...."

[63] Hargis, *Communist America... Must It Be?* (*op. cit.*), p. 101, "Regardless of what the Negroes think, regardless of what the entire South thinks, segregation and racism have become one of America's great 'social crises,' one of the most artificial of all such social crises, instigated by the Communists within America to add racial hatred to class hatred...." In part American Communists are themselves responsible for this view. Cf. the editorial in the July, 1963 issue of *Political Affairs*, which says that the current civil rights struggle is "the key to all other struggles" in the fight to conquer the United States.

[64] Hargis, *Threats To Christian Education* (Christian Crusade Pamphlet, n.d.).

[65] Hargis, *How the Communists Influence American Elections* (Christian Crusade Pamphlet, n.d.).

[66] Hargis, *Communism and American Labor* (Christian Crusade Pamphlet, n.d.).

[67] Hargis, *Communism, The Total Lie!* (*op. cit.*), p. 45.

[68] *Ibid.*, p. 15. Despite this deep pessimism, Hargis concedes that "a nation-wide campaign on every radio station, in every newspaper and on every television channel might spare us" from Communist victory.

[69] Hargis, *Communism, The Total Lie!* (*op. cit.*), p. 68.

is that America must nevertheless avoid 'social reforms,' for they indicate shrewd Communist plotting and nothing else.

Another frequent charge is that the United States government is power-hungry, or even power-mad. Hargis's discussion of the 1964 Civil Rights Bill, which has since become law, illustrates the point. In a feature article he asks, "Is Civil Rights a Moral Issue?" His answer is as follows.

> Any open-minded study of the facts will show the Civil Rights Bill to be primarily a political power grab instead of a moral issue. The struggle over this legislation is primarily between those who believe in an all-powerful federal government and those who believe in the concepts of freedom left us by our wise founding fathers.[70]

In another article the point is made even more forcefully: "The issue is not civil rights but is a power grab for an unbelievably dictatorial extension of federal power."[71]

Hargis has frequently been angered by specific government actions, especially as they affect him and his operations, but never more so than by a Federal Communications Commission "Public Notice" of July 26, 1963, which apparently was intended to curb the influence of certain Rightist spokesmen, including Hargis.[72] Explaining the situation to the faithful, he states: "This has nothing to do with any law, you understand. The FCC is actually a gang of federal outlaws, operating with impunity inside the invisible machinery of the Kennedy dictatorship."[73]

Government corruption may in part be credited to a loss of honor. But for a good Christian-American honor is no small thing.

> And honor might well be the story of the U. S. Government in recent years — a lack of it — a lack that has grown to such proportions that American leaders seem to thrive on it. The Government today has two principal concerns — the collection of taxes from its citizens, for whatever purposes it can invent, and the appeasement of its enemies, whoever and wherever they may be.[74]

Hargis also attacks dereliction, and worse, in foreign affairs. "This small group of liberals in Washington control [sic] our destiny and that of the entire free world. Though not card-carrying com-

---

[70] Hargis, *Weekly Crusader,* Vol. 4 (June 26, 1964), p. 3.

[71] Hargis, *Weekly Crusader,* Vol. 4 (April 3, 1964), p. 3.

[72] A discussion of the FCC "Public Notice" and of the Reuther Memorandum in which Hargis is named is found in the *Weekly Crusader,* Vol. 3 (September 20, 1963).

[73] Hargis, *Weekly Crusader,* Vol. 3 (September 6, 1963), p. 5.

[74] Hargis, *Weekly Crusader,* Vol. 3 (February 8, 1963), p. 2.

munists, many of the men in our government seek to paralyze our defense against the communist attack."[75] Secretary of Defense Robert McNamara is singled out for special derision. He is accused of not authorizing "a single new weapon system" and of "slowing down our technological progress deliberately."[76] The "gross ignorance and naiveté" of Washington "brass" make Hargis extremely frustrated:

> The almost complete blindness on the part of some U.S. policy makers to the realities of Communism was demonstrated in the idea that Laos is a test of the Soviet Union's coexistence policy. Their coexistence policy has existed for years, even before the words peaceful coexistence were ever used. When the Communists speak of peaceful coexistence, they are merely speaking of a different tactic of war.[77]

Many of the specific charges relate to the Supreme Court and especially Chief Justice Earl Warren. The Court is probably the most criticized part of "the entire federal government octopus." It is held mainly responsible for the "fact" that the United States is now a "government of men" instead of a "government of laws."[78] Hargis charges that under Warren the Court "has rendered sufficient decisions against America as to make it almost possible for the Communists to take over the nation without firing a shot."[79] Even worse, "Chief Justice Earl Warren has" personally "voted 92%...in favor of the enemies of America."[80] Hargis repeatedly urges "loyal" Americans to act against the obvious threat. "Let's get something done about decisions of our Supreme Court which have paralyzed opposition to the conspiracy in America. There is more than coincidence in these decisions."[81]

Writing in August, 1963, on the New York school prayer case, Hargis says,

> As I contemplate the recent decision of the United States Supreme Court regarding prayer and Bible reading in our public schools, my

---

75 Hargis, *Weekly Crusader*, Vol. 2 (June 1, 1962), p. 7.

76 *Weekly Crusader*, Vol. 3 (April 26, 1963), p. 4. Hargis quotes from the April 15, 1963 issue of *Washington Report*, a publication of the American Security Council.

77 Hargis, *Weekly Crusader*, Vol. 3 (May 3, 1963), p. 1.

78 Hargis, as stated in various radio lectures.

79 Hargis, *Communist America...Must It Be?* (*op. cit.*), p. 110. Note also his statement in *Weekly Crusader*, Vol. 2 (July 13, 1962), p. 1, "it is my earnest conviction that every member of the United States Supreme Court who either voted to outlaw prayer in the public schools, or was a party to this decision by silence should be impeached. Justice demands it."

80 Hargis, *Communist America...Must It Be?* (*op. cit.*), p. 114.

81 Hargis, *Christian Crusade*, Vol. 15 (February, 1963), p. 6.

own feeling for that which has come to pass by their action can only be described by one word, shameful. I regard it as shameful that we have permitted these judicial appointees, most of whom have no past judicial experience and are certainly not qualified to serve on the highest tribunal in our land, to wipe God from the pages of American history with the stroke of a pen.[82]

Any Supreme Court decision which in some way thwarts the fundamentalist concept of Christianity is attacked, regardless of what the reasoning of the Court might be. When the Court disallowed a section of Maryland's constitution which required public office-holders to believe in God, Hargis rose to take on Goliath. He wrote, "There are other areas," not only the obviously pro-Communist rulings, "which point up very clearly this suicidal road our nation is traveling. For example, during 1961, a public official was installed in the state of Maryland who does not believe in God and this was the first time in history that such had happened."[83]

As Hargis sees it, the state of affairs in Washington is rapidly deteriorating. What is his evidence? It is perfectly obvious for all who care to see it. The situation is now so critical that, "because of rulings of the Supreme Court . . . it is no crime in America to teach or advocate the violent overthrow of the government."[84] The believers nod and tremble.

---

[82] Hargis, *Christian Crusade,* Vol. 15 (August, 1963), p. 26. For the National Council of Churches stand on school prayer see *The News Release,* published by the National Council of Churches Office of Information, April 29, 1964, and *The Churches and the Public Schools,* an official National Council of Churches Policy Statement dated June 7, 1963.

[83] Hargis, *Weekly Crusader,* Vol. 3 (June 7, 1963), p. 4.

[84] Hargis, *Communist America . . . Must It Be? (op. cit.),* p. 111.

3. CONSERVATISM AND "THE FAR LEFT"

IT IS CUSTOMARY FOR HARGIS TO INTRODUCE HIMSELF AS A TRUE conservative. Since he also presents himself as a true Christian, it is revealing to see how he relates the two. Describing an upcoming lecture series, he states, "I plan to point up clearly, for every American to see and understand, that there is a sound scriptural basis for the position taken by the political conservative."[1] In the lectures themselves the usual assertions are repeated: property rights, patriotism, free enterprise, and limited government are described as being biblical. In view of that "fact," "Bible-believers" must necessarily be conservative in politics.[2] Here, again, it is not a matter of reasoning, but a matter of "seeing the truth," the "Biblical facts."

The identification is total. Conservative Christianity and political conservatism are not just overlapping ideologies; they are two sides of one and the same coin. "Christ is the heart of the Conservative cause," says Hargis. "We conservatives are fighting for God and Country."[3] How God's cause can simultaneously be universal as well as American, and how Christians inclined toward liberalism in politics fit into this scheme, are not explained.

The important question for Hargis remains — is an individual on God's side and God on his? The question is crucial; "if the conservative cause is of God and right, then the people who fight it are fighting God." Then come the words of assurance: "Those of us who have been in this fight against communism know beyond a shadow of a doubt that what we do is of God, and those who oppose this conservative effort are not fighting us — they are fighting

1 Hargis, *Christian Crusade*, Vol. 15 (October, 1963), p. 10.
2 Hargis, statement on KAIL-TV, Fresno, October 25, 1964.
3 Hargis, *Christian Crusade*, Vol. 14 (October, 1962), p. 14.

God."[4] Who wants to be fighting God? Couched in these terms, there is only one option — Christian conservatism. Again the question becomes simply one of obedience, not of rational choice.

Since God is an ally, the cause cannot fail.[5] Men of action are needed, men who will stand and fight. "I feel that this is the time," observes Hargis, "to hit communism and its allies, political and religious liberalism, our hardest blow. These common enemies of New Testament Christianity and Constitutional government, are justly concerned about the conservative revival in full sway throughout the nation."[6]

Of course, the "fact" that God is one's partner does not guarantee victory right away. As every fundamentalist knows, God at times delays victory, and may even seem to prevent it, for reasons known only to Him; His ways "are past finding out."[7] But the disciple's task is not to question, but to obey. That is Hargis's conviction, and he does not moderate it as he transfers his religious orientation to the political arena. There is also the further point that the forces of righteousness, God's forces, are to expect to be a minority. This point is emphasized in order to sustain interest and activity. The fundamentalist image in this respect is that of a faithful few persevering on a narrow and steep trail while the deluded masses merrily and blindly drift along on a broad highway that leads to doom.[8] Hargis frequently casts himself and his followers in the role of the faithful few, the faithful remnant. "I am convinced," he says, that "it is the Christian conservative that is the true nonconformist, the persecuted minority."[9] Given this outlook and this identification, persecution becomes both a sign of approval and proof of authenticity.

Being somewhat successful in political affairs is important for the righteous remnant, but it is not the most important thing —

---

[4] Hargis, *Weekly Crusader,* Vol. 3 (January 18, 1963), p. 6.

[5] Cf. Hargis, *This I Believe (op. cit.),* p. 4, "These mistaken ones can conceivably destroy their critics now, but tomorrow they will reckon with God, and I have no doubt who will win in that conflict." Compare also Hargis, *If Our Foundations Be Destroyed* (Christian Crusade Pamphlet, n.d.), p. 2, "Were it not for our confidence that truth will ultimately conquer, we would all be discouraged and give up. But, we dare not give up. Truth is on our side. We are on the side of God and His Holy Angels."

[6] Hargis, *Weekly Crusader,* Vol. 2 (June 1, 1962), p. 8.

[7] Romans 11:33.

[8] Matthew 7:13-14.

[9] Hargis, *Christian Crusade,* Vol. 15 (January, 1963), p. 3. Hargis goes on to compare his situation with that of the Apostles described in Acts chapter 5.

faithfulness is. Accordingly, defeat, as in the presidential election of 1964, is readily accepted. The forces of righteousness may not win each battle, but some day, in God's good time, they will win the war. And, after all, that is what really counts. "Ultimate victory is assured." Hargis writes,

> We are claiming the promise of II Chronicles 7:14. "If my people, which are called by my name, shall humble themselves, and pray, and seek my face, and turn from their wicked ways; then will I hear from Heaven, and will forgive their sin, and will heal their land." As one Crusader put it: "We have God's promise that if we return to Him, He will save us. It is only by the grace and mercy of God that this fight can be won."[10]

Over whom is this victory assured? Over the forces fighting God. And who are these forces? They are the forces of liberalism, socialism, and Communism, "The Far Left" in Hargis's view; and he has much to say about these "sinister" forces of "corruption." "A giant gangster conspiracy threatens to take away our freedoms and enslave us all," he says,[11] a conspiracy of evil that is universal in scope and unbelievably complex in nature; it is both domestic and external.[12] But the greatest threat "is not so much from the outside as it is from the inside"; and even there, "our greatest threat is not internal communism per se ... the greatest threat to freedom ... is the powerfully entrenched Liberal Establishment."[13] What is the nature of this establishment? "The Liberal Establishment," says Hargis, "is a sinister brotherhood that reaches into the fields of education, politics, religion, labor and management — dedicated men

---

10 Quoted from a personal letter to the author, October 26, 1964.

11 Hargis, *We Have Been Betrayed* (Christian Crusade Pamphlet, n.d.), p. 4. Hargis is frequently accused of downgrading the external threat of Communism. The *New York Times,* August 6, 1961, quotes him as saying, "We conservatives all agree on one thing — that our problem is almost entirely from internal subversion." But this type of statement must be correctly understood. Hargis is not saying that there is no foreign threat. In fact, his view of it is much the same as that of the average American. His reason for saying what he does is twofold: in the first place, he is convinced that the domestic threat is much more immediate and much more subtle than the external; in the second place, he does not see the domestic and external threats as separate phenomena. It is all perceived as part of a single plot in which domestic agitation, penetration, and "internal decay" are given top priority.

12 Hargis, *Communism, The Total Lie!* (*op. cit.*), chapter 8.

13 Hargis, *Christian Crusade,* Vol. 14 (September, 1962), p. 6. Cf. Eastman, *Reflections on the Failure of Socialism* (New York: Grosset and Dunlap, 1955, Universal Library Edition, 1962), pp. 23, 24. "Almost everyone who cares earnestly about freedom is aroused against the Communists. But

determined to abolish the free enterprise system and bring about a world government of socialist nations."[14] They are, he continues, men "who distrust democracy because they feel the people are not capable of governing themselves.... With this hatred of the less educated masses . . . the Liberal Establishment works feverishly to enslave us all."[15]

In Hargis's lexicon the label "liberal" represents the epitome of all that is reprehensible. "Left-wing liberals," we are told, are under "a satanic influence."[16] As a matter of fact, "the entire left-wing movement is of the devil."[17] Communism and liberalism are cut from the same cloth; the shading may vary but the weave is constant. "There is no sense in kidding ourselves," says Hargis, "Socialism and Communism are one and the same thing. The socialist views that they [the liberals] hold and Communist views, are the same."[18] The entire Left, the whole "vicious poison of liberalism"[19]— all is of the devil. "Today," writes Hargis, "we find Satan incarnate in international Communism and in its offshoots in the United States, the 'Far Left.'"[20]

Anything liberal is inherently anti-Christian from Hargis's vantage point. "It is Adam defying God all over again. The underlying reason for the liberals' defiance of the historic American way and orthodox New Testament Christianity, is their disbelief in God and the Bible."[21] Believers are conservatives and non-believers are liberals; it is almost as simple as that. Hargis notes, "The Word of God says, 'The vile person shall be no more called Liberal' (Isaiah 32:5)."[22] Thus the argument is clinched.

Perhaps the most disturbing leftist pursuit of the day, in Hargis's view, is the campaign to "throw God out of the U.S." Liberals are held accountable for the entire affair, and their methods and motives are spelled out fully. Hargis describes, for

---

it is not only the Communists, it is in a more subtle way the Socialists who are blocking the efforts of the free world to recover its poise and its once-firm resistance to tyranny." Eastman feels that "in America as elsewhere it is the socialist ideal, as surely as the communist implementation of it, that is working against freedom."

[14] Hargis, *Christian Crusade*, Vol. 14 (September, 1962), p. 6.
[15] Hargis, *If Our Foundations Be Destroyed (op. cit.)*, p. 1.
[16] Hargis, *The Far Left (op. cit.)*, p. 216.
[17] *Ibid.*, p. 8.
[18] Hargis, *Communist America . . . Must It Be? (op. cit.)*, p. 58.
[19] Hargis, *Weekly Crusader*, Vol. 2 (April 6, 1962), p. 1.
[20] Hargis, *The Far Left (op. cit.)*, p. 16.
[21] Hargis, *This I Believe (op. cit.)*, p. 4.
[22] Hargis, *Communism, The Total Lie! (op. cit.)*, p. 73.

example, the various tactics allegedly employed by liberals to kill the 1964 Becker Amendment, which was an effort on the part of conservatives to legalize prayer and Bible reading in public schools on a voluntary basis.[23] He finds the whole pursuit despicable. Referring to certain inferences made by some of these liberals, he says, "This, of course, is gutter-type warfare, but the liberals will use it again and again in order to put across their satanic, godless schemes."[24]

Interestingly enough, no less an eminent liberal than Arthur Schlesinger, Jr., lends at least a modicum of credence to these charges of anti-Christian agitation. Writing in the *Partisan Review* several years ago, he said,

> Official liberalism ... dispensed with the absurd Christian myths of sin and damnation and believed that what shortcomings man might have were to be redeemed, not by Jesus on the Cross, but by the benevolent unfolding of history.[25]

Hargis's standard presentation of liberalism is that, while being the halfway house to Communism, or even continuous with it, it nevertheless is at least less barbarous. But on occasion the argument takes a new twist. The suggestion then is that liberalism is the broader category; that it is the genus of which Communism is a species. For example, commenting on the 1964 presidential election, Hargis states that Communists were planning "to work with various other liberal forces. . . ."[26]

Alleged inconsistencies — the "liberal double-standard" — are also unveiled. To illustrate this point Hargis discusses certain activities of the AAUP, the American Association of University Professors. He contends that this group quickly blacklists schools for firing self-proclaimed Communists, but shows no concern for academic freedom if an anti-Communist is fired. Cited is the case of Professor Herbert Fuchs.[27]

---

[23] For a concise analysis of the Becker Amendment and a summary of the major points of view, see Leo Pfeffer, "The Becker Amendment," *A Journal of Church and State*, Vol. 6 (Autumn, 1964), pp. 344-349.

[24] Hargis, *Christian Crusade*, Vol. 16 (July, 1964), p. 21.

[25] Hargis, *American Socialism . . . Moving America Downhill* (*op. cit.*). The Schlesinger statement cited here continues, "Tolerance, free inquiry, and technology, operating in the framework of human perfectability, would in the end create a heaven on earth, a goal accounted much more sensible and wholesome than a heaven in heaven."

[26] Hargis, *Weekly Crusader*, Vol. 4 (August 14, 1964), p. 3.

[27] Cited in Hargis, *The Far Left* (*op. cit.*), pp. 256f. Some additional startling instances are described in William Buckley, *Up From Liberalism* (New York: Hillman Books, 1961), pp. 26f., 42f., 91f.

The self-righteousness and arrogance of the Left Wing is especially galling to Hargis. He seems to be particularly sensitive on this point, perhaps because he lacks a secular higher education. And "sophisticated" references to him as a "hillbilly evangelist" seem to have just enough truth to the charge to make it sting. No doubt Hargis agrees fully with William Buckley's judgment[28] when the latter laments that "American Liberals are reluctant to co-exist with anyone on their Right"; that they give the impression that they have "given conservatism a terminal audience." "The Liberals' implicit premise," according to Buckley, "is that intercredal dialogues are what one has with Communists, not conservatives, in relationship with whom normal laws of civilized discourse are suspended."[29]

The Left is frequently charged by Hargis with taking America down the road to ruin. We are told that "for years, in America, the social planners, whom American citizens were deceived into believing were working for their welfare, have been about the evil business of converting free and blessed America into the ugly pattern of the Soviet Union."[30] Who are these "ugly planners"? They are the "so-called liberals and progressives."[31] They are the Schlesingers, the Rusks, the McNamaras, the Goldbergs, the Kennedys, and the whole "Harvard crowd."

The gamut of leftist subterfuge, for Hargis, is almost endless and takes many forms, but much of it is perpetrated in the guise of federal control. We read,

> Federal control of education (which will make total Communist control easy), minimum wages and hours, socialized medicine, federal housing, government loans and grants, civil rights, human rights, mental health, and endless schemes for the spending of money and the piling on of more power — these so-called "social reforms" are the internal traps Communists use to shape America after the Soviet pattern.[32]

---

[28] Buckley, *op. cit.*, p. 141.

[29] *Ibid.*

[30] Hargis, *Communism, The Total Lie!* (*op. cit.*), p. 32.

[31] *Ibid.*

[32] *Ibid.*, p. 66. Note the incident reported in Hargis, *Mental Health* (Christian Crusade Pamphlet, n.d.), p. 18, in which Dr. Richard Hofstadter told a Los Angeles press conference on March 20, 1964, that isolation of "overprincipled man" was needed to keep the United States on "the sane road of moderation." He stated that he was referring to Right Wing extremists. He added, "We certainly cannot commit them all to mental hospitals" but suggested that some kind of therapy must be undertaken.

As Hargis sees it, the mass media are the worst offenders in this whole plot. "It is my contention that the majority of the American newspapers are actively promoting the communist line,"[33] he asserts. In support of his belief Hargis cites the case of the York, Pennsylvania, *Gazette and Daily*, which refused to accept advertising for Republican presidential candidate Barry Goldwater because he was too far to the right.[34] The radio and television networks also are guilty. They are "wide open for the clever, delicate nuances of liberal commentators, slyly injecting the Marxist narcotic; open for the dramatic performance insidiously low-grading nationalistic patriotism"; open for "the comedies making fools of army officers and police; and open for the sex shows making light of marriage and sound American life. A most vicious campaign, my friends, and it is working."[35] One of the worst, according to Hargis, is columnist Walter Lippmann. "In the opinion of Christian Crusade," he writes, "there is no more vicious leftwinger in the United States than Walter Lippmann."[36]

While usually described as an integral part of the Communist conspiracy, liberals are also described as ignorant dupes. Informed conservatives have long since seen what is happening; liberals have not. They have presumably been blinded by their fellow-travelling Communist cousins. The fact of the matter, says Hargis, is that "the communists depend upon the mistakes of the liberals. The liberals, oblivious to the end result of their socialistic schemes, continue to drag America downward to a communist grave."[37] If only the liberals would wake up, if only they would realize that "the communists wait like buzzards for the corpse of capitalistic United States to fall...."[38] Can Harvard graduates be so blind as not to see that "the success of world communism is not due to the

---

[33] Hargis, *Communist America... Must It Be?* (*op. cit.*), p. 30. See also p. 23.

[34] See UPI news release of October 25, 1964, as carried in the *Fresno Bee,* Fresno, California.

[35] Hargis, *Highlights of the Anti-Communist Leadership School* (Christian Crusade Pamphlet, 1962), p. 2 of Hargis's address. See also Hargis, *The Ugly Truth About Drew Pearson* (Christian Crusade Pamphlet, n.d.).

[36] Hargis, *Christian Crusade,* Vol. 14 (September, 1962), p. 5.

[37] Hargis, *Christian Crusade,* Vol. 14 (September, 1962), p. 6. Cf. Hargis, *This I Believe* (*op. cit.*), p. 4. "The Communists have found a valuable champion of their rights and activities, in the camp of the liberals, that stretches from the lofty peaks of 'religious agnosticism' alias 'higher learning,' to the wastelands of 'anti-Americanism' alias 'academic freedom.'"

[38] Hargis, *If Our Foundations Be Destroyed* (*op. cit.*), pp. 1-2.

effectiveness of Marxist dialectics, but instead, is due to the failures of our own liberal leaders?"[39]

Hargis is deeply concerned about the millions who feel that the United States is safe as long as foreign attack is not imminent. To these he says, "but why should the Communists attempt to capture America by a two-ocean invasion, or by atomic warfare, when there are more than enough people inside the country willing to hand over the nation peacefully?"[40]

How much time remains for the attempt to save the nation? Not much. One could hardly expect the situation to be otherwise, since "there are more Communists in New York City today than in Moscow. . . ."[41] Hargis notes that Dr. Revilo P. Oliver, professor of classics at the University of Illinois, "a keen student of the times," "has seen fit to observe that America could go down before the Communist tide within four years from March, 1959."[42] Fortunately that date is now safely past, but Hargis himself is hardly a cautious prophet. "So successful has . . . subversion within America been," he says, "that the capture of the world's freest and richest nation lacks only another shove or two."[43] When he does cite numbers, however, he is careful to hedge — predictions are attributed to others. "Some of the nation's best informed conservative and patriotic Christian-American citizens believe that unless there is an awakening among American people quickly . . . Communism will take over the nation in five to ten years at the most."[44] These statements were written in 1960. Anticipating great liberal opposition in the 1964 election, Hargis challenged his readers in the March, 1964, Newsletter as follows: "It is 'do or die' in 1964. If we don't break this liberal yoke in '64, forget about freedom and liberty. It will become but a memory in the hearts of an enslaved people."

---

[39] *Ibid.*, p. 2.
[40] Hargis, *Communist America . . . Must It Be? (op. cit.)*, p. 17.
[41] *Ibid.*, p. 144.
[42] *Ibid.*, p. 19.
[43] *Ibid.*
[44] *Ibid.*, pp. 16f. At times Hargis's mood is highly pessimistic. Cf. *Christian Crusade*, Vol. 14 (April, 1962), p. 3, "The question is no longer 'CAN the Communists overthrow us,' but 'WHEN will they overthrow us?'"

4. THE COLD WAR AND AMERICAN FOREIGN POLICY

THE COLD WAR, FOR HARGIS, CONSISTS OF THE TOTAL CONFRONTA-tion of right with wrong: conservatism versus leftism, the United States versus the Soviet Union, and God's cause versus the Anti-christ's cause. It has devious and complex dimensions; it is fought in churches,[1] in the press, in education, in politics, and in society generally. "The fight" involves blood, bullets, and ballots — the Cold War is everywhere.

Since the Cold War includes all the efforts of "the conspiracy," it is both external and internal. In advertising his national "Mid-night Ride" with General Walker, Hargis emphasized that his aim was "to alert the public to the enemy within and without."[2] Since various critics had accused him of minimizing the foreign threat, this writer put the question to Hargis directly. His response was an emphatic, "very definitely," the external threat must not be underrated.[3] Yet at other times Hargis has taken a quite different line, saying that the only real threat is internal. "The inescapable and damning truth is that the real power of Communism is right here in our own land."[4] Says Hargis, "Clean up Communism INTERNALLY and America's problem with Communism INTER-NATIONALLY will be solved."[5] The supposed superiority of the internal threat comes as no surprise to Hargis, for have not Com-

---

[1] Hargis, *The Facts About Communism and Our Churches* (*op. cit.*), especially the first three chapters.

[2] Hargis, *Christian Crusade*, Vol. 14 (February, 1963), p. 1.

[3] Hargis, in an interview with this writer, October 25, 1964.

[4] Hargis, *Communist America ... Must It Be?* (*op. cit.*), pp. 134f.

[5] Hargis, *What's Wrong With America?* (*op. cit.*), p. 3.

munists always said that the United States would be taken from
within?[6]

Whatever the relative significance of the various types of
threats may be, the frightening aspect of the entire phenomenon is
the retreat of the free world. "Look about you in the world," says
Hargis; "the Communists win every battle they engage in."[7] He
continues, "We must remember always this awful truth: Our country, and the Western World, has not won a single victory over
Communism, either on the battlefield or at the conference table,
since the Bolshevik Revolution in 1917. Not one."[8] A major cause
of this failure is the allegedly erroneous conception our government has of the nature of the encounter. Goldwater's statement on
this issue coincides with Hargis's views. The former senator writes,
"Our enemies have understood the nature of the conflict, and we
have not. They are determined to win the conflict, and we are not."[9]
Hargis finds the situation incredible and the actions of the Western
leaders incomprehensible. "Like a bird paralyzed before a snake,
the civilized world stands transfixed as the international boa con-
strictor known as Communism swallows first this portion and then
that portion of the earth."[10]

Most of the blame for this situation is charged to the "leftist,
Harvard crowd" which is thought to be dominating the American
State Department — "the dupes, stupes, and traitors."[11] Hargis is
particularly critical of the 1961 Department of State Publication
No. 7277 entitled, "Freedom From War: The United States Program for General and Complete Disarmament in a Peaceful World."
As he sees it, its authors and promoters stand condemned on two
counts. In the first place, disarmament is bad because it would
"invite attack," and in the second place, the document has "a strik-

---

6 See Hargis, *Communist America . . . Must It Be?* (*op. cit.*), especially
Chapter 3.

7 *Ibid.*, p. 8.

8 Hargis, *Christian Crusade*, Vol. 14 (January-February, 1962), p. 20.

9 Barry Goldwater, *The Conscience of a Conservative* (New York: Macfadden Books, 1960), p. 91.

10 Hargis, *Communism, The Total Lie!* (*op. cit.*), p. 36.

11 Hargis, *What's Wrong With America?* (*op. cit.*), p. 5. Note his state-
ment about "the Institute of Pacific Relations, organized to orient American
Far Eastern policies toward Communist objectives. . . ." *Communist America
. . . Must It Be?* (*op. cit.*), p. 93. Note also his views on the Peace Corps,
"Many Americans are looking beyond the appealing altruistic motives of the
Peace Corps, looking for the real ulterior motive." He suggests that it might
be to promote racial intermarriage and thus world government. *Weekly
Crusader*, Vol. 3 (May 24, 1963), pp. 1f.

ing resemblance" to Red proposals, and anything which parallels "the Commie line" is by definition totally corrupt.[12]

Instead of disarmament, Hargis advocates a militant stance, a readiness to fight. There must be no more retreating. "We dare not give up another INCH to the international Communist conspiracy, whether it is in West Berlin or Viet Nam or Matsu or Quemoy"; and the risks, he assures us, are not as great as our "duped" and "fear-stricken" leaders would have us believe. "I am convinced," says Hargis, "that Khrushchev or, presumably, a successor will not risk a major war to get the West out of West Berlin."[13] Somewhat surprisingly, his argument is that Soviet leaders are too realistic and rational to retaliate with a full military effort. "We should be on the offensive," he says; "We should be insisting that the Communists live up to their agreement for free elections. ... We should shout to the world" about communist-controlled nations. "We should encourage these enslaved people to overthrow their communist dictators."[14] That would be true Americanism in action. In a typical statement in which he perceives only two alternatives, he asks, "Should we surrender to Castro or SMASH him?"[15] His unequivocal answer is, "truth demands the liquidation of Fidel Castro. Honor demands the liberation of Cuba from the hands of this godless despot."[16]

Hargis is deeply dismayed by the fact that the majority of his countrymen, as he sees it, have not understood the nature of the Cold War. "Don't let anyone tell you," he cautions, that it is only a "political conflict far from it. It is a spiritual war — the 'end-time battle' spoken of by Christ and the Apostles."[17] Hargis continues, "Whether we like it or not, we are all in this struggle between the forces of Satan and truth."[18] And, of course, the blame lies all on one side. "Let our reaction be determined by this simple fact: The only 'tensions' that exist between East and West have been

---

[12] Hargis, *Weekly Crusader*, Vol. 3 (June 28, 1963), p. 3.

[13] Hargis, *What's Wrong With America?* (*op. cit.*), p. 4.

[14] *Ibid.*, p. 5.

[15] This is the title of a Christian Crusade pamphlet written by Hargis. See also his lead article in *Weekly Crusader*, Vol. 4 (October 30, 1964), in which he stresses that there are only two alternatives in foreign policy, "to rely on American military strength" or "to rely on Communist promises."

[16] Hargis, *What's Wrong With America?* (*op. cit.*), p. 6.

[17] Hargis, *Communism, The Total Lie!* (*op. cit.*), p. 24. Hargis quotes I John 2:18.

[18] Hargis, *The Far Left* (*op. cit.*), p. 288.

created, and deliberately so, by the Communists."[19] The statement is by Senator Goldwater, but it is also Hargis's view. America and the West are thus totally guiltless.

A special appeal is addressed to Christians. "Because of the nature of the struggle," claims Hargis, "the church should be in the forefront in the fight against Communism. . . ."[20] "I am convinced that Communism is winning World War III without firing a single shot or losing a single soldier, and the apathy and lethargy of God's people are responsible."[21]

What is needed most of all is a will to fight and confidence of victory. "Victory is assured the Christian in battle," says Hargis, thus why fear to fight![22] "The people of America should be reminded," he continues, "that God gave us victory in two great world wars. . . . We have the greatest opportunity of any nation in history to lead the nations of the world in righteousness and strength."[23]

Negotiation and compromise are ruled out from the start. "You can't do business with the communists; you can't trust a communist. America should quit trying."[24] Might the nuclear age have changed this situation? Is there not a chance that the Reds might conclude that a negotiated compromise might be to their advantage, and might they then not act accordingly? Might American and Soviet national interests coincide? Apparently not. As Hargis sees it, "Negotiating and reaching agreements with murderers, rapists, bank robbers and other criminals to 'relax the tensions' makes just as much, if not more, sense than negotiating and reaching agreements with these international, lying murderers." Hargis's position is absolute. "Any negotiations and agreements with them are stupid. . . ."[25] Apparently, in Hargis's view, the notion of negotia-

---

19 Goldwater, *op. cit.*, p. 105.

20 Hargis, *Communist America . . . Must It Be?* (*op. cit.*), p. 7.

21 *Ibid.*, p. 111. In a rather unusual application of Scripture, Hargis writes, "The Apostle Paul wrote in Romans 13:11, 'and that, knowing the time, that now it is high time to awake out of sleep.' No verse in the New Testament is more appropriate for this hour. . . . Whatever the reason may be for their apathy and complacency, it is nevertheless a fact, America is asleep. Paul's words ring down through the corridors of time — 'It is high time to awake out of sleep.'" *What's Wrong With America?* (*op. cit.*), p. 3.

22 Hargis, *Communism, The Total Lie!* (*op. cit.*), p. 86.

23 Hargis, *Communist America . . . Must It Be?* (*op. cit.*), p. 129.

24 Hargis, *Communism, The Total Lie!* (*op. cit.*), p. 3.

25 Hargis, *Weekly Crusader*, Vol. 3 (June 28, 1963), p. 6.

tions is itself of Red origin: "negotiation is the most successful weapon of war the Communists have ever devised,"[26] we read. For this reason, if for no other, even to contemplate an eventual rapprochement between the Big Two is "suicidally ridiculous reasoning."[27]

Not only negotiation is denounced, but so is almost every other form of contact and interaction with the Communist bloc. "For America, or any other nation, to have diplomatic relations, exchange visits, and summit meetings with communist leaders is to have diplomatic relations, exchange visits, and summit meetings with representatives of the devil."[28] If that is the case, then "why does America negotiate with Russia?" The response is straightforward. "Mainly for one big reason, which the American people must grasp or America soon will be lost — Soviet Russia has become able to dictate American foreign and internal policies almost to the point of total control."[29]

Can the situation still be saved? If so, what should be done? For one thing, says Hargis, "we should break off diplomatic relations with the Soviet Union and the Communist satellites."[30] More than that, we should fully and finally "end American recognition of Russia."[31] This step would at least eliminate much of the temptation to negotiate. Recognition and its denial are crucial in Hargis's view; "Mr. Roosevelt recognized Russia in 1933 and one-half the world went Communist. If Mr. Kennedy is persuaded . . . to recognize Communist China . . . we cannot keep the other half of the world from going Communist."[32] What is needed most, and here Goldwater again expresses Hargis's views, is a return to the good old ways. "The ancient and tested truths that guided our Republic through its early days will do equally well for us."[33] Complicating factors, such as the new international role of the United States since 1900 and the complex nature of the modern world, are presumably inconsequential.

A government undertaking which is not included in the rubric of "ancient and tried truths," and is therefore unjustifiable,

---

[26] Hargis, cited in Adams, *op. cit.*, p. 192.
[27] Hargis, *Weekly Crusader*, Vol. 3 (June 14, 1963), p. 3.
[28] Hargis, *Communism, The Total Lie!* (*op. cit.*), p. 29.
[29] *Ibid.*, p. 44.
[30] *Ibid.*, p. 67.
[31] Hargis, *Christian Crusade*, Vol. 15 (February, 1963), p. 6.
[32] Hargis, *What's Wrong With America?* (*op. cit.*), p. 11.
[33] Goldwater, *op. cit.*, p. 3.

is the foreign aid program launched by President Harry S. Truman in 1947. "Americans are horribly deceived into thinking their foreign aid money benefits the oppressed and strengthens the free world against the oppressor." This view is wrong, says Hargis. "Nothing is farther from the truth. Nothing!"[34]

Basically, foreign aid is opposed for six reasons: it has produced inflation; it is draining away American gold; it has not thwarted Communism; it has advanced the cause of Communism; it is being wasted and squandered; and, it is un-Christian.[35] "Christian America," we read,

> must demand a national referendum on foreign aid, or by some other means cut off the flow of money to anti-Christian enemies. America must stop financing its own destruction. America's hands must be washed by the blood of Jesus Christ from the guilt of financing the slavery of nearly one-half the people in the world today and the brutal torture and murder of untold millions.[36]

Sometimes it seems that Hargis opposes even that foreign aid which was given to allies during wartime[37]; at other times he would seem to tolerate "proper aid." Emphatically he insists that "all foreign aid to any country that will not stand with us 100% in the fight against communism" must end.[38]

Foreign aid has failed completely to halt Communism in any way, as Hargis sees it. After citing Brazil as a case in point, he continues,

> Of course, case after case could be cited of such failure of the foreign aid theory of fighting communism. This asinine theory merely serves as an escape hatch for diplomats and government officials who do not want to face up to the realities of the nature, methods, and objectives of the international communist conspiracy.[39]

He argues that, if foreign aid were indeed as effective in combating Communism as its proponents claim it to be, then it would

---

[34] Hargis, *Communist America... Must It Be?* (*op. cit.*), p. 144. For a detailed criticism of foreign aid, see Hargis's feature article in *Weekly Crusader,* Vol. 5 (January 22, 1965).

[35] Hargis, *Weekly Crusader,* Vol. 2 (April 13, 1962), p. 7.

[36] Hargis, *Communist America... Must It Be?* (*op. cit.*), p. 148.

[37] Hargis, *Christian Crusade,* Vol. 14 (May, 1962), p. 24.

[38] Hargis, *Communism, The Total Lie!* (*op. cit.*), p. 67. Cf. Dean Smith, *Conservatism: A Guide to its Past, Present and Future in American Politics* (New York: Hearst Corporation, 1963), p. 193, "The Conservative position on foreign aid is that such aid should be given only where it bolsters our allies in the global battle against Communism."

[39] Hargis, *Weekly Crusader,* Vol. 3 (April 5, 1963), p. 5.

be reasonable to expect strong opposition from the Kremlin. He finds such opposition to be lacking.

Agricultural and technical assistance given to the Polish, Yugoslav, and other Communist governments comes in for the harshest indictment. "Foreign aid to Communist Countries is sin," says Hargis.[40] "The Bible absolutely forbids me to participate in a foreign aid program to an atheistic government. Try as hard as you may, you can not erase from the pages of the Bible the commandment 'NEITHER BID THEM GODSPEED.' "[41] Accordingly, "We are actually guilty of persecuting the Believers in Yugoslavia, Poland, Hungary, even the Soviet Union, because we financed the godless despots who declared war against God's remnant in those countries."[42]

Besides supporting atheism and religious persecution, the extension of assistance to "bloc" countries presumably has another detrimental effect, this time on America itself. "They take American money and use it to fight on the side of the Kremlin. Because such money is used by anti-Christian forces, the God and Father of the Lord Jesus Christ can not continue to bless the nation — for to do so would be to bless evil besides good."[43]

It is that simple; God cannot pour out His full blessing on His favorite nation because that nation is guilty of giving assistance to Communists. God's Israel has mingled with Canaanitish people. "The prayers of the Christian people of America are hindered," the account continues, "because their money goes to anti-Christian nations dedicated to the destruction of Christianity."[44]

What, asks Hargis, can one say about the promoters of such ventures? There is only one thing to say, he answers, "What word can describe such conduct except TREASON."[45]

---

[40] Hargis, *This I Believe* (*op. cit.*), p. 5.
[41] *Ibid.*
[42] *Ibid.*
[43] Hargis, *Communist America ... Must It Be?* (*op. cit.*), p. 142.
[44] *Ibid.*
[45] Hargis, *Communist America ... Must It Be?* (*op. cit.*), p. 138.

5. COMMUNISM
AND THE SOVIET UNION

HARGIS ONCE MENTIONED TO THIS WRITER THAT "NOTHING IS MORE important in our day" than "the fight against Communism." What does he mean by that term? How does Hargis perceive Communism? He is eager to let us know. In short, it is total and absolute evil. "All the corruptness of mankind was gathered together into one document, known as the Communist Manifesto. . . ."[1] In his widely circulated book, *Communism, The Total Lie!*, he asserts that "Communism is distortion, perversion, despotism, suspicion. It is deadly, venomous, intolerant, arbitrary, implacable, relentless, savage, ruthless, brutal, monstrous, bestial, murderous, deceitful, false, corrupt, evil, wicked."[2] His condemnation is boundless. Marx, Communism's notorious founder, is given special attention. "Of all the writings which have been since the world began," says Hargis, "the writings of Marx are the dullest and the most pedantic. . . . His creation emerged out of the depth of the ages dripping with all the slimy evil which has ever afflicted mankind. . . ."[3] Both Hargis's fundamentalist orientation and his non-historical perspective are revealed clearly in his further contention that Communism

---

[1] Hargis, *Communism, The Total Lie!* (*op. cit.*), p. 13. In view of the unqualified denunciation of Soviet Communism characteristic of the Far Right generally, the statement by Roy V. Peel, "The Wackacobi: Extremists of Our Own Times," *Western Political Quarterly*, Vol. 16 (September, 1963), p. 577, about the Wackacobi's "ambivalence of attitude respecting Russian Communism" is incorrect.

[2] Hargis, *Communism, The Total Lie!* (*op. cit.*), p. 28.

[3] *Ibid.*, p. 14. Note the statement on p. 8, "Stalin was one of history's most wicked men, and he was one of history's champion liars. Lenin was a greater liar than Stalin, but the greatest liars of all were the authors of the gospel of Satan, Karl Marx and Friedrich Engels."

is worldliness at its worldly worst. It is as ancient as the human, worldly race itself, having its beginnings in the first rebellion of Adam and Eve against the commandment of the Lord in the Garden of Eden. Although Communists claim Communism is new and wonderful, it is old and terrible, and it has had many names throughout the ages besides Communism.[4]

Lest anyone attribute any good thing to Communism, Hargis declaims, "Communism has destroyed more human life and more of the world's benefits than all of the [other] evil systems put together since the world began."[5]

For Hargis, Communism is a very broad category. "The American people," he believes, "need to see Communism for what it really is, whether disguised as liberalism, socialism, progressivism, or modernism."[6] "There is no sense in kidding ourselves, Socialism and Communism are one and the same."[7]

While a gradation of evil is admitted — "socialism, social reforms, liberalism, progressivism" are termed "embryo stages" of Communism[8] — this differentiation is much less important for Hargis than the "fact" that "leftism" represents the depth of conceivable depravity. Using the terms socialism and Communism interchangeably, Hargis analyzes history and predictably finds all the evidence on one side. "Socialism," we are told, "has wrecked the economy of every nation that has tried it."[9] Unfortunately, no statistics are cited. But the fact that Hargis means to include non-Communist countries, and that he intends the term "socialism" to refer to even fully democratic systems, is made clear by the following statement.

> Socialism, which is the drawing room name for Communism, has had more than a fair trial in England. The result was to be expected. England's socialistic government asserted over the worker the right to say where he should or should not work. The government asserted the right to throw the farmer off his farm if he did not comply with its directives.[10]

As indicated in an earlier chapter, Hargis sees Communism as the unequivocal antithesis of Americanism. He also sees it as the

---

[4] *Ibid.,* p. 13.
[5] Hargis, *Communist America . . . Must It Be?* (*op. cit.*), p. 165.
[6] *Ibid.,* pp. 21f.
[7] *Ibid.,* p. 58.
[8] Hargis, *Communism, The Total Lie!* (*op. cit.*), p. 6.
[9] Hargis, *The Facts About Communism and Our Churches* (*op. cit.*), p. 139.
[10] Hargis, *Communism, The Total Lie!* (*op. cit.*), p. 71.

opposite of Christianity.[11] From this perspective he asserts that "Communism is not a system of government, it is a religion."[12] Or, perhaps more correctly, it is irreligion. Hargis states that he believes "with all my heart" that "atheism is three-fourths of the way to Communism."[13] Thus Hargis concludes that atheism is virtually synonymous with Communism and that Christianity is equal to anti-Communism.

Sometimes, however, the analysis shifts to the level of economics. In that case Communism is, of course, depicted as the ultimate antithesis of capitalism. In his first major book, Hargis says that the only alternative to capitalism is Communism, "which is really nothing more than a moth-eaten theory which has been discredited before the Pyramids were built."[14] Modifications and halfway points are ignored.

Eric Hoffer has well said, "Mass movements can rise and spread without belief in a God, but never without belief in a devil."[15] The religious Far Right, as exemplified by Hargis, lacks nothing in this respect. Not only is God real and vivid, but there is a very real devil. In fact, there are two devils, the religious, the Satan of the Bible, and the political, Marx and his doctrines, and the two ultimately merge into one, for Marxism is seen as a manifestation of Satan. Communism is satanic, is "of the devil." Such phrases ring forth almost endlessly, and they are obviously not meant to be taken symbolically. "Without a doubt," says Hargis, "Communism has been conceived in the brains of the devil, spawned in hell, and receives its inspiration and direction from Satan." He then quotes Ephesians 6:12.[16] And again, "It is apparent upon examination that Communism cannot be of human origin, for human beings are of

---

[11] For Hargis, Communism seems to be the negative component of all important dualisms. He sees it as the opposite of Christianity, Americanism, capitalism, freedom, conservatism, God, happiness, progress, and much more. Very little mention is made of any evil without it being somehow related to Communism.

[12] Hargis, *Communism, The Total Lie!* (*op. cit.*), p. 65.

[13] Hargis, *Christian Crusade*, Vol. 15 (June-July, 1963), p. 4.

[14] Hargis, *Communist America... Must It Be?* (*op. cit.*), p. 94.

[15] Eric Hoffer, *The True Believer* (New York: New American Library, 1951), p. 86. Cf. Hoffer's view (p. 22) that "faith in a holy cause is to a considerable extent a substitute for the lost faith in ourselves." The present writer believes that this is not a true depiction of Hargis.

[16] Hargis, *Communism, The Total Lie!* (*op. cit.*), p. 25. Ephesians 6:12 states, "For we wrestle not against flesh and blood, but against principalities, against powers, against the rulers of the darkness of this world, against spiritual wickedness in high places."

themselves incapable of total corruption. Only Satan could inspire in human beings complete dedication to utter folly, unspeakable horrors, and total untruth. Only Satan can be the inspiration for Communism. . . ."[17]

The identification of political phenomena with the religious is complete and unqualified, and to Hargis the fact is perfectly clear. "As Jesus plainly said in John 8:44 (of such as Communists to-day)[18] 'Ye are of your father the devil, and the lusts of your father ye will do. He was a murderer from the beginning, and abode not in the truth, because there is no truth in him. When he speaketh a lie, he speaketh of his own; for he is a liar, and the father of it.' "[19] But the fact that Communism is empowered with all the forces and wiles of Satan is not as disconcerting as it might be, since the corollary is that Jesus came "to destroy the works of Satan." It follows that "Communism, which is satanic, is also doomed for destruction by Christ."[20]

This satanic dimension of Communism is significant also in relation to recognizing conspiratorial activities. Presumably, only a Christian filled with the Holy Spirit is properly equipped to recognize the workings of "the unholy spirit." Spirit-filled, he perceives what others cannot. Thus Hargis is not surprised that many people, including most sophisticated intellectuals, disagree with much of his diagnosis. This situation makes sense to him; popularity with sophisticated people would suggest that he was deviating from the truth. Educated persons cannot be expected to see what he sees. His ability in detecting evil is simply a result of his greater spirituality, as it is also a proof thereof.

In his depiction of Communism as a religion antithetical to Christianity, Hargis fills in many details and draws some interesting parallels. As already suggested, his initial premise is that "Communism is the essence of evil, directly opposite to Christianity which is the essence of good. One is the doctrine of hell, the other the doctrine of heaven; one of Satan, the other of God."[21] He continues, "Israel" (and by inference, America) "was called in love to be the chosen people of God. Russia was forced in hate to be the chosen people of Satan."[22] As Matthew, Mark, Luke, and John were moved

---

17 *Ibid.*, p. 7.
18 The bracketed statement is in the original.
19 Hargis, *Communism, The Total Lie!* (*op. cit.*), p. 29.
20 *Ibid.*, p. 26.
21 *Ibid.*, p. 15.
22 *Ibid.*, p. 10.

by the Holy Spirit to record the Gospel of Christ, so Marx and
Engels "were moved by the unholy spirit to write the gospels of
Satan."[23]

Sometimes the parallel is shifted slightly. We read, for example,
"As dedicated as Paul was to Christ, just as dedicated was Marx to
Satan."[24] Harking back to the Old Testament account, Hargis de-
claims, "as Moses needed Aaron, Marx needed Engels."[25]

The identification of Communism as the Antichrist occurs
frequently. I John 4:3 is cited as proof; "and this is that spirit of
Antichrist, whereof ye have heard that it should come; and even
now already is in the world." The Marxist dialectic and theory
of inherent contradictions are related to the statement in Revelation
13:11 that the Antichrist will be counterfeit and will exhibit many
forms of contradiction; for example, although a lamb, he will have
horns. Furthermore, does not Revelation 12 state that in John's
vision "there appeared a great red dragon, having seven heads and
ten horns, and seven crowns upon his heads. And his tail drew the
third part of the stars of the heaven"?[26] Obviously there is much
room for analogy here. Quoting the editor of the *Baptist Bible
Tribune,* Hargis answers the question, "What is the spirit of the
Anti-Christ?" "It is the spirit of internationalists and one worlders
demanding, in the name of unselfishness, humility, and peace, that
the constitutional sovereignty of the American people be sacrificed
to a universal atheistic state."[27] Hargis laments that "the world has
sought other explanations for Communism than a spiritual explanation" — "the world has looked to man for an explanation of Communism instead of to God."[28]

This perception of Soviet Communism as the Antichrist movement prophesied in the Bible, a movement that will cunningly de-

---

23 *Ibid.,* p. 3.
24 *Ibid.,* p. 13.
25 *Ibid.,* p. 14.
26 For extensive treatment of Russia in prophecy, from the fundamentalist
perspective, see one of the editions of Rev. Gerald B. Winrod's 10-volume
study of prophecy. He identified the Gog of Ezekiel as the Soviet Union
and stated, "Every genuinely informed student of eschatology knows that
Gog will eventually make war with the nations of the Western world. For
this reason it is asinine to think of the United States entering upon a permanent merger of interests with Russia." This excerpt is quoted in G. Myers,
History of Bigotry in the United States (New York: Random House, 1943),
p. 420.
27 Hargis, *Communism, The Total Lie!* (*op. cit.*), pp. 25f.
28 *Ibid.,* p. 29.

ceive millions, accounts for at least some of the fanaticism of fundamentalist anti-Communism. These believers, convinced that because of their faith they will recognize this eschatological manifestation of evil, are not distressed by others who disagree. After all, does not the Bible plainly teach that many nominal believers will be caught up themselves in the spell cast by the Antichrist and will rush to aid his cause?[29] From this viewpoint, then, the greater the opposition experienced by fundamentalist anti-Communists, the more credible their cause seems to themselves and the more strenuous will be their efforts to "fight for righteousness."

Naturally, Hargis completely condemns the Soviet Union. As the headquarters of the global "satanic" conspiracy, it is by definition totally corrupt. "The Soviet Union since 1917," he observes, "has been a hell on earth."[30] Communist doctrine has been the total undoing of the country, and Communism itself has prevented all progress. "The Soviet Union has the worst educational system in world history."[31] "Illiteracy and ignorance have become plagues of Russia, for millions of people since 1917 have had no education in truth and very little education in anything."[32] Hargis never attempts to explain how a society in such educational poverty has managed to become the second most powerful country in the world and the recognized leader in several areas of the new space sciences. Nor is any recognition given to the very impressive advances in living standards. Indeed, Hargis argues that "in spite of their vast resources of slave labor, communist lands have the world's lowest standards of living,"[33] and that the Soviet Union itself has "one of the world's lowest."[34] Communism not only causes stagnation, but actual deterioration, even in education.

Hargis is especially upset by accounts which purport to show Soviet educational achievements and which are critical of certain American practices. To him it is obvious that

> such an educational system as the Communists do have could not produce anything but human robots, who can be used to kill, to destroy, to rape, to murder, to confiscate, to liquidate, and to enforce the ruthless will of their slavemasters.... Yet, the Amer-

---

[29] See I John 2:18-22; I John 4:3; II John 7f.; II Thessalonians 2:9-12.
[30] Hargis, *Communism, The Total Lie!* (*op. cit.*), p. 15.
[31] *Ibid.*, p. 67.
[32] *Ibid.*, p. 68.
[33] *Ibid.*, p. 171.
[34] *Ibid.*, p. 134.

ican people are disturbed and confused by claims of American educators that Russia is in the lead.[35]

The black versus white, Russian versus American analysis continues. "There is no freedom of any kind in the Soviet Union."[36] "All people under Communism are slaves — whether inside or outside prison walls, and the role of women is the same, whether inside or outside prison walls. The only escape is death."[37] Oblivious to the fact that scores of churches are currently functioning in the Soviet Union (although the number is admittedly small and their freedom restricted), Hargis claims that no one is "permitted to worship God either in St. Basil's or any other place inside the Kremlin walls or anywhere else inside the Soviet Union."[38]

Although Hargis rarely indulges in personal ridicule, he is unrestrained in his description of former premier Nikita Khrushchev, the "ugly roly-poly paragon of Satanic Communism...."[39] More typical is his complaint that "the Soviet Union ... has abolished ... nationalism, or love of country, abolished the family unit...."[40]

This tirade of derision brings to mind Eric Hoffer's comment about the *True Believer,* for whom "the ideal devil is a foreigner," and that "to qualify as a devil a domestic enemy must be given a foreign ancestry."[41] Whether Hoffer is altogether correct or not, the Soviet Union fits the description perfectly. For Hargis, the Soviet Union's connection to the domestic conspiracy is unassailable, and everything is frighteningly vivid.

---

[35] *Ibid.,* p. 69.

[36] Hargis, *Communism, The Total Lie!* (*op. cit.*), p. 5. He adds, "any worship which exists is entirely underground."

[37] *Ibid.,* p. 17.

[38] *Ibid.,* p. 19. See Paul B. Anderson, "Religious Liberty Under Communism," *A Journal of Church and State,* Vol. 6 (Spring, 1964).

[39] *Ibid.,* p. 54.

[40] Hargis, *Communist America ... Must It Be?* (*op. cit.*), p. 13.

[41] Hoffer, *op. cit.,* p. 87. Peel, *op. cit.,* p. 576, argues that the Wackacobi are anti-Communist because Communism is foreign, not because of any intrinsic quality of Communism. The evidence does not justify this conclusion.

6. THE UNITED NATIONS

"The United Nations is the beginning of the end for the
United States,"[1] says Hargis; "the enemy marches on our shores from
the United. Nations. . . ."[2] The United Nations organization is an
evil plot, as evidenced first by its origin.

> The United Nations, which severely threatens the sovereignty of
> our nation, was conceived in subterfuge and was clearly the re-
> sult of careful Kremlin planning. . . .
>
> Many well informed persons have reason to believe that the
> United Nations charter was written by Alger Hiss and Molotov.
> In essence, it is taken almost entirely from the phoney constitu-
> tion of the Soviet Union. . . .[3]

Hargis believes that by now it must be clear to all who look at "the
facts" that "the United Nations is the result of a declaration from
Moscow, and is becoming itself a Moscow declaration."[4]

The major difficulty with the United Nations, says Hargis, is
that it rests on false premises and false assumptions. For one thing
"the present day concept of the brotherhood of all men is not a
Christian principle"; properly understood, the concept refers to
Christians only.[5] Then, too, the de-emphasis of nationalism is

---

[1] Hargis, on KAIL-TV, Fresno, October 25, 1964.

[2] Hargis, *Christian Crusade*, Vol. 13 (February, 1961), p. 18. Concerning
the United Nations and its activities, Hargis does not logically analyze the
merits of United Nations aims, but postulates American goals — as he perceives them — as "given" and then asks whether the United Nations supports
these American goals.

[3] Hargis, *The United Nations* (Christian Crusade Pamphlet, n.d.), pp.
2, 3, 6.

[4] Hargis, *Communist America . . . Must It Be?* (*op. cit.*), p. 119.

[5] Hargis, *The Facts About Communism and Our Churches* (*op. cit.*), p.
145. The verses he refers to include I Peter 2:17 and Galatians 4:1-4.

dangerously un-Christian. "If this Republic is to be saved, we must
... rebuild the broken walls of nationalism."[6] This is not the time,
argues Hargis, for international "do-goodism" and sentimental internationalism. "The primary threat to the United States is internationalism,"[7] and, conversely, as a supporter puts it, "it is the
United States and not the United Nations that is the hope of free
men."[8] Thirdly, of the international law promoted by the United
Nations Charter, Hargis says, "actually, there is no such thing as
international law...."[9] And the report that the chairman of the
United Nations' International Law Commission is looking forward
to an "increasing...role of international law in international relations" reveals only the chairman's ignorance. The sad fact is, Hargis adds, that "some misinformed Americans look forward to the
same thing."[10]

From any viewpoint, claims Hargis, the United Nations is bad
for America. "The hideous glass House that Hiss built" poses a real
threat. "The United Nations exists to take away from America even
its right to determine where its own money shall be spent, by whom
it shall be spent, and whom it should benefit."[11] Shame on Christians who support this monstrosity, says Hargis. "Instead of prayers
for the U. N. America's churches should appeal in their prayers for
protection of our nation from the terrible fate toward which the
United Nations is leading it."[12] A model prayer is presented:

> Let us pray: Our Heavenly Father, may we never be guilty of
> betraying Christ as did the disciples years ago.... May we stand
> and fight for America, regardless of the consequences, realizing
> that America is God's greatest nation in this world.[13]

A significant part of Hargis's animosity toward the United
Nations is based on his conviction that it represents the final attempt
at world government ostensibly predicted in biblical prophecy. The
view that this world dictatorship will be established by the Anti-

---

[6] Hargis, *Christian Crusade,* Vol. 13 (June, 1961), p. 20.

[7] Cited in *The Fall 1962 Guide to Current American Government* (Washington, D.C.: Congressional Quarterly Service, 1962), p. 64.

[8] Charles M. Crowe, *Christian Economics,* Vol. 15 (March 19, 1963), p.
1. Hargis frequently expresses similar sentiments, especially on his radio
programs.

[9] Hargis, *The Facts About Communism and Our Churches (op. cit.),* p.
206.

[10] Hargis, *Weekly Crusader,* Vol. 4 (September 4, 1964), p. 2. See also
his further comments on page 3.

[11] Hargis, *Communist America...Must It Be? (op. cit.),* p. 122.

[12] Hargis, *Weekly Crusader,* Vol. 3 (November 8, 1963), p. 6.

[13] Hargis, *Christian Crusade,* Vol. 13 (February, 1961), p. 18.

christ presumably dovetails with the notion of Communism as the Antichrist's ideology. Since the empire of the Antichrist is identified with Communism, and the United Nations as part of the Communist plot, the United Nations is viewed as a phenomenon of the Antichrist. For this reason more than any other the fledgling "Parliament of man" must be denounced as part of the total satanic plot against God. What began with Lucifer's rebellion in heaven will culminate in a world government propounding enmity with God. "By the total exclusion of God, [sic] United Nations is atheistic. By its inclusion of Communist nations, [sic] United Nations is Anti-Christ,"[14] says Hargis. What began as a theory is soon depicted as fact. The exact nature of Hargis's views on the eschatological interrelationship of Communism, the United Nations, and world government is revealed in the following excerpt from his book, *Communist America... Must It Be?*

> In Revelation 13 ... John saw through the spirit of prophecy a great world dictator arising in the end-time, one world government. In verse 7 we read: "...and power (authority) was given him over all kindreds, tongues, and nations." This great world dictator does not acquire this world power by force of arms, but it is "given him." There is only one way that such a world dictatorship could be given any one man, and that is by the representatives of the nations of the world sitting in legal session in a one world government.... This is exactly how it will come about, according to Bible prophecy.
>
> This great world dictator over a one world government will be the very devil incarnate... "and the dragon (Satan, the devil) gave him (world dictator, Antichrist) his power, and his seat, and great authority...." The United Nations gives every indication of fulfilling Bible prophecy concerning the end time.[15]

Thus the United Nations is the diabolic agency through which a world dictator will emerge. The implication is that the Secretary-General's post will emerge as the world presidency.

Quite apart from the matter of prophecy, the United Nations is incompatible with Christianity on the basis of its record, says Hargis. "Scripture warns us to test every spirit to see if it is good, if

---

[14] Hargis, *Communist America... Must It Be?* (*op. cit.*), p. 132.

[15] *Ibid.*, pp. 131f. Cf. Wilbur M. Smith, *This Atomic Age and the Word of God* (Boston: Wilde, 1948), p. 195, where the author says that "at the end of this age there will appear on this earth one great, powerful, final world ruler, a hater of God and a persecutor of God's people, the Scriptures clearly testify...." For a discussion of "The World Dictator of Daniel and Revelation" see pages 195-208.

it is of God or of Satan. Test the Spirit of the United Nations, to
see whether it is good or evil, of God or of Satan. You will find
that it is of Satan — against America."[16] The evidence is there for all
to see; "the United Nations has never recognized God. Indifferent
to the atheism of Russia and the heathenism of other countries, we
turned our backs on God, without even a bold demand for open
recognition of God in United Nations chambers." That was one of
the biggest and most revealing mistakes of all, argues Hargis. "The
God of our Fathers who granted us victory in World War II has
been ignored in the United Nations chambers." This policy is
"morally wrong," insists Hargis. "As a Christian, I protest this shabby
treatment of the most important source of peace ... Almighty
God."[17]

Related to the indictment for not revering God is the charge
that the United States is sinning by being "yoked together" with
"ungodly" member states. The "UN bears the curse of God for its
inclusion of godless nations." Hargis claims that the majority of the
nations are ungodly and thus, "from its beginning, the United
Nations has deliberately ignored the Lord God Almighty and the
Lord Jesus Christ."[18] The conclusion is categorical; "participation in
the United Nations is sin," says Hargis. "As a Christian," he adds,
"I have no choice. ... God commands in Psalm 1: 'Blessed is the
man that walketh not in the counsel of the ungodly.' God has
spoken once and for all."[19]

Again we encounter the antipathy to all compromise and
negotiation. "In peaceful coexistence between opposing ideologies,
the more sinister and subversive of the two will triumph. This is a
law of God. You can't do business with the devil."[20] There is no point
even in attempting it. "If Jesus Christ couldn't co-exist and work
harmoniously with the forces of evil, why do our present leaders
think they can?" he asks. "It's rather presumptuous to say the
least."[21] Interestingly, this logic is not applied to the ultimate conflict between God and Satan. The inconsistency is not explained.

The Specialized Agencies, the various service departments, and

---

16 Hargis, *Communist America ... Must It Be?* (*op. cit.*), p. 133.

17 Hargis, *This I Believe* (Christian Crusade Pamphlet, n.d.), p. 6.

18 Hargis, *Communist America ... Must It Be?* (*op. cit.*), p. 130. See also
page 97, where Hargis accuses the Communists of "changing traditional
Christmas decorations into heathen 'United Nations — We Believe' themes."

19 Hargis, *This I Believe* (*op. cit.*), pp. 5-6.

20 Hargis, *This I Believe* (*op. cit.*), p. 6.

21 *Ibid.* See also Hargis, *Communist America ... Must It Be?* (*op. cit.*),
p. 19.

individual United Nations leaders are objects of shrill criticism. Americans must be alert, warns Hargis, because United Nations-sponsored attacks are subtle and numerous. For example, several agencies are guilty of trying to undermine the Christian faith by "substituting the psychiatrist for the preacher!"[22] UNICEF is seen as a sinister scheme; its Halloween collections as a clever deception. "Unless you and I put a stop to this Unicef Trojan horse," Hargis claims, "our children will become tools of one world international-ists now and ultimately become the slaves of the communist dictators of the future."[23]

In terms of notoriety, no agency surpasses UNESCO, in Har-gis's opinion, for it has furthered Communism more than any other agency. How could results be other than what they are, in view of the "fact" that "UNESCO is polluted with communists, pro-communists, fellow travellers, sympathizers, dupes and world govern-ment dreamers."[24] In his pamphlet, *UNESCO, The Snake in Our Schoolroom, We Put It There*, Hargis elaborates his charges that this agency is the propaganda arm of the United Nations, and that its main function is to brainwash the American public.[25]

Judgments passed on various United Nations Secretaries-General are equally denunciatory. "Why the first head of the United Nations should not have been a loyal, patriotic Christian-American is one of the mysteries of the ages," as far as the Tulsa evangelist is con-cerned.[26] Why did it have to be "the communist conspirator, Alger Hiss"?[27] The reference presumably is to Hiss's role at the San Francisco founding conference. In a passage on Trygve Lie, Hargis illustrates that like certain other "true believers," he too can see relationships where none, in fact, exist. He says,

> The second Secretary-General...was Trygve Lie...who, some-time before January 28, 1921, negotiated a secret agreement on behalf of the Norwegian Labor Party, pledging unconditional obedience to the Comintern in Moscow. Lie visited Moscow in May, 1950, and the Korean War broke out just one month later.

22 Hargis, *Communist America...Must It Be?* (*op. cit.*), p. 127.
23 Hargis, *Weekly Crusader*, Vol. 1 (September 22, 1961), p. 8.
24 Hargis, *Communist America...Must It Be?* (*op. cit.*), p. 128.
25 Hargis, *UNESCO, The Snake in Our Schoolroom, We Put It There* (Christian Crusade Pamphlet, n.d.). See this for a very interesting descrip-tion of certain UNESCO publications.
26 Hargis, *Communist America...Must It Be?* (*op. cit.*), p. 123. Hiss served as a secretary at the founding conference; he never was a duly elected Secretary-General of the United Nations.
27 *Ibid.*

Lie resigned suddenly and unexpectedly on November 10, 1952, just when the patriotic Senator Pat McCarran was getting started with his exposures of Communist spies within the United Nations.[28]

Hargis can pin nothing specific on Dag Hammarskjold, but he does observe that "Hammarskjold called himself a Socialist 'but not a Communist.' In just what manner his 'Socialism' differed from Communism, he did not make clear."[29]

The current officeholder, U Thant, is labelled a "pro-Communist" who is constantly making "dictatorial demands."[30] The main charges against him stem from a speech which Thant delivered at Upsala University in Sweden, on May 6, 1962. Hargis alleges that the Burmese statesman "attacked the precious American heritage called the 'sovereign state,'" that he "referred to national sovereignty as a myth," and that he urged "member states to give up the concept of the absolute sovereign state."[31] What further evidence is needed — Thant is pro-Communist!

Hargis is equally critical of the Security Council and the General Assembly. He claims that "every decision of the United Nations... seems to help advance the cause of aggressive-godless Communism."[32] But then, what else can one expect; the United States "is now outvoted by a group of Africans not far advanced from savagery...."[33] The official American policy and its widespread acceptance confuse Hargis. "We cannot understand by what process some of the finest brains in all of Christianity have become so confused, so soft, that they would subvert this nation to the will of the polyglot that makes up the United Nations." He continues, "We are asked to surrender ourselves, our freedoms, our dreams, to the will of non-believers, to ignoramuses barely emerging from the Dark Ages...."[34] Hargis seems to harbor nothing but contempt for the new African members, for he states, "Included in recent admissions to the UN were 13 newly created African nations, most of

---

[28] *Ibid.*

[29] *Ibid.* For a true depiction of a deeply religious man, see Dag Hammarskjold, *Markings* (New York: Knopf, 1964).

[30] Hargis, *Is Freedom of Speech Dead in the US?* (Christian Crusade Pamphlet, January, 1963), p. 3.

[31] Hargis, *Christian Crusade,* Vol. 15 (January, 1963), p. 14. See also Julian William's article in *Weekly Crusader,* Vol. 3 (October 4, 1963), p. 4.

[32] Hargis, *Communist America...Must It Be? (op. cit.),* p. 8.

[33] Hargis, *Weekly Crusader,* Vol. 2 (April 13, 1962), p. 7.

[34] Hargis, *The Far Left (op. cit.),* p. 233.

which were only slightly removed from cannibalism, and which have strong pro-communist leanings."[35]

Obviously, any American aid or technical assistance for struggling new nations should be rejected. The only help which Hargis would endorse is that which contributes to "American military purposes."[36] All else should be eliminated because it is socialistic. This philosophy is summed up tersely by Howard Kershner, a Rightist economist often praised by Hargis: "If the United Nations achieves the ideal of many of its supporters — more and more equalization of wealth — civilization will disappear."[37]

Some unusual opinions are expressed by Hargis about the United Nations police action in Korea and the Congo. It is categorically stated, for example, that the United Nations "Military Staff Committee . . . was responsible for the strategic direction of the United Nations armed forces" in Korea,[38] and that the United States could easily have won the Korean War were it not for the fact that America's "hands were tied."[39] It is stated that "through membership in the United Nations . . . the United States surrendered its right to win a war," and "was forced to settle on Communist terms."[40] These are the facts, as Hargis sees them; "the United Nations refused America the victory."[41]

Concerning United Nations activity in the Congo and the United Nations Congo Police Force specifically, we read, "The action in Katanga is nothing short of lunacy. . . . The United Nations . . . sent troops into the Congo to prevent self-determination of a civilized and Christian province which did not want to be part of a Communist-controlled Congo."[42] The fact that this same United Nations' relief activities rescued hundreds of Protestant and Catholic missionaries in late 1964 and 1965 is ignored.

The United Nations is even held responsible for the disastrous Cuban Bay of Pigs affair. Writing in Hargis's *Weekly Crusader,* Congressman James B. Utt, a close co-worker with Hargis, declares, "Our defeat in the abortive Cuban invasion can be laid on the

[35] Hargis, *The United Nations* (Christian Crusade Pamphlet, n.d.), p. 5.
[36] Hargis, *A Call to Action to Every Real American* (Christian Crusade Pamphlet, n.d.), p. 5.
[37] Howard E. Kershner, *Socialism — Reversal of God's Design* (Christian Freedom Foundation Pamphlet, n.d.), p. 12.
[38] Hargis, *Communist America . . . Must It Be?* (*op. cit.*), p. 125.
[39] *Ibid.,* p. 124.
[40] *Ibid.*
[41] Hargis, *Communism, The Total Lie!* (*op. cit.*), p. 69.
[42] James B. Utt, *Weekly Crusader,* Vol. 3 (January 4, 1963), p. 7.

doorstep of the United Nations, as the United Nations treaty pro-
hibits us from engaging in any military operations without the con-
sent of the Security Council...."[43] How the United States managed
to give even its limited support to the invasion, how it presumably
hoodwinked the entire Security Council, how it did so in good
conscience, and on what grounds this partial flouting of the alleged
Charter injunction was justified, is not explained. Apparently the
United Nations is also responsible for the initial establishment of
the Castro regime. Hargis himself writes, "because of United Nations
restrictions, we could not prevent the victory of atheistic communism
in Cuba."[44] The restrictions are not identified.

An additional criticism of the United Nations relates to its
presumed role in the expansion of the Red Empire in Africa and
Asia. Hargis writes that the United Nations has been instrumental
in "decrying the colonialism of Western nations while fostering increased Communist colonialism."[45] In a polemic directed against
"UN propagandists," Hargis asserts that "they fail to remind themselves and others that during the UN lifespan, the International
Communist conspiracy has grown from a slave empire of 200 million
to almost 1 billion."[46] He continues, "The enslavement of the human
race has been progressing steadily since the world's peace-keeping
activities were assigned to the United Nations."[47] The inference of
direct causality is obvious, but no supporting evidence is produced.
As Hargis sees it, this great expansion of Communism, attributable
to the United Nations, is a major reason why "Khrushchev and his
fellow international communist gangsters are not working to destroy
the United Nations." In fact, that is why "they want to retain and
strengthen it."[48]

There seems to be widespread agreement among Hargis and
his associates that the United Nations is a major headquarters of
Soviet espionage. James Utt insists that it is the "biggest fifth
column in the world."[49] Hargis expands on this assertion, saying
that because of UN diplomatic immunity, "these foreign agents [i.e.
UN delegates] — many of whom are saboteurs — have complete

---

[43] *Ibid.*
[44] Hargis, *Weekly Crusader*, Vol. 2 (April 13, 1962), p. 7.
[45] Hargis, *The United Nations (op. cit.)*, p. 6.
[46] *Ibid.*, p. 5.
[47] Hargis, *Weekly Crusader*, Vol. 3 (November 8, 1963), p. 1.
[48] *Ibid.*, p. 4. Hargis does not explain why the Soviet Union does not
pay its assigned dues, or why it insults United Nations officials, etc.
[49] James B. Utt, *op. cit.*, p. 5.

access to our ports, railroads, airlines, communications, industrial plants, and defense installations."[50] A strange judgment, to be sure, but it is not the only one. We also encounter the unqualified insistence that "there are no provisions for amending the UN charter...."[51]

Despite all of the above denunciation, Hargis at times does agree that a greatly revamped United Nations might perhaps serve some useful functions. Of course, "as it is now, the United Nations is the cruelest hoax ever perpetrated on freedom-loving people."[52] But if, in keeping with Psalm 1, verse 1, "you could move the communists out and God in, the United Nations could be a workable affair."[53] Purged and reconstituted in this manner, it might have some limited usefulness. Recent travels have shown him, says Hargis, that "a working alliance of free nations is needed."[54] Thus, apparently, he would like to see the United Nations become an enlarged NATO to be used not to reduce friction between the two blocs, but as a marshalling device for one of them.

His harder line, however, is more representative of him, even after his travels. "There is not a respectable liberal in the United States," he wrote in 1963, "that can give one good reason why the United States should retain its membership in the United Nations."[55] It is "nothing more than a sounding board for communist propaganda and a mechanism for war instead of peace."[56] "Exposure" of the United Nations and resistance to it are the only honorable responses.

In summary, then, as Hargis sees it, the United Nations stands for centralization, world government, internationalism, foreign entanglements, atheism, un-Americanism, overt Communism, covert Communism, espionage, secularism, Social Gospel, compromise, and the Antichrist. The evidence, from his vantage point, is all on one side. He is convinced that the United States has only one alternative. It must "withdraw from the United Nations.... Conservative groups should support a bold and positive measure to get the US out of the UN and the UN out of the US."[57]

---

[50] Hargis, *Communist America ... Must It Be? (op. cit.)*, p. 119.
[51] *Ibid.*, p. 120.
[52] Hargis, *Communism, The Total Lie! (op. cit.)*, p. 37.
[53] Hargis, *This I Believe (op. cit.)*, p. 6.
[54] Hargis, in an interview with this writer, October 25, 1964.
[55] Hargis, *Christian Crusade*, Vol. 15 (January, 1963), p. 14.
[56] Hargis, *Weekly Crusader*, Vol. 2 (April 13, 1962), p. 7.
[57] Hargis, *Christian Crusade*, Vol. 14 (April, 1962), p. 15.

7. PHILOSOPHY OF GOVERNMENT

THE AIM OF THIS CHAPTER IS TO DELINEATE HARGIS'S BASIC POLITI-cal values, and his views on the role and nature of government in general. Evaluation is not the major purpose at present; a critical analysis follows in the next chapter.

In an interview with this writer, Hargis stated, "My philosophy is dogmatic." As one reads his books and articles it soon becomes evident that "dogmatic" is a correct label. Always resolute, he has categoric views on most issues and does not hesitate to voice them. Although he has had no university education in government or political theory, he exudes the confidence of a seasoned expert.

In answer to the basic question, What is government?, he answers unequivocally. "Government is force," and government is oppression.[1] Accordingly, "We believe the BEST governed are the LEAST governed,"[2] and the only way people can keep themselves free is "to keep their own government financially poor."[3] Nowhere does he describe a positive role for government, nowhere does he see it as a cooperative venture to enable all of society to accomplish what the individual members could not possibly do for themselves. His stand is clear. "Government does not create, it only takes by coercion and attempts to redistribute that [which is] created by others. This is what government does when it ventures outside the useful government function of administering justice among a cre-

---

[1] Hargis, *Communist America... Must It Be?* (*op. cit.*), pp. 138f.
[2] Hargis, *Weekly Crusader,* Vol. 2 (March 9, 1962), p. 8.
[3] Hargis, *Communist America... Must It Be?* (*op. cit.*), pp. 138f.

ative people."[4] Hargis quotes James B. Utt approvingly on this point. "Our founding fathers were well aware that man's eternal enemy was government, whether that government was a dictatorship, a benevolent monarch, a democracy, or a republic."[5]

The de-emphasis on governmental authority agrees with Hargis's basic assumption that political institutions and human laws function as inferior substitutes for divine government and divine laws — a true theocracy — and that the challenge and ultimate goal is to bring the former into alignment with the latter. Undoubtedly, Hargis would agree with the statement that "the better that men learn the profound truth of the lessons Christ taught, the more clearly they see that man-made laws are a poor substitute for the universal and eternal truths which make it possible for men to be free."[6] On several occasions Hargis deprecates human government to the extent that it is portrayed not as a laudable component of a greater divine order but as its opposite. Thus we are informed that "Satanic" Communism "has come along with insistence that America no longer look toward God, but instead toward government."[7]

Nevertheless, he also argues that human government is a highly praiseworthy endeavor and that it functions as a direct agent of God with primary responsibility to Him. Lamenting the trends of this century, Hargis observes, "Thus has the welfare of a great Christian nation been committed to 'sons of disobedience' instead of to the holy and perfect will of God."[8]

As suggested above, Hargis is very critical of the concept of a dynamic or an evolving constitution. He holds that "each step away from the principles upon which this nation was founded is another step towards cruel dictatorship."[9] Hargis attributes ultimate ideals to the founders of our country, and a permanent adequacy to the earliest political institutions. He accepts the "pre-

---

[4] Hargis, *American Socialism . . . Moving America Downhill* (Christian Crusade Pamphlet, n.d.), p. 2. Cf. "Let us never forget that when government planners seize power and dollars from the people to promote the people's welfare, they make the situation worse." Hargis, *Uncle Sam M. D.?* (Christian Crusade Pamphlet, n.d.). It would be interesting to see whether pensioners and disabled persons now receiving government assistance would agree with him. See also *Weekly Crusader*, Vol. 3 (July 5, 1963), p. 1.

[5] *Christian Crusade*, Vol. 15 (June-July, 1963), p. 5.

[6] *Aims and Procedures* (Christian Freedom Foundation Pamphlet, n.d.), p. 2.

[7] Hargis, *Christian Crusade*, Vol. 15 (June-July, 1963), p. 12.

[8] Hargis, *Communism, The Total Lie!* (op. cit.), p. 81.

[9] Hargis, *Weekly Crusader*, Vol. 3 (January 4, 1963), p. 2.

formation" thesis, which holds that a complete political theory was received via revelation from God. Hargis implies that the essential principles of all sound political institutions exist in the Divine Mind prior to all written forms and derivative laws, and that it is foolish for mere human beings to try to improve upon principles which originated with God. How can the created improve on the thought of the Creator? In support of his view, Hargis invokes no less a figure than the great emancipator himself. "Lincoln said, 'Our safety, our liberty, depend upon preserving the constitution of the United States as our Founding Fathers made it, inviolate. The people of the United States are the rightful masters of both Congress and the courts, not to overthrow the Constitution, but to overthrow the men who pervert the Constitution.' "[10] Hargis seems to subscribe fully to Joseph De Maistre's contention that a contract in itself does not make authority legitimate — Providence alone can establish legitimacy.[11] The Philadelphia Convention may have produced a contract, but from Hargis's viewpoint it is important to remember that the constitutional contract, like the Commandments at Sinai, was dictated by God.[12]

The evil which results if society strays from the original, undefiled principles is illustrated, as Hargis sees it, by the progressive income tax and its effects.

> Most of the devil's brew, mixed up by the Moscow clinic to slide us painlessly into the mental coma which is communism, has two basic ingredients, (1) the progressive income tax and (2) foreign aid.
>
> By far the more potent of these nostrums is the income tax. ... It gave us the flat, flabby dropsy of a bulging bureaucracy. It has left us a drooling hypochondriac, grasping at any and all Liberal-Socialist medicines.... Practically all our ills stem from this little pill, rolled for us in 1913 by the Marxist specialist.[13]

---

10 Hargis, *Christian Crusade*, Vol. 15 (May, 1963), p. 34.

11 Elisha Greifer, ed., *Joseph De Maistre: On God and Society* (Chicago: Regnery, 1959), p. xv. Note also the following statement by De Maistre (p. 63): "The history of all ages contains not one fact to contradict these maxims. No human institution can endure unless supported by Him who supports all — that is to say, unless it is specifically consecrated to Him at its origin."

12 See Hargis, *America, Let's Get Back TO GOD!* (Christian Crusade Pamphlet, n.d.).

13 Hargis, *Weekly Crusader*, Vol. 2 (March 30, 1962), p. 8. The single-factor analysis of all evil is, of course, not a new phenomenon on the American scene. For example, William Jennings Bryan, a former Secretary of State and three-time presidential candidate, stated in 1924, "All the ills from which

The progressive income tax and the "big government" with which it is associated are unequivocal evils, to be resisted to the utmost. "Bureaucracy," says Hargis, "is a disease, exactly like cancer. If its growth is not arrested in time, it is fatal."[14]

Hargis would like to see power revert back to "the people." "The source of government authority is the people of the United States. They delegate this authority to the federal government in the Constitution, but they delegated no authority other than that which is specifically described in the Constitution."[15] Hargis is convinced that "the hope of America is in its common people where the Faith of Our Fathers still is strong." In his emphasis on the common people and their native virtue, however, Hargis is not fully consistent. The notion that the will of the people is a manifestation of the will of God is rejected by Hargis, at least by implication, whenever "the people" disagree with him, as when Senator Goldwater was rejected for the presidency. Nonetheless, Lincoln is again invoked, "I have faith in the common People. Tell the people the truth and the Nation will be saved."[16] Speaking about the contemporary American situation, Hargis asserts that "the answer to the smears of deceived liberals is the voice of a free people whose loyalty is to God and Constitutional Government, not political parties."[17] The implication is that political parties and big government, or simply government, are directly responsible for thwarting the virtuous behavior of the common people and their natural propensity to establish God's Kingdom on earth. However, exaltation of the masses as the channel of God's political direction and the hope of political redemption runs counter to another frequently mentioned political dictum, namely, "America is not a democracy, but a Republic."[18] The contradiction is apparently not recognized. In any event, the dilemma is left unresolved.

America suffers can be traced back to the teaching of evolution. It would be better to destroy every other book written and save just the first three verses of Genesis." This statement is cited in Myrnard Shipley, *The War on Modern Science* (New York, 1927), pp. 254f. See also p. 130.

[14] Hargis, *Weekly Crusader*, Vol. 3 (February 8, 1963), p. 5. Cf. "Movements in recent years proposed to make the government of the United States bigger and bigger, have been Communist inspired, so that it will be easier for the communists to control the people once the government is taken over completely." *Communism, The Total Lie!* (*op. cit.*), p. 63.

[15] Hargis, *Weekly Crusader*, Vol. 4 (October 9, 1964), p. 3.

[16] Hargis, *Communism, The Total Lie!* (*op. cit.*), p. 8.

[17] Hargis, *Christian Crusade*, Vol. 14 (May, 1962), p. 6.

[18] Hargis, *Communism, The Total Lie!* (*op. cit.*), p. 43.

"Welfarism" is another favorite target. We read, "In spite of the attitude of left-wing liberal clergymen, there is nothing in the Holy Bible to justify turning the responsibility of caring for the needy over to the government."[19] Moreover, Hargis continues, government charity should be eliminated, because it is impersonal, it is credited to the wrong people, it soon is taken for granted and abused, it is cunningly used to buy votes, it produces more immorality and illegitimacy, it is given to the non-needy, and it tends to burgeon beyond all reasonable proportions. Hargis asks, "Did Jesus originate the 'Welfare State'?" to which he answers in the negative and offers biblical "proof." Passages such as Luke 12:13-15, Ephesians 4:28, and Galatians 6:2 are cited.[20] The first passage is a denunciation of covetousness, the second is a denunciation of stealing and an exhortation to generosity, the third urges the faithful to "bear one another's burdens." How these statements can be taken as a condemnation of government aid is not explained. But for Hargis, "welfarism" is thievery; "demanding money from the federal government is nothing more than demanding money from our fellow citizens."[21] The indictment continues, "under the welfare state philosophy, individual Americans are considered to be generally incapable of managing their own affairs. . . ."[22] Government assistance has not and will not work, it only aggravates problems. History, Hargis says, has shown that "the standard of living of the people under welfare state socialism will tend to go down and down, until nobody has anything except the rulers who run the government dictatorship."[23]

The only other legitimate function of government besides national defense[24] appears to be the restraint of evil. Force is needed to restrain the selfish interests of sinful men. Law, from this perspective, is seen not as a form of collective positive action, but mainly as an imposed restraint necessitated by the Fall. Hargis believes, on the basis of Romans 13 and other similar passages, that God did indeed establish civil power, but he is also convinced that this authorization included very specific, rigid limits. The power to restrain must itself be rigidly restrained.

---

[19] Hargis, *Weekly Crusader,* Vol. 2 (July 6, 1962), pp. 7f.

[20] *Ibid.,* pp. 1f.

[21] Hargis, *The Facts About Communism and Our Churches (op. cit.),* p. 138.

[22] Hargis, *Weekly Crusader,* Vol. 3 (January 4, 1963), p. 1.

[23] *Loc. cit.*

[24] Defense is seen as being only a negative action. Hargis seems to have no place for defense by preventive action, by cooperation, or by compromise.

"The thing that is needed," Hargis declares, "is a gradual turning back." All "programs which contain compulsion should be made voluntary."[25] That poverty and misery will then be constant ills is not denied, but simply considered unimportant. Scripture is again invoked, not as commanding charity and humanitarianism, but as justifying official inaction.

> Of course, anyone who believes in the Word of God knows that it is impossible to eliminate poverty. Our Lord and Savior Jesus Christ told us that the poor would be with us always. In the long run, much more could be done for the poor if it was taken out of the hands of the government and left to religious and charitable private organizations as it was in the past.[26]

One wonders if Hargis would be content with the poverty and disease which were commonplace before the inauguration of government welfare programs.

What Hargis favors, here as elsewhere, is conformity to traditional norms; he wants laissez-faire economics. He believes that "under a government based on Christian principles people can fail or succeed according to their own initiative and ability."[27] It seems as if shades of Darwinism have influenced his theology. He endorses the statement by the Reverend Mr. Mahaffey, another notable anti-Communist pundit, when he says, "Socialism stands condemned as opposed to Christianity.... Capitalism, on the other hand ... is the system that is in accord with Christianity."[28] As Hargis sees it, "When you lose the profit motive you lose the initiative."[29] It is as simple as that. In a flourish of adulation he declaims, "America's free enterprise system is the best form of industrial and political economy that the human mind has ever devised. Every civilization that has adopted the 'welfare' state philosophy of the communists has gone down to oblivion. It is no accident that America, with only a comparatively small land area, outproduced all the rest of the world many times over."[30] This quotation is particularly interesting because, in advancing the argument that the economic system of free enterprise is the cause of political freedom, Hargis seems to be accepting the Marxist doctrine of economic determinism, albeit in an inverted fashion.

---

25 Hargis, *Weekly Crusader,* Vol. 3 (July 5, 1963), p. 2.

26 Hargis, *Weekly Crusader,* Vol. 3 (April 19, 1963), p. 6.

27 Hargis, *The Facts About Communism and Our Churches (op. cit.),* p. 217.

28 Hargis, *Communism, The Total Lie! (op. cit.),* p. 74.

29 Hargis, on KAIL-TV, Fresno, October 25, 1964.

30 Hargis, *Communist America ... Must It Be? (op. cit.),* p. 91.

Hargis categorically rejects any notion that large, complex societies may necessarily require economic and political modifications. He states that some "Big Government" enthusiasts argue that

> the free market economy will work in a smaller, less complex society but will not work where the society of a nation becomes more complex as in present day, industrialized America. Actually, the truth is that the larger the economy grows, [the] greater is the need for the free market. As population grows the number of individual business transactions grow accordingly. Obviously, the difficulty of a relatively few individuals controlling the economic activities of millions of people increases as the population increases.[31]

Hargis's traditionalist stance on the questions of welfarism and free enterprise is reflected further in his views on civil liberties and freedom generally. He is constantly clamoring for full "constitutional freedoms," but what he means by this term is not altogether clear. Although at one point he asserts, "We are against censorship,"[32] and even argues convincingly for that view, this statement is not representative of his overall position. His definitions of liberty and freedom are not those of John Stuart Mill. For example, in his pleas for religious freedom the emphasis is not on freedom of religion, but on the "preservation of Christian freedom."[33] That the difference is fundamental is illustrated in his criticism of certain civil rights enthusiasts. He asks, "Whose 'civil rights' are the critics [of the House Un-American Activities Committee] defending?"[34] His main concern seems not to be "which" rights but "whose rights." One can conclude only that freedom is not an essential "good" in its own right and therefore to be given equally to all, but that it is a "good" only insofar as it advances the "right" cause. Hargis's underlying assumption concerning human freedom is that, since creation, the true believer is a free moral agent and can exercise his will, but that after he has made a commitment to "follow Christ" his freedom consists only of choosing "the right."

Occasionally Hargis implies that he considers the advocating of views with which he disagrees to be an abuse of freedom.[35] He asserts, "Academic freedom, however, was never intended to include the right to . . . peddle atheism in [the] public schools [i.e. universities]

---

31 Hargis, *Weekly Crusader*, Vol. 3 (January 4, 1963), p. 3.
32 Hargis, *Weekly Crusader*, Vol. 2 (March 9, 1962), p. 6.
33 Hargis, *Christian Crusade*, Vol. 14 (May, 1962), p. 6.
34 Hargis, *Communist America . . . Must It Be?* (*op. cit.*), p. 45. See also his statement in *Communism, The Total Lie!* (*op. cit.*), p. 70.
35 Hargis, *Communism, The Total Lie!* (*op. cit.*), p. 84.

of America. Therefore the return of academic freedom to the American campuses, as reported by Dr. Fine, is something to oppose rather than applaud."[36] Should a pro-Christian bias be required in political offices as well? Indeed it should, says Hargis. "We can and should deny the right of any individual to hold office who does not believe in God." Having quoted this view from another source, Hargis adds the unequivocal judgment, "Truer words could not be spoken."[37]

One reason given by Hargis for his view that there should be a pro-Christian emphasis everywhere is that neutral secularity is a myth; it can not and does not exist in education, in government, or anywhere else. It is nothing more than a figment of the imagination of certain liberals. "There can be no neutrality toward God," he insists. "A state system of education which leaves out the Bible and prayer is not neutral toward the Word of God, but is definitely against it."[38]

This is a direct application to the political arena of the simple good-evil dichotomy inherent in fundamentalist Christianity. Those who think they are neutral are not really neutral at all and are deceiving themselves. "He who is not with me is against me."[39] The prior question, whether this transfer of non-neutrality from the individual to the societal level is at all logical, is not asked. For Hargis the matter is clear, "To have no conviction about God is to guarantee a working by Satan for evil."[40] Translated into political terms, this opinion might read, "Not to be a dedicated patriot who manifests patriotism and Americanism whenever possible is to guarantee a working for leftist dreamers and the eventual victory of the international Communist conspiracy."[41]

The very concept of secularity, as distinguished from its desirability, is totally rejected. The idea that certain realms of societal activity can be seen as temporal and non-religious, and thus can be distinguished from the spiritual realm, does not exist for him. He sees two alternatives: either Christianity infuses all of a society's essence and activity, or it does not, in which case that society is displeasing to God.

---

36 Hargis, *Communist America . . . Must It Be?* (*op. cit.*), p. 72.
37 *Weekly Crusader*, Vol. 3 (June 7, 1963), p. 4.
38 Hargis, *Communist America . . . Must It Be?* (*op. cit.*), p. 65.
39 Matthew 12:30.
40 Hargis, *Communism, The Total Lie!* (*op. cit.*), p. 81.
41 For a more extended formulation of precisely this view see Hargis, *The Facts About Communism and Our Churches* (*op. cit.*), Chapter 1.

The substitute term for secularism is paganism, with its connotation of primitive and non-Christian jungle rituals. Hargis asks,

> Shall we sit meekly by and accept the anti-God decisions of the
> liberals that rule God out of public life or shall we obey the Lord
> as commanded in Isaiah 53:13, "All Thy Children shall be taught
> of the Lord"? Public education must be Christian — not pagan.
> We will go the way of France and the way of Great Britain if
> this trend is not soon stopped.[42]

The simplistic dichotomy is all-inclusive. "As God is totally
good, Satan is totally evil. Whatever is good is of God, and whatever
is evil is of Satan.... Neutrality towards God is impossible. Neutrality towards Satan is also impossible. Neutrality towards communism is impossible."[43] Neutrality does not exist.

Another facet of this rigid thought pattern is that religion
and politics are viewed as part of the same order; more specifically,
politics is an extension of religion. Thus we read, "religion and
politics cannot be separated or set off against each other."[44] The
argument is not that the tenets of the former produce guiding principles for the latter, but that the two are part of an all-inclusive
whole. Hargis's point is not that he necessarily desires it to be so,
but that God in His infinite wisdom has decreed it. The political
order, like the family and the church, is another of the God–man
relationships in which man's role is submissive obedience and
wholehearted adulation of God.

At the level of practical significance, Hargis's central argument
for a fusion of Christianity and government — he does not advocate a fusion of the state with a particular denomination — is that
"there is no freedom without God."[45] Christianity is posited as
a necessary and perhaps even a sufficient condition for liberty, at
least for the kind of liberty Hargis advocates. A non-political biblical statement in which the term "liberty" occurs is cited as supporting evidence. " 'Where the spirit of the Lord is, there is liberty,'
says the Scripture. This means that where the spirit of the Lord
is NOT, there is NO liberty."[46] Shifting to the offensive, Hargis
denounces "socialists" and fellow-travellers who say that "the rights
of the people stem from the state rather than from the true source
of all rights — Almighty God."[47]

---

[42] Hargis, *Christian Crusade*, Vol. 15 (August, 1963), p. 26.
[43] Hargis, *Communism, The Total Lie!* (*op. cit.*), p. 27.
[44] Hargis, *Weekly Crusader*, Vol. 2 (April 13, 1962), p. 3.
[45] Hargis, *Christian Crusade*, Vol. 14 (April, 1962), p. 3.
[46] Hargis, *Communism, The Total Lie!* (*op. cit.*), pp. 65f.
[47] Hargis, *Weekly Crusader*, Vol. 3 (January 4, 1963), p. 2.

Hargis's contention appears to be that a fusion of Christianity and government would pose a solution to all problems of state. "When America seeks the Lord with its whole heart, America will find Christ — and when Christ is found, there will be found also the perfect solution to all of America's problems — even the solution to Communism."[48] What that solution will be and how it will be implemented is not explained. The implication, however, is that the Soviet Union will be laid low and that the United States will receive its due reward of greatness and preeminence.

Since, for Hargis, the cause of God and the cause of country are properly one, patriotism becomes a cardinal Christian virtue. We read, "Patriotism and Christianity are very close to each other. It is impossible to be a true Christian and not be a true patriot. One who loves God also loves his country."[49] The reverse is argued as well, namely, "You cannot love the United States unless you first love God."[50] Since God and country are thus inseparable and constitute the greatest possible object of love and adoration, patriotism becomes another form of worship, and nationalistic fervor becomes evidence of true piety.

In view of all his ideological pronouncements, it is interesting to note Hargis's conception of the political spectrum and his place in it.[51] The extreme Left, in Hargis's opinion, includes not only Communists and Communist sympathizers but also Fascists and Nazis because, as he says, "they all follow basically the ideology of Karl Marx." Since all three supposedly rest all power in the hands of dictators, and since location of power is the basic criterion for him, Hargis places them in the same class. The only differences which he sees between Communism and Nazism-Fascism are: (1) Communism is international socialism while Nazism-Fascism is national socialism, and, (2) Under Communism, the government owns the means of production, while under Nazism-Fascism these means are formally under private ownership, but the governments "own the owners" and make "the vital decisions." The distinguishing trait is lack of freedom.[52] Movements and individuals, such as the British Labour Party and Western-style socialists, who have re-

---

48 Hargis, *Communist America . . . Must It Be? (op. cit.)*, pp. 165f.
49 Hargis, *Christian Crusade*, Vol. 15 (June-July, 1963), p. 12.
50 Hargis, *Christian Crusade*, Vol. 15 (October, 1963), p. 10.
51 This entire paragraph is based on Hargis's feature article in *Weekly Crusader*, Vol. 4 (December 20, 1963).
52 Hargis, *The Far Left (op. cit.)*, p. 106.

nounced violence and who hedge on other points of doctrine or method, constitute less extreme elements of the Left.

The extreme Right, says Hargis, would have to be those whose ideas are in greatest contrast to those on the extreme Left. "This is anarchism," where freedom is absolute and unfettered, "and no conservatives favor anything remotely resembling anarchism." However, the argument continues, left extremism and right extremism, if pushed far enough, tend to share certain outlooks, and this similarity, says Hargis, explains the actual occurrence in history of at least temporary alliances between Communists and anarchists as well as Fascists and anarchists.

The middle of the spectrum, the area of true moderation, is occupied "primarily" by "the type of freedom established by our founding fathers." Here we have "Constitutional law under which the government protects the lives, liberties and property of the people and does not interfere with them otherwise." To the extent that one wants more or less regimentation and control of society by government, one places oneself to the left or right of center. According to this criterion, "liberalism" is placed well to the left, because on the issues of government interference, regulation, and control "the policies of Fascism and ultra-left liberalism have many points of similarity."

At times, for the benefit of the millions who do not understand the political spectrum "correctly," Hargis describes himself as a member "of the so-called ultra-right."[53] But he much prefers being labelled a moderate, as defined above. It is, he says, the only proper designation. Referring to the conventional view of political ideology, he exclaims, "This entire scheme of classing anti-communist conservatives into the same camp with Fascists or Nazis is utterly ridiculous. No thinking American who has the slightest knowledge of the basic elements of Socialism, Communism, Fascism or Nazism should be deceived by such idiotic nonsense." What is needed is an all-out campaign of "education and truth."[54]

---

[53] Hargis, *Christian Crusade,* Vol. 14 (January-February, 1962), p. 2.
[54] Hargis, *Weekly Crusader,* Vol. 4 (December 20, 1963), p. 4.

8. AN ANALYSIS OF HARGIS'S POLITICAL THOUGHT

IN THE FOREGOING CHAPTERS WE HAVE SURVEYED HARGIS'S VIEWS and opinions on politics and government. We turn now to an evaluation of these views and an analysis of his political thought in general. It is not my intention to respond in detail to each of Hargis's claims and assertions; that would require undue repetition. Rather, my aim is to analyze a representative selection of Hargis's statements in each of the major subject areas discussed in the preceding chapters. These responses constitute Section I of this chapter. Section II is an analysis of Hargis's procedural techniques: consistency, accuracy, and overall methodology. Section III is an evaluation of Hargis's political thought taken as a whole.

I

How valid or correct is the view of American origins which Hargis presents? The evidence indicates that much of his description is factually correct, but that many of his inferences and conclusions are faulty. While it is true that "the aim of the religious believers who first arrived on the New England Coast was to create an ideal society, both civil and ecclesiastical, for Europe to copy,"[1] it is not at all definite that they succeeded. Moreover, it is not fully known what they meant by the term "ideal." Hargis apparently assumes that the term meant "ideally Christian." That there was official endorsement of Christianity is clear — this subject will be analyzed in Chapter 13 — but whether early American society actually functioned in accordance with Christian principles,

---

[1] George E. Probst, *The Happy Republic* (New York: Harper and Brothers, 1962), Harper Torchbooks edition, p. 222.

especially as defined by modern fundamentalism, is at best doubtful. Franklin Littell writes,

> The whole image of early America as a "Christian nation" (i.e. Protestant-controlled) is a lie which must be struck down: America was, in her colonial period — like continental Europe — officially religious and in fact characterized by "baptized heathenism"; in her early years as a nation she was overwhelmingly churched and heathen, regardless of pretensions and public claims.[2]

> In the colonial period, state churches were maintained at public expense.... The time of the founding fathers was not an age of Christian virtue.... The course of American history has been marked, by and large, by the effort to win a people back to the churches they had frankly abandoned when support ceased to be compulsory.[3]

Hargis also claims that early colonial America, even though it did not hesitate to use the state as the coercive arm of the church, nevertheless simultaneously gave America true freedom. Of this analysis of freedom and liberty in the Puritan era, George M. Waller states:

> The belief that the Puritans came to the New World in the cause of religious freedom is, of course, completely erroneous. The battle for toleration in this country was won in the face of their bitter opposition. It would have seemed to Mary Dyer, William Robinson, Marmaduke Stevenson and William Leddra, as they went to their fate on the gallows, ironical indeed that three centuries later their executioners should win applause as champions of religious freedom.[4]

Norman Cousins, in a slightly less harsh verdict, asserts that "it is one of the ironies of human history that what was to be a religious haven in the New World turned into an arena of fierce religious competition and discrimination."[5] Most experts agree that

---

[2] Franklin H. Littell, *From State Church to Pluralism* (Garden City, New York: Doubleday, 1962), p. xx.

[3] *Ibid.*, p. x.

[4] George M. Waller, ed., *Puritanism in Early America* (Boston: Heath, 1950), p. 111. Note also Littell's statement that "in the colonial period we have the whole theory and practice of 'Christendom,' precisely as found then in Europe. Religion was maintained at law; it was enforced by jailings and even by the death penalty; and little hesitancy was felt in compelling persons of no conscience or bad conscience to go through the motions of it." Franklin Hamlin Littell, "Religious Liberty in American History," *A Journal of Church and State,* Vol. 6 (Autumn, 1964), p. 322.

[5] Norman Cousins, *"In God We Trust," The Religious Beliefs and Ideas of the American Founding Fathers* (New York: Harper and Brothers, 1958), p. 11.

the political rights in which the Puritans and their immediate successors were most interested were not the rights of the individual, but independence from an antagonistic religion. "Their great aim was to secure a form of civil government under which their religious system could be best maintained. . . . They showed no great enthusiasm for political equality, and were not given to doctrinaire ideas about popular sovereignty."[6]

On the question of American origins, then, Hargis is perhaps correct in stressing the Christian motivation of the early colonists, but wrong in asserting that they advocated full religious freedom.

What about Hargis's view on the separation of church and state? Does he reflect the colonists' view of this principle? Evidence indicates that he is at least close to it. James E. Wood, Jr., has pointed out[7] that for the colonists the principle of separation never meant a repudiation of the concept of America as a Christian state. Bela Bates Edwards illustrates this viewpoint and speaks for his fellow colonists when he says, "Perfect religious liberty does not imply that the government of the country is not a Christian government." In his carefully documented study of early America, Winthrop Hudson has convincingly shown that the colonist's concept of separation of church and state was not derived from any abstract philosophical ideas about human freedom and equality. It was, he says, a distinctly religious principle reflecting the teaching of Romans 13, which was taken to mean that both church and state are intended to serve God, albeit in different ways.[8]

The colonist's unequal treatment of non-believers tends to corroborate Hargis's views. He is probably correct in attributing to the colonists the conviction, which he also holds, that "a nation could not prosper and retain freedom if God was separated from its national life."[9] Hargis also suggests that the First Amendment limitation of Congress clearly was not meant to imply that state legislatures, local school bodies and state boards of regents should not have the right to make laws respecting the establishment of reli-

[6] Raymond G. Gettell, *History of American Political Thought* (New York: Appleton-Century, 1928), pp. 68f. Note Chapter III, "Colonial Political Thought" and Chapter IV, "Political Thought of the American Revolution."

[7] James E. Wood, Jr., "Editorial," *A Journal of Church and State*, Vol. 6 (Autumn, 1964), pp. 277-284.

[8] Winthrop Hudson, *The Great Tradition of the American Churches* (New York: Harper and Row, 1953), pp. 42-49, esp. p. 42.

[9] Hargis, *Weekly Crusader*, Vol. 4 (December 27, 1963), p. 1.

gion.[10] He is probably correct. It is certainly true that Puritan theology, and much of Protestant theology in general, made no distinction in the eighteenth century between the secular and the spiritual. Life on this earth was little more than a brief episode in
the continuing struggle between God and Satan. Norman Cousins
states that early American leaders "connected their spiritual beliefs
to political action. They saw no walls separating science, philosophy, religion, and art."[11] Perry Miller explains, "By starting with the
proposition, 'the Magistrate hath a co-active power to compel the
Church to execute the ordinances of Christ,' the founders aligned
themselves with the then universal premise of Europe. As a matter
of fact, their peculiar ecclesiastical program obliged them to give to
this thesis a heightened and sharpened prominence."[12] Another
authority, James Bryce, sums up as follows:

> Someone has said that the American government and constitution
> are based on the theology of Calvin and the philosophy of Thomas
> Hobbes. This at least is true that there is a hearty puritanism in
> the view of human nature which pervades the instrument of
> 1787. It is the work of men who believed in original sin and
> were resolved to leave open for transgressors no door which they
> could possibly shut....[13]

In essentials, Hargis agrees with Cousins, Miller, and Bryce on the
issue of early American views on separation of church and state.

In this connection we need to remember that, even centuries
after the Reformation, the idea of close cooperation between church
and state was still widespread. Early Protestantism gave great reverence to the state, no doubt partly because of events which occurred during the period of antagonism between secular and papal
authorities. Indeed, the modern Western state is largely Protestant
in origin. The early reformers and their patrons aspired to establish
nation-states adhering as closely as possible to the Christian Way
as they saw it. It was generally agreed that manifestation of religion,

---

10 Hargis, *Weekly Crusader*, Vol. 3 (June 7, 1963), p. 1. For a scholarly
statement of a similar view, see Stokes and Pfeffer, *op. cit.*, pp. 91f.

11 Cousins, *op. cit.*, p. 1. Cf. pp. 10-14. Consider Alexis de Tocqueville's
observation, "Puritanism, as I have already remarked, was almost as much a
political theory as a religious doctrine." *Democracy in America*, Vol. 1 (New
York: Vintage, 1945), trans. Henry Reeve, p. 36.

12 Perry Miller, *The New England Mind: From Colony to Province* (Boston: Beacon, 1953), p. 119.

13 James Bryce, *The American Commonwealth*, Vol. 1 (New York: Putnam
edition, 1888), p. 306.

at least outwardly, was essential to national unity.[14] Hargis is simply reiterating this view and correctly asserting that it once was generally accepted. The somewhat surprising fact is not the nature of the view itself or its lingering popularity in some circles, but that it should be propounded by a fundamentalist who, when preaching "the Gospel," denounces formalistic and nominalistic Christianity as the cardinal sin of hypocrisy.

Even now, recent Supreme Court decisions notwithstanding, the traditional interpretation of this doctrine continues. In 1959 the Supreme Court of Oklahoma stated,

> It is a well-settled principle and philosophy of government that we should preserve separation of church and state, but that does not mean to compel or require separation from God.... It is well-settled and understood that ours is a Christian nation, holding the Almighty God in dutiful reverence.... All of our 50 state constitutions as well as the national constitution recognize the existence of God, and that we are a Christian nation and a Christian state....[15]

An even stronger statement comes from a well-known Protestant minister.

> By prohibiting the Congress from making any law respecting an establishment of religion or prohibiting the free exercise thereof, the states gave constitutional guarantees to the freedom of Christian religion. They had no intention of giving constitutional guarantees to atheism or any other religious system. They knew better. They knew it was impossible. To guarantee toleration of Christians means to outlaw all works that are anti-Christ.[16]

Evidence indicates that even such a narrow view as the above was not altogether unpopular in the 1780's. After all, Locke himself, the chief theoretician of the American constitution, did not extend toleration to Catholics and atheists.[17]

Hargis emphasizes that the American constitutional system, in its mature form, was revealed once and for all as the divine model for human society, and that our political aim should be to reconstruct and maintain that system. Hargis's view on this point is fairly close to the mainstream of traditional American thought.

---

[14] Evarts B. Greene, *Religion and the State* (Ithaca: Cornell University Press, 1941), Great Seal Book, 1959, esp. pp. 6-15.

[15] In *Weekly Crusader*, Vol. 4 (December 27, 1963), p. 2. For a summary of the surprisingly long list of Supreme Court statements supporting this view, see Stokes and Pfeffer, *op. cit.*, pp. 562f. and 568f.

[16] T. Robert Ingram, *Weekly Crusader*, Vol. 4 (March 20, 1964), p. 3.

[17] J. Salwyn Schapiro, *Liberalism: Its Meaning and History* (Princeton: Van Nostrand, 1958), p. 20. See also Reading No. 8.

As Boorstin has noted, "Perhaps never before, except conceivably in the modern state of Israel, has a nation so firmly believed that it was founded on a full-blown theory and hence that it might understand itself by recapturing a particular period in its past."[18] The whole notion of "givenness," of attributing mature political theory and philosophy of government to the founding fathers, of relying on the past to explain the present, is central to the traditional and the continuing creed of Americanism.

A word needs to be said about Hargis's comments on the Supreme Court. Operating on a double standard, he praises decisions with which he agrees, and denounces not only decisions but also the justices and the entire court system when he disagrees with its judgments. His statement, that "it does not make the slightest difference what nine political experts who are called Supreme Justices say," is an amazing assertion in the light of United States history or the history of any other government. Hargis is revealing the fact that he does not understand the role of the judiciary in a constitutional democracy. Apparently he believes that the judiciary should not be fully independent, that it should be, instead, the defender of an orientation, essentially religious in nature, which is advocated by certain groups within a society. His freedom-undermining argument is that, if the majority identifies with the "right" religious outlook, then the courts should grant that outlook legal sanction and support, even if such action means that the dissenting minority would thereby lose rights and freedoms guaranteed by the Constitution itself.

A further weakness in Hargis's analysis of America is his fusion of Americanism with Christianity. In the first place, he creates a dilemma for himself in that his political ideology contradicts his fundamentalist theology. The definitions of "Christian" which are implied in his various nationalistic-political and theological arguments cannot all stand. Hargis cannot point to the merely formal rituals, the nominalism, and the external paraphernalia as evidence of "being Christian" and at the same time define "becoming a Christian" in terms of the usual fundamentalist prerequisites of repentance, confession, conversion, and personal faith. The two criteria are incompatible, no matter how much this fact is glossed over. Unconsciously, Hargis admits this, for in his various roles he shifts from one standard to the other. When he speaks about Communism and political issues, the emphasis is on Christian-Ameri-

---

[18] Daniel J. Boorstin, *The Genius of American Politics* (Chicago: University of Chicago Press, 1953), Phoenix Books edition, pp. 11-12.

canism — thus West Germany was occupied by "Christian American soldiers"[19]— but when preaching as an evangelist he quickly returns to his narrow, fundamentalist categories. He asserts, "The American people do not know God, they do not know Christ."[20] "Statistics prove that 80 percent of this nation never go to church, never read the Bible, never attend a religious service, and likely would never have a religious thought were it not for these religious holidays."[21] This basic inconsistency is nowhere analyzed or explained.

In the second place, Hargis's Christian-Americanism is open to criticism because its essence is chauvinistic nineteenth-century nationalism. In a world threatened with self-destruction because mankind has not yet learned to live in peaceful brotherhood, Hargis advocates an even more divisive and jingoistic tribalism. He overlooks the fact that nationalism breaks the first two commandments, committing idolatry by worshipping nationalistic symbols, and by assuming that a given civilization, or even a given country, is the bearer of the meaning of history.[22] Furthermore, he also errs in assuming that nationalism and internationalism are necessarily incompatible, and that American nationalism, whatever its merits, inevitably requires a determined effort to discredit the United Nations.

Hargis's claim that the United States is God's greatest nation, chosen by Him to lead the world, must surely be an affront to many Christians. The fact that this view is still held by a significant sector of American Christendom makes it no more tenable, for Hargis eliminates the New Testament doctrine of a separated, supra-national Christian Church and replaces Christ's teachings with a vague, sentimental religion of temporal and nationalistic expediency. Littell harshly charges that the false image of America, exemplified by Hargis, has made possible an almost imperceptible decline of much of true Christianity into a tribal religiosity.[23]

---

19 Hargis, *Communism, The Total Lie!* (*op. cit.*), p. 169.

20 Hargis, *Communist America... Must It Be?* (*op. cit.*), p. 169.

21 Hargis, *Christian Crusade*, Vol. 14 (December, 1962), p. 3. For an interesting discussion of the relation of Christianity to the American political system, see Wilbur G. Katz, *Religion and American Constitutions* (Evanston, Ill.: Northwestern University Press, 1964).

22 See John Howard Yoder, *The Christian Witness to the State* (Newton, Kansas: Faith and Life, 1964), pp. 15f.

23 Littell, *op. cit.*, p. 127. See also John Edwin Smylie's "The Christian Church and National Ethos" in Paul Peachey, ed., *Biblical Realism Confronts the Nation* (Scottdale, Pa.: Herald, 1963), Chapter 2.

Reinhold Niebuhr says much the same thing about the present state of American Christianity by noting that "here we are in the twentieth century at once the most religious and the most secular of Western nations."[24] He, too, feels that misguided preachers and pundits have contributed to this state of affairs.

Readers will recall that Hargis severely criticized Supreme Court rulings on official prayer in public schools. He viewed these rulings as a sinister attack on "the Christian-American heritage." Virtually all of the leaders of the larger denominations view these developments in a different light. A number of reports by the National Council of Churches and some statements by member constituencies carefully delineate the opposing view. One of these releases, *Questions and Answers on the Supreme Court and Public School Religion,* authorized by the Baptist Joint Committee on Public Affairs, Washington, D.C., summarizes the arguments well. Dr. C. Emanuel Carlson, the author of the pamphlet, shows that it is not God and the Bible who have been "eliminated" from the schools, but rather, a state requirement of a formal religious exercise, and that the new policy does not infringe upon freedom or promote secularism. This type of argument is not answered by Hargis, perhaps because he seems not to distinguish between instruction in religious knowledge, a proper function of the state educational system, and instruction in religious practice, properly

---

24 Reinhold Niebuhr, *Pious and Secular America* (New York: Scribners, 1958), p. 1. At this point someone will surely ask: But did not other nations committed to liberal-democratic values develop the same superiority complexes and identification with the Christian cause? The answer is that they did, but not in the same way. Hans Kohn (*op. cit.*), p. 9, says, "The American self-identification with innocence was not shared by the British or the Europeans; they could not claim to have been born in Rousseauan virgin forests." Niebuhr writes, "Every nation has its own form of spiritual pride.... [Examples] of American self-appreciation could be matched by similar sentiments in other nations. But every nation also has its peculiar version. Our version is that our nation turned its back upon the vices of Europe and made a new beginning." Niebuhr, *The Irony of American History* (*op. cit.*), p. 28. Finally, Boorstin explains Americanism and its uniqueness this way: "The tendency to gloss over differences and construct a kind of generalized American religion, and the tendency to talk a great deal about what we believe without feeling the obligation to sharpen our definitions — both of these express a unity in American Life.

"When we have broken down the boundaries between public and private life, between community values and personal belief, between political philosophy and religious faith, we have prepared ourselves to make the agreed-upon community values do for a religious doctrine." Boorstin, *op. cit.*, pp. 157f.

a responsibility of the family, the church, and the many religiously oriented voluntary organizations.

Much of Hargis's discussion of contemporary American politics consists of sweeping claims unsupported by any evidence. His insistence that all of America's social crises are traceable to Communist agitation and manipulation is a case in point. He fails to distinguish between possible Communist exploitation of a crisis and the cause of the crisis itself. Similarly, his description of the 1964 Civil Rights Act as a "power grab" is stated as fact, not as opinion. He cites no evidence. The same is true of his statement that, "what civilization there is now in the world is due to the missionaries sent out from America." His unqualified assertion that "the FCC is actually a gang of federal outlaws" is another example of unwarranted generalization. No responsible political scientist, after reviewing the history of the Federal Communications Commission, could possibly agree with his judgment. A final example of the dangerous allegations which Hargis permits himself is his charge that, "because of rulings of the Supreme Court . . . it is no crime in America to teach or advocate the violent overthrow of the government."[25]

The shortcomings evident in Hargis's discussion of American origins, government, and politics appear again in his treatment of political ideology. Careful use of evidence, reasoned analysis, and qualified judgments are in short supply.[26] His repeated assertion that Christianity and political conservatism are correlatives reminds one of the saying, "What I say three times is true!" No serious attention is given to alternate points of view. Conservatism is of God and the whole "Left" is of the devil!

Hargis ignores the most basic distinctions; socialism, liberalism, progressivism, Marxism and Communism are often treated as one single phenomenon. At best, much of his analysis of "Conservatism" and "Leftism" is naive and uninformed, and some of it is ludicrous. One cannot but conclude that Hargis's intemperate scathing of the "Left" does not constitute a contribution to coherent political discussion.

Next we turn to Hargis's views on the Cold War and American foreign policy. We note that he shows little understanding of the radically changed nature of war resulting from the development of

---

25 Hargis, *Communist America . . . Must It Be?* (*op. cit.*), p. 111.

26 Note his generalization, completely unsupported by evidence, that Communists "have revised and rewritten school textbooks and are about the labor of completely rewriting American history." *Ibid.*, p. 71.

nuclear weapons. For him, even total war is a legitimate means of settling international disputes,[27] and there are victors even in an all-out nuclear conflagration. It is this belief, together with his messianic complex, which encourages Hargis to reject all negotiation and bargaining.[28] He has more or less accepted the hard-line Marxist thesis that violent conflict is inevitable.

Hargis's uncompromising stand on war is reflected also in his view on foreign aid. Granted, there has been waste and mismanagement, but these facts are not the main reasons for his criticism. He denounces all aid which does not produce immediate military benefit to the United States. His criterion is self-regarding nationalism. He has nothing to say about supra-national altruism or humanitarianism, let alone supra-national Christian love. His perception of the current international situation is equally faulty. Some of his "facts" are false and, as indicated earlier, he assumes causal connections where none are apparent and indulges in dangerous over-simplification.

The analysis of Communism and the Soviet Union is also inadequate. Hargis ignores the very impressive social achievements of Communism. Conflicting evidence is ignored and we are given glib, often absurdly inaccurate, generalizations, but no evidence. On what basis does Hargis claim that "Communism has destroyed more human life and more of the world's benefits than all of the other evil systems put together since the world began"? Does he really think that people will believe his claim that Communism "is really nothing more than a moth-eaten theory which had been discredited before the Pyramids were built"? Hargis implies that he has examined history carefully, but there is no indication that he has subjected himself to its discipline. For example, nowhere does he treat social injustices as a factor in protest movements, be they

---

[27] In this connection, note the following statement by Reinhold Niebuhr in E. W. Lefever, ed., *The World Crisis and American Responsibility* (New York: Association, 1958), p. 34, "The development of atomic weapons to the point of the hydrogen bomb for the sake of exercising our responsibilities toward the free world is the measure of our growing political and moral maturity. We know now that we cannot be responsible without guilt. . . . The ultimate exercise of responsibility may involve the guilt of the destruction of life."

[28] In a way, given his assumptions about his camp and that of the enemy, Hargis's belief in eventual all-out war makes some sense, but only if one ignores the nuclear factor. As George F. Kennan has written, "A war fought in the name of high moral principle finds no early end short of some form of total domination." *American Diplomacy, 1900-1950* (New York: New American Library, 1953), p. 99.

socialist, Populist, Marxist, or anarchist. Hargis's assertion that under socialism British workers lost all choice of employment is false; a Labour government which was tied to the larger labor unions would hardly have succeeded in such an authoritarian policy and did not attempt to do so. Furthermore, a survey of British farm policy under the Attlee government (1945–1951) indicates that there was confiscation of land only for defaulting on taxes and expropriation according to the standard principles of eminent domain, both of which are commonplace throughout the free world. The main point, however, and one which Hargis apparently misses entirely, is that democratic socialism does not deny political freedom and that it can be, and has been, terminated by democratic procedures.

Finally, we turn to Hargis's view of the United Nations. His antagonism toward it is boundless — all is Communist and devilish. UNESCO, UNICEF, and the World Health Organization are roundly condemned. His omissions, misconceptions, and distortions are glaring. The statement that Secretary-General Lie was a Moscow agent who resigned suddenly when Senator McCarran began his exposure of Communists is an amazing tale. Why would Soviet leaders have boycotted the Security Council during the first half of 1950, giving their disgust with Lie as the reason, if he was their ally? And if the Soviets had plotted the Korean War with him, why were they absent when the crucial vote was taken to initiate United Nations resistance to the advancing forces of Communist North Korea? If Lie was so sympathetic to the Soviets, why did they totally ignore him for more than two years after the Korean War broke out? The fact of the matter is, of course, that Lie's resignation hardly came as a surprise, and that it came not because of Senator McCarran's "exposures," but because of the Soviet boycott.

Furthermore, Hargis's insistence that "the world government's Charter cannot be changed or amended" is patently incorrect. In the first place, the United Nations is not a world government. In the second place, amendment is provided for by Articles 108 and 109 of the Charter. In fact, amendments are being passed; the Soviet Union was the first major power to ratify Charter amendments expanding Security Council membership from 11 to 15 and Economic and Social Council membership from 18 to 27.

Hargis, and others as well, have overlooked or ignored the fact that the various United Nations agencies are trying to solve the same problems — war, hunger, disease, and injustice — which supposedly disturb the Christian conscience. They have not realized that most of the world's major problems have become internationalized, that no nation can successfully ignore these problems, and that a joint effort is required to cope with them. They seem not to appreciate assistance as a mutually beneficial undertaking, even from a secular humanitarian point of view. Neither does Hargis recognize the ill will which prolonged economic disparity necessarily generates in an increasingly informed world. Viereck rightly observes that "the Christian religion itself, so basic to conservatives, is by definition inter-nationalist."[29]

Much more could be said about Hargis's view of the United Nations and his fear of its spreading influence. Perhaps the most telling rebuttal is the fact that the Nobel Committee awarded the 1965 Nobel Peace Prize to UNICEF.

II

We turn now to a brief analysis of Hargis's procedural devices, consistency, accuracy, and overall methodology.

One of Hargis's major flaws is his inconsistency. He insists, for example, that most, if not all, Americans are Christians — but he also holds the opposite to be true. He cannot have it both ways. His definition of a Christian is in itself confusing in that sometimes he employs a broad, inclusive meaning, and at other times insists on a narrow, fundamentalist one. He states that the American government is ultimately accountable to God, but also asserts that in this "Constitutional Republic" the government is ultimately responsible to the common people. Taken to their logical conclusions, as Hargis duly takes them, these two emphases seem not to be entirely compatible. Related to this problem is his fundamental ambivalence on the question of whether or not this nation ought to be a democracy. On the one hand, he places the utmost confidence in the judgment of "the people," but on the other hand he claims that this country is not, and must not become, a democracy; it must remain a "Republic." Furthermore, within one sentence he indicates his contradictory views on the matter of sovereignty. "Christian Crusade," he writes, "believes in state sov-

---

29 Peter Viereck, *Conservatism* (Princeton: Van Nostrand, 1956), p. 23. See also Robert Lawson Slater, *World Religions and World Community* (New York: Columbia University Press, 1963), who in his final chapter discusses the ways in which religion can contribute to the perfection of the world community.

crcignty, national sovereignty, and constitutional government."[30] In the rigid sense that Hargis uses the word sovereignty, this statement is meaningless.

An interesting inconsistency arises from his views on freedom. He apparently sees no conflict between his enthusiastic support of the most rigid immigration laws[31] and his unqualified adoration of the freedom cult. In similar fashion he condemns all statism and "big government," yet he praises the regimes of Vorster, Franco, Salazar, and the erstwhile establishments of Trujillo and Batista. He wants to keep the government poor, but he also wants the United States to be strong militarily. He also insists that unregenerate, "unsaved" man is bestial and evil, but simultaneously argues that "the less government the better" is a good slogan for all societies everywhere.

An example of contradiction involves a *New York Times* report. In a certain issue of his *Weekly Crusader*, Hargis photographically reproduces the article in question, written by Donald Janson. He calls it "the true story of Christian Crusade as it relates to our constant financial struggle. . . ."[32] Yet on the very same page he speaks of "this *Times*' intended smear. . . ."

Another example of this kind of contradiction, and the last to be cited here, is the most glaring. The April 28, 1962, number of the *Saturday Evening Post* carried a feature article on Hargis and the Christian Crusade. In the next issue of his monthly magazine he commented on it, gushing praise and appreciation.[33] "During its 14 years of anti-communist activity, Christian Crusade seldom has had an opportunity to thank a great national magazine for its valuable and cooperative publicity," said he. "We now have that chance. . . ." The *Post* was praised as "that shining pillar of genuine Americanism." Hargis described the article itself as "an excellent and inspiring outline." "How Mr. Martin got his story past the advertising department puzzles us," wrote Hargis, "but we are not going to look a gift horse in the mouth"; there "will be no rejection of $207,760.00 worth of publicity in a circulation of 6,624,-866!" Personal appreciation for Martin's diligence is indicated. Hargis stated that words could hardly express his feelings about "these precious pages." "If only *Life, Look* and the *New York Times* could now do as well by us, we've got it made."

---

[30] Hargis, *Christian Crusade*, Vol. 15 (June-July, 1963), pp. 11, 12 and 71.
[31] See *Christian Crusade*, Vol. 15 (September, 1963), p. 21.
[32] Hargis, *Weekly Crusader*, Vol. 3 (August 23, 1963), p. 8.
[33] Hargis, *Christian Crusade*, Vol. 14 (May, 1962), p. 2.

Letters to the *Post* started flowing in; most were critical of Martin's article. By September, *Christian Crusade* itself was singing a different song.[34]

> Among the "past-masters" at vicious, tongue-in-cheek smear, we must admit the *Saturday Evening Post* has the greatest effect. Since Christian Crusade was the object of such treatment several weeks ago [it was actually several months], we feel qualified to pass on to our readers many of the reactions to their unfairness. It is truly a testimony to the potency of an aroused citizenry. *Christian Crusade* herewith presents excerpts from many of the letters written regarding the *Saturday Evening Post* abortion.

Then follow the letters attacking Martin.

A second general category of inadequacy is outright error. Various examples have already been given. The equating of democratic socialism with Communism is obviously false, and even worse is the statement that "from this day forward, my friends, it (i.e. Christian Crusade) will equate liberalism and socialism with communism...."[35] A number of erroneous statements concern living standards in foreign countries. Citing statistics compiled by Harding College, a fundamentalist college in Searcy, Arkansas, Hargis argues that "the citizens of socialist nations have living standards one-third to one-sixth as good as ours in America, and the greater [the] amount of socialism a country has, the lower its living standard becomes."[36] The experiences of a half-dozen European countries as well as of Australia and New Zealand are brushed aside. The quotations given earlier about education in the Soviet Union illustrate the many erroneous views held about the actual situation in that country.

Concerning the United States, Hargis disseminates inaccurate information about the amount of its agricultural production in relation to that of the rest of the world, and about its supposed uniqueness in the religious freedom it affords. Hargis also errs when he suggests that the extent of Christian influence in the United States, at least in terms of church membership, is declining.[37] Furthermore, a number of the statements describing the current American political situation are either untrue or problem-

---

34 *Christian Crusade*, Vol. 14 (September, 1962), p. 2.
35 Hargis, *Weekly Crusader*, Vol. 2 (April 13, 1962), pp. 7-8. Cf. Matthew 12:30, "He that is not with me is against me....".
36 Hargis, *Communism, The Total Lie!* (*op. cit.*), p. 71.
37 Murray S. Stedman, *Religion and Politics in America* (New York: Harcourt, Brace and World, 1964), p. 6.

atic. Some have been cited earlier, but here is an additional example: "I know that federal aid to education is the entering wedge to federal control of the minds of our young people — because the man who pays the fiddler calls the tune — and under this law the tune would be communist."[38] Probably the most striking example of all is the statement that "because of rulings of the Supreme Court . . . it is no crime in America to teach or advocate the violent overthrow of the government."[39]

The false statements about the United Nations should not be overlooked.[40] The roles which Hargis gives it in Korea and Cuba, to name but two instances, are not true to historical fact. The United Nations was not responsible for the United States' setbacks in those foreign affairs.

A third category of weakness is inconsistency between Hargis's clearly enunciated theological tenets[41] and his political principles and postulates. His fundamentalist claim that all men are equal before God contradicts his insistence on the supremacy of all things American. His rejection of Christian pacifism in any form, and the concomitant depiction of Jesus is puzzling, to say the least.[42] Hargis writes, "There is no such thing as a Pacifist Christian. A Christian is a fighter, or he is nothing. Jesus was a fighter."[43] He continues, "The Christian, above all . . . is a fighting man, whether the battle is one of words with the danger as ridicule by one's fellows, or whether the battle is one of hydrogen weapons with danger of complete annihilation."[44] It is difficult to see how a clergyman can arrive at such a conclusion, in view of Jesus' meekness, love for his enemies, and death on the cross, not to mention his reprimand to sword-swinging followers.[45] A third inconsistency relates to Hargis's conception of God's will in political matters. Hargis writes,

> Christians have not been as militant as God would have them be. They have neglected their duties. They have not followed the leadership of the Holy Spirit and fought to preserve freedom,

---

[38] Hargis, *Weekly Crusader,* Vol. 2 (April 13, 1962), p. 7.

[39] Hargis, *Communist America . . . Must It Be? (op. cit.),* p. 111.

[40] *Ibid.,* p. 132.

[41] As stated in *What's Wrong With Jesus?* (Christian Crusade Pamphlet, n.d.), and many other writings.

[42] See William Klassen's "Love Your Enemy! A Study of New Testament Teaching on Coping with an Enemy" in Paul Peachey, ed., *Biblical Realism Confronts the Nation* (Scottdale, Pa.: Herald, 1963).

[43] Hargis, *Communism, The Total Lie! (op. cit.),* p. 83.

[44] *Ibid.,* pp. 82f.

[45] Matthew 26:51f.

orthodox Christian principles of Constitutional Government, as God would have them do.[46]

As a fundamentalist theologian, he frequently cites the biblical statement that "God's ways are past finding out"; they are inexplicable.[47] Yet on political matters he claims to have fully comprehended these "ways."

On the question of becoming a Christian, Hargis seems to be inconsistent in his theology. Fundamentalism stresses the personal experience of a conscious conversion. Yet, when expounding the theme of Christian-Americanism, Hargis can concur with the view that "Americans are Christians whether they know it or not." Hargis's patriotic fervor also gets him into difficulty on another count. In a manner which must strike even many fundamentalists as heresy, Hargis makes God into an ardent nationalist. "It is a tribute to God," he writes, "that he approves of love of country; of patriotism. . . ."[48] No biblical or other evidence is cited.

In his use of the Bible, Hargis appears at times to be careless and illogical. Reference has already been made to his argument that "the Word of God says, 'The vile person shall be no more called Liberal' (Isaiah 32:5)."[49] Another false, out-of-context application is made when II Chronicles 7:14 is applied directly to the United States as a political entity.[50] The Bible is invoked to support arguments of all kinds. We read, "God is still on the Throne. . . . God is still concerned with the destiny and future

---

[46] Hargis, *Christian Crusade*, Vol. 14 (June, 1962), p. 3.

[47] Romans 11:33, "O the depth of the riches both of the wisdom and knowledge of God! How unsearchable are his judgments, and his ways past finding out."

[48] Hargis, *Communism, The Total Lie!* (*op. cit.*), p. 83.

[49] The word "liberal" occurs frequently in this chapter but is nowhere capitalized. Hargis's use of the capital "L" is unexplained. For a discussion of the dangers in misusing Scripture, see William Cunningham, *Christianity and Politics* (New York: Houghton Mifflin, 1915), pp. 87f.

[50] Hargis, *Communist America . . . Must It Be?* (*op. cit.*), p. 38. The verse in question is, "If my people, which are called by my name, shall humble themselves, and pray, and seek my face, and turn from their wicked ways; then will I hear from heaven, and will forgive their sin, and will heal their land." The historical reference is, of course, to ancient Israel. It is true that most evangelicals agree that there is some prophetical significance to this verse, but they apply it to the universal mystical church, not to the United States. Most Christian writers firmly believe that God no longer deals with favored nations as He apparently did in Old Testament times.

of the United States."[51] Hargis urges his readers to turn to Isaiah 41:10, 21-33, and then proceeds to apply this passage to contemporary political conservatism. "God says, 'Don't fear this liberal crowd.' God says, 'Don't let them arrest your action.' God says, 'Don't let them unnerve you': as He promises, 'I will strengthen thee; I will help thee; I will uphold thee.' "[52] Another instance of misapplication involves Titus 3:3-5. After having quoted these verses,[53] Hargis says, "Now let us listen to what God has to say and then let us purpose in our heart to do something about it. 'For we ourselves also were sometimes foolish....' Yes, we have been foolish. We have failed to do our best in the fight to save this country."[54] The Bible is also used — or abused — to trigger emotional and economic response for the benefit of Christian Crusade. "In the words of St. Paul: 'Now is the accepted time; behold, now is the day of salvation.' If we permit this hour to pass, the bottomless pit of communism is not far distant. Please send your help to Christian Crusade, Tulsa 2, Oklahoma."[55]

Hargis and his associates have failed to see that a central quality of Christianity is its universality, its supra-national appeal. A noted writer, the conservative Mennonite leader Carl M. Lehman, states, "To put my country and my God on an equal basis... is... blasphemy."[56] Commenting on this tendency, the Presbyterian missionary M. Richard Shaull observes, "God is not necessarily on *our* side; he is on the side of justice and concern for all men."[57] Hargis's apparent unconcern for the physical plight of foreigners, not to

---

[51] Hargis, *Weekly Crusader,* Vol. 3 (October 11, 1963), p. 7. A statement by Maritain is relevant here. The philosopher observes, "there is an atheism which declares that God exists but which *makes an idol of God himself,* because by its acts, if not by its word it denies the nature and the attributes of God and His glory of a people or State *against* all others, or as the daimon of the race." Jacques Maritain, *True Humanism* (New York: Scribners, 1950), p. 278.

[52] Hargis, *Weekly Crusader,* Vol. 3 (October 11, 1963), p. 7.

[53] "For we ourselves also were sometimes foolish, disobedient, deceived, serving divers lusts and pleasures, living in malice and envy, hateful, and hating one another. But after that the kindness and love of God our Saviour toward man appeared, not by works of righteousness which we have done, but according to his mercy he saved us, by the washing of regeneration, and renewing of the Holy Ghost."

[54] Hargis, *Christian Crusade,* Vol. 14 (June, 1962), p. 3.

[55] Hargis, *Weekly Crusader,* Vol. 2 (April 13, 1962), p. 8.

[56] Hershberger, *War, Peace, and Nonresistance (op. cit.),* p. 57.

[57] M. Richard Shaull, *Encounter With Revolution* (New York: Association, 1955), p. 66.

mention fellow Americans, is relevant here. One notes a failure
to express the Christian virtues of love and charity, especially in
terms of aiding the Afro-Asian multitudes directly or in supporting
institutions, such as the United Nations and its agencies, which
work toward that end. This continuing agitation against non-military aid is deplored by many conservative critics, critics who do not
share Prentiss L. Pemberton's apparent regret that fewer Chinese
may be starving. Pemberton states, "Economic developments in
China also present disturbing evidence of progress under communist rule."[58]

Surveying the phenomenon of the religious Far Right as a
whole, one observer suggests that "political movements of the extreme right, which use God as a support for the status quo, may
in the end do much greater damage to faith in God than a movement that has no room for God in its philosophy."[59] The statement warrants careful consideration, as does the following comment:

> The idea of God's activity in the world and his judgment upon
> all human attainments has surprising political consequences. It
> warns us that no system is absolute and eternal, and that all the
> structures of our collective life now stand under judgment and
> must be reformed. It reminds us that God may not be quite as
> concerned as we are about the idols we have set up. He may not
> be so anxious to preserve Western supremacy nor the superior
> position of the white race. He may not . . . desire to fight commu-
> nism in just the same way we do. He might even will radical
> changes in certain institutions we cherish, as the only way by
> which his plan for the world can go forward.[60]

The same writer also emphasizes that since men "always tend
to make idols of the systems that sustain their life, especially when
these systems are under attack,"[61] contemporary Americans, and
Christians generally, ought to be particularly cautious about what
kind of crusades they support.

Besides these several categories of inconsistency, error, and
misuse of the Bible, there is much that is simply illogical and naive.
Thus we read that "with all United Nations Internationalists, the
thought of religion is repugnant."[62] Some assertions are best described as ludicrous: "It is reported that Europe is being taken over

[58] Prentiss L. Pemberton, *Christians Face the Total Menace of Communism* (Chicago: Hudson, 1962), p. 39.

[59] Shaull, *op. cit.*, p. 32.

[60] *Ibid.*, p. 65.

[61] *Loc. cit.*

[62] Hargis, *Weekly Crusader*, Vol. 1 (September 22, 1961), p. 7.

by the Communists by telephone. . . ."[63] Or, "Nikita Khrushchev . . . would never have come to America if the American government were not already largely shaped after the Soviet pattern. . . ."[64]

A tendency to assume that events which are sequentially related are therefore also causally related appears frequently in Hargis's writing and speaking. Reference has already been made to the view that the expansion of the Communist empire since the United Nations was founded is the result of United Nations activity. Readers may recall also that Hargis said, "Mr. Roosevelt recognized Russia in 1933 and one-half the world went Communist."[65]

Hargis seems to assume that all evil emanates from one source, "satanic Marxism," and then goes on to assume that anything in opposition to Communism is therefore inherently good. He is convinced, he writes, that "the antidote to every communist intrigue is to do the opposite."[66] The reasoning seems to be that anything favored by the Reds is automatically bad, and that the intrinsic quality of the proposal is of no importance. He applies this type of reasoning to the current civil rights controversy, to the issue of nuclear test ban agreements, to United Nations decisions, and other current affairs. A related tendency is Hargis's belief that any change from the status quo implies a definite step, although one not necessarily or immediately obvious, toward Communism.

It is clear from Hargis's discussion of the Cold War that he sees the entire phenomenon simplistically: what one side gains the other must lose. He implies that there cannot be a time when it might be in the Communists' interest to negotiate in good faith, that real progress for both sides might result from honest compromise, or that the United Nations might serve as a neutral catalyst and forum. Least of all does he envision any situation in which American and Soviet interests might coincide. The experience of the Suez Canal Crisis of 1956, the test ban treaties, and the establishment and functioning of the United Nations itself are ignored.

The final inadequacy to be noted here is the simplistic dichotomy which underlies many of Hargis's conclusions. He rarely envisions more than two options. Accordingly, non-Communist nations are by definition free: Franco's Spain is free; Batista's Cuba

63 Hargis, *Christian Crusade*, Vol. 15 (February, 1963), p. 5. See also *Christian Crusade*, Vol. 14 (January-February, 1962), p. 20.

64 Hargis, *Communism, The Total Lie!* (*op. cit.*), p. 64.

65 Hargis, *What's Wrong With America?* (*op. cit.*).

66 Hargis, *Communist America . . . Must It Be?* (*op. cit.*), p. 38.

was free; Duvalier's Haiti is free; Vorster's South Africa is free; Salazar's Portugal is free; and China in 1943, under Chiang Kai-shek, was "then totally free."[67] Hargis sees only two ideologies in the world. "The world is split in a struggle for the minds of men and women," he asserts; "If you THINK communist, you are a communist. If you THINK American, you are American and anti-communist. It's as simple as that."[68] Again, one sees a possible correlation with fundamentalism. The absence of a neutral zone, the depreciation of moderation ("luke-warmness"[69]), and the all-encompassing duality have recognizable roots.[70]

In general, Hargis quickly dismisses all others, including other Protestants, who disagree with him. Identifying himself and his cause as "Christian Conservatism" and denying any basic distinction between political conservatism and religious conservatism,[71] he proceeds to lump critics with a liberal theological orientation together with those having a liberal political orientation, calling them "allies of communism,"[72] and accusing them of "fighting God."[73] This crude analysis is supposedly supported by Scripture; for example, Matt Cvetic, a writer in Hargis's monthly, insists, "we can take our guidance from Jesus Christ who said: He who is not with me is against me. Never were these words of Jesus more appropriate."[74] Seldom has the use of Scripture been more revealing.

III

Hargis's thought cannot be described as a philosophy, for Hargis is no political philosopher. The basis of this statement 'is not primarily the nature of his views, but his failure to elucidate his premises and clarify his inconsistencies. "Hargisism" lacks depth and is not a coherent, let alone well-ordered, system of thought.

---

[67] *Ibid.*, p. 121.

[68] Hargis, *Christian Crusade*, Vol. 14 (April, 1962), p. 24.

[69] Cf. Revelation 3:15-16, "I know thy works, that thou art neither cold nor hot: I would thou wert cold or hot. So then because thou art lukewarm, and neither cold nor hot, I will spew thee out of my mouth."

[70] Carl McIntire goes even farther than Hargis in this regard. His categories cannot be simplified any further. "You either agree with McIntire or the Devil. Take your choice." The statement is cited in Forster and Epstein, *op. cit.*, p. 100.

[71] Hargis, *New England Rally For God and Country* (Christian Crusade Pamphlet, n.d.), p. 2.

[72] Hargis, *Weekly Crusader*, Vol. 2 (June 1, 1962), p. 8.

[73] Hargis, *New England Rally For God and Country (op. cit.)*, p. 2.

[74] Cited in *Christian Crusade*, Vol. 14 (September, 1962), p. 17.

This inadequacy is significant, because Hargis posits his views as a respectable, viable alternative to the present philosophy of the United States government.

Probably the most striking and most important feature of Hargis's political thought is his "religification" of politics itself. To put it another way, the very concept of politics, with its overtones of moderation, compromise, relativism, and interminable revision, is denied. The notion of democratic processes being separable from individual religious pursuits is rejected. Rather, Hargis's view is that man, total man, must lead an integrated life in which procedures and goals, private piety and public law, all form part of a single larger whole. "Religification of politics" or "politicization of religion," the result is basically the same, namely, the distinction between the two kingdoms disappears. Politics practiced according to secular norms, to the extent that the phenomenon persists at all, is something that non-believers undertake; Christians who undertake what appear to be similar activities are not "in politics" but are only "obeying God." They are faithfully building His kingdom, via church, state, or better still, both.[75]

It is this "religification" of many traditional ultra-conservative values, rather than any inherently new ideas, which characterizes Hargis and the rest of the contemporary Far Right and makes them the significant movement they are at present. Conservatives in America and in Western democracies in general have traditionally opposed what they termed a "hasty progressivism," but they did not question the propriety of the political framework itself. The major new ingredient which the Far Right has injected into the American body politic is nothing less than a frontal assault, in the name of Christianity, on the democratic political perspective, on its intrinsic secularity, and on its legitimization of conflict. In a sense, this new theory is little more than an up-dated version of medieval and early modern notions of theocracy and divine right. The point bears repetition, since the Far Right has not so much brought in radically new ideas as it has made a religion out of some traditional ones. Long-familiar political concepts, some of which hark back to Edmund Burke and even earlier writers, have now

---

[75] An awareness of Hargis's ideological presuppositions in this area is essential for a true understanding of the following statement in his April, 1964, Newsletter. "I think the criticism of me that is most unjust and most unfair, instigated by our pro-red enemies, is that I am engaged in political, not Christian activities."

been made absolute, and subsequently canonized.[76] From a theological viewpoint, the phenomenon can also be described as the
difference between the clergy merely advocating certain ideals by
labelling them pro-Christian, and the inclusion of these ideals in
the Christian creed itself.

The full implication of this transformation is virtually in-
estimable. The whole nature of the battle has changed. New
criteria are applied to both goals and methods. Nationalism, capitalism, capital punishment, opposition to the income tax, Americanism,
state sovereignty, and constitutional infallibility are notions which
the religious Far Right has raised in status and included in its
concept of Christianity's essence. Since each of these concepts has
been made an absolute, it follows that for members of the Far Right
even to think critically about these concepts produces feelings of
guilt and apostasy. Furthermore, a compulsion for total partisan
victory has replaced the desire merely to restrain somewhat the
excesses of an otherwise acceptable evolution of society. In keeping
with the above, a political opponent is no longer one who differs
in degree; he is a total enemy — a traitor. Not only a difference in
personal judgment but the whole realm of motives, loyalty, and
commitment is now involved. The result is that almost any controversy involving capitalism or disarmament, the United Nations or
cultural exchange, immediately takes on the quality of a holy war.
Each controversy constitutes a skirmish in the crusade to prevent
the forces of evil from de-Christianizing a supposedly Christian
society; each battle is Armageddon in microcosm.

Nevertheless, the passing centuries, and especially the last
few decades, have brought momentous changes. As Professor Ernest
Barker has clearly shown, the historical, and historic, impact of early
Christianity was to split the human community, separating government and the state from voluntaristic society. He argues that in
the field of social and political theory, "this was the great result of
the teaching of Christ. . . . The effect of Christianity was the emergence of the doctrine of the two ends — the temporal end, which
alone belongs to the State, and the eternal end which belongs to,

---

[76] Edmund Burke was strongly in favor of a "Christian Commonwealth,"
which would embrace both church and state with the latter being more or
less subordinate to the former. See, for example, his "Reflections" in *Works
of Burke,* World Classics Edition, Vol. 2, pp. 100f. Hargis, it appears, is
not familiar with Burke's views.

and is the prerogative of, the Church."[77] With the concepts of "Christian Conservatism" and "Christian-Americanism" as found in Hargis's writings, we have now come full circle. Hargis's goal is to fuse again that which early Christianity split asunder. Thomism, Gelasianism, and the other classic statements concerning the separateness of the two kingdoms all fall by the wayside. They are, however, not vanquished by sound argument, just conveniently ignored.

Another major result of the "religification" of politics is a blurring of the distinction between law and morality, a distinction which is central to the entire Christian view of man and the world. What is the basic difference? We turn again to the stimulating analysis of Professor Ernest Barker. Law, as Professor Barker has said, is the major technique of the state through which it controls external behavior.[78] Law, properly viewed, is a uniform rule of action binding on all men. It establishes a moral norm in the sense that external compliance can be called moral. Compliance is not identical with morality, since the morality of an act, from the Christian perspective, is determined strictly by its motive, a factor which is quite irrelevant when considering legality alone. Christian morality is ultimately a matter of the conscience and the heart, and thus is not susceptible to legal enforcement. Resting on conviction, it is necessarily voluntary. Hargis, it is evident, wants the state to translate religious convictions into legal prescriptions. The coercion of the state is to undergird the persuasion of the church, and thus cooperate in ushering in the Kingdom. He argues that this joining of forces is nothing other than majority rule, but the basic points to note are that such a fusion is fundamentally impossible and that the majority which he has in mind is a constant, unshifting one which divides society into irreconcilable ideological factions with the dissenting minority permanently suppressed.

Honorable as Hargis's motive may be, the scheme he advocates never works. True Christianity and state enforcement are incompatible. As Barker puts it,

> The standards of religion can only be applied in the area of voluntary life which lies outside the State; and the quality of behavior which they involve can only be achieved if it is sought freely and without any shadow of legal compulsion. If the State attempts to draw religious standards, and the quality of behavior

---

[77] Ernest Barker, *Principles of Social and Political Theory* (New York: Oxford, 1961), p. 7.

[78] *Ibid.*, pp. 45-47. See also page 69.

which they involve, into the area of the legal association, and to enforce them as the prescriptions and by the sanctions of law, it simply fails.[79]

A responsible ethics resting on individual initiative is the first casualty; toleration is usually the second. The ideal is never realized.

Incidentally, in Hargis's view, the state is important not only as a sanction to ensure morality. It is also a dynamic, living organism possessing moral qualities in its own right. The state emerges as omnipotent and omni-virtuous. It is not only the foremost inculcator of the majority's religio-political culture-creed, but is itself the locus of true virtue. The state, says Hargis, is the creation of God to which all merely man-made individualistic as well as internationalistic institutions must yield authority. Harking back to certain notions first developed in classical Greece, Hargis believes that man developes his full potential and fulfills his purposes only as a totally committed citizen of a state. But the state which Hargis has in mind is not the free, democratic ideal of Pericles or Aristotle. It resembles the state described by Hegel and Herder, where glorification is both a privilege and a duty.

The near-deification of the state, particularly the American state, and Hargis's views on public morality are paralleled by an equally vigorous defense of individualism in the realm of property rights and free enterprise. Individualism is endorsed as a teaching of the Bible. Any infringement on the fullest possible rights in the economic realm is termed "collectivism" and therefore labeled Communist. In Hargis's lexicon unconditional freedom or unconditional statism are the only options we have.

The creed of individualism, however, must not be confused with a concern for individual welfare. This emphasis is notably lacking. There is little indication of any desire that abuses of society should be corrected so that underprivileged individuals might also learn what individual freedom means. Hargis favors human rights, but his concept turns out to be little more than the freedom of privilege.

Hargis offers no plan, program, or social ideal. Abstract individualism is the single principle. All we can do is resist the civil rights movement, cooperative federalism, Fair Employment Practice laws, the graduated income tax, the United Nations and other forms of "socialism in disguise." Anything that limits freedom must be

---

[79] *Ibid.*, p. 105. Daniel Bell has suggested that "the historic contribution of liberalism was to separate law from morality." "Interpretations of American Politics," in Daniel Bell, *op. cit.*

resisted. Mental health programs, fluoridation of drinking water, collective bargaining, and the minimum wage law are all denounced not primarily because they are ineffective, or even because of their actual effects, but because they are believed to be plots against individualism. Not an inch is to be yielded to the foe. Collectivism or Christ, these are the options. Anything that enhances individualism is good; anything that circumscribes it is bad. That, in brief, is the essence of Hargis's views on economic and social justice.[80]

It was stated above that "Hargisism" includes no new positive political doctrine. But there is a new negative one which should be mentioned — a total, unqualified anti-Communism. Hargis's anti-Communism is a matter of absolute principle. It is based not on a systematic point-by-point analysis of Marxism with reference to relative strengths and weaknesses, achievements, failures, or crucial flaws, but on a layman's familiarity. Its essence is implacable enmity and repeated invective. Hargis's point of departure and unchanging criterion, here as elsewhere, is the traditional "Christian–American" norm as perceived by himself.[81]

---

[80] Interesting and informative discussions of the relationship of Christianity to social reform are found in the following works: John C. Bennett, *Christian Ethics and Social Policy* (New York: Scribners, 1946); C. H. Dodd, *Gospel and Law* (New York: Columbia University Press, 1951); E. C. Gardner, *Biblical Faith and Social Ethics* (New York: Harper & Brothers, 1960); Alfred E. Garvie, *The Christian Ideal for Human Society* (New York: Richard R. Smith, 1930); George A. Graham, *Morality in American Politics* (New York: Random House, 1952); Carl F. H. Henry, *Aspects of Christian Social Ethics* (Grand Rapids: Eerdmans, 1964); John H. Hutchison, ed., *Christian Faith and Social Action* (New York: Scribners, 1953); Halford Luccock, *Christian Faith and Economic Change* (New York: Abingdon, 1936); Reinhold Niebuhr, *An Interpretation of Christian Ethics* (New York: Harper & Brothers, 1935); Justin Wroe Nixon, *Responsible Christianity* (New York: Harper & Brothers, 1950); Albert T. Rasmussen, *Christian Social Ethics* (Englewood Cliffs: Prentice-Hall, 1956); Harvey Seifert, *The Church in Community Action* (New York: Abingdon-Cokesbury, 1952); D. R. Sharpe, *Call to Christian Action* (New York: Harper, 1949); W. A. Visser 't Hooft and J. H. Oldham, *The Church and Its Function in Society* (Chicago: Willett and Clark, 1937); and Ernst Troeltsch, *The Social Teaching of the Christian Churches*, Volumes I & II (New York: Harper & Brothers, Harper Torchbooks, 1960).

On the relationship of Christianity to foreign affairs see: Chapter VI, "Internationalism" in Garvie, *op. cit.*; George F. Kennan, "Foreign Policy and Christian Conscience," *Atlantic Monthly*, Vol. 203 (May, 1959), pp. 44-49; J. T. McNeill, *Christian Hope for World Society* (Chicago: Willett and Clark, 1937); John Courtney Murray, *Morality and Modern War* (New York: The Church Peace Union, 1959); Harvey Seifert, *Ethical Resources for International Relations* (Philadelphia: Westminster, 1964); and Kenneth

W. Thompson, *Christian Ethics and the Dilemmas of Foreign Policy* (Durham, North Carolina: Duke University Press, 1959).

On the specific topic of Christianity and human rights see: K. W. MacArthur, *The Bible and Human Rights,* revised edition (New York: The Woman's Press, 1949); O. C. Quick, *Christianity and Justice* (London: Sheldon, 1960); H. Schrey, H. Walz, and W. Whitehouse, *The Biblical Doctrine of Justice and Law* (London: SCM, 1955).

The Papal Encyclicals, such as *Mater et Magistra* (1961) and *Pacem in Terris* (1963), as well as the earlier ones which deal with social issues should also be consulted.

[81] For a representative sampling of writings on Christianity and Communism, consult the following titles. Works somewhat sympathetic to Communism include: Emil Fuchs, *Marxismus und Christentum* (Leipzig, 1953); Josef L. Hromadka, *An der Schwelle des Dialogs zwischen Christen und Marxisten* (Frankfurt am Main: Stimme Verlag, 1964); Marcus Bach, *God and the Soviets* (New York: Crowell, 1958, 1961).

Works more or less neutral include: John C. Bennett, *Christianity and Communism Today* (New York: Association, 1960); Edward Rogers, *A Christian Commentary on Communism* (New York: Praeger, 1952); Charles C. West, *Communism and the Churches* (New York: Macmillan, 1958).

Works "crusading" against Communism include: Thomas O. Kay, *The Christian Answer to Communism* (Grand Rapids: Zondervan, 1961); Charles W. Lowry, *Communism and Christ* (New York: Morehouse-Gorham, 1953); Prentiss L. Pemberton, *Christians Face the Total Menace of Communism* (Chicago: Judson, 1963).

An interesting study of the contemporary upsurge of Christian anti-Communism is Russell L. Mast, *Christianity and Communism* (Newton, Kansas: Faith and Life, 1962).

PART TWO

AN EXPLANATION OF "HARGISISM"

"The mentality of fundamentalism is dominated by ideological thinking. Ideological thinking is rigid, intolerant, and doctrinaire; it sees principles everywhere, and all principles come in clear tones of black and white."

Edward John Carnell, The Case for Orthodox Theology, *p. 114.*

"Nationalist demagogy, whether McCarthy style or John Birch style, would never have become such a nuisance if liberal intellectuals and New Dealers had earlier made themselves the controlling spearhead of American anti-Communism with the same fervor they showed when spearheading anti-fascism."

Peter Viereck in Daniel Bell., ed., The Radical Right, *p. 194.*

"The concept of destiny has been an ever deepening current in American thought. Conviction that America has a mission to mankind was perhaps never stronger than today."

Daniel J. Boorstin, The Genius of American Politics, *p. 163.*

9. ORTHODOX CHRISTIANITY AND LIBERAL DEMOCRACY

So far we have described and analyzed some of Hargis's major political views. In the next three chapters we will try to ascertain the sources of "Hargisism." Chapters 10 and 11 will deal with the forces acting upon and contributing to "Hargisism." The aim in the present chapter is to determine whether "Hargisism" can be explained, at least in part, as the consequence of a tension between orthodox Christianity and liberal democracy. Is there a basic tension between these two orientations which periodically spawns reactionary or ultra-rightist movements, and which, for various reasons, does so frequently in our age?

Initially, we need to define our terms. Edward John Carnell states, "Orthodoxy is that branch of Christianity which limits the ground of religious authority to the Bible. No other rule of faith and practice is acknowledged. Orthodoxy is friendly toward any effort that looks to Scripture; it is unfriendly toward any that does not."[1] While the term technically includes fundamentalism — Carnell says that "fundamentalism is orthodoxy gone cultic" — the two are posited here as separate phenomena.[2] It is admitted at the outset that "orthodoxy" is a relative term. Lord Byron's witty comment that "Orthodoxy is my doxy, Heterodoxy is another man's doxy," contains some truth. Even so, the term has taken on a sufficiently

---

[1] Edward John Carnell, *The Case for Orthodox Theology* (Philadelphia: Westminster, 1959). The term "Orthodox" is seen as a subcategory of "Evangelical"; "Fundamentalism" can be viewed as either a subcategory of "Orthodox" or of "Evangelical" and thus a parallel to "Orthodox." This writer prefers the latter. Carnell's book is accepted here as the best concise statement on Christian orthodoxy. More specialized works are cited by Carnell. The quotation is from page 13.

[2] *Ibid.*, p. 113.

113

distinct coloration, especially in recent decades, to make it a useful label. Any Christian who claims that the Bible taken literally is not the sole source of religious authority is unorthodox, according to the definition employed here. Thus, all Roman Catholics and most liberally oriented Protestants are excluded.

By the term "liberal democracy" is meant the basic premise and the actual operative principles common to most of the Anglo-American states, among others, and exemplified in the United States and Great Britain.[3] The term is not used in any narrow or technical sense; it is not meant to denote direct, as contrasted with indirect, self-government. The emphasis is on a spirit of equality and an acceptance of equal rights and privileges. In a previous era liberalism and democracy may have been antithetical; the concept employed in this chapter is of the contemporary fusion of the two.

Renowned experts have disagreed sharply on the problem of orthodoxy's relation to liberal democracy. Responsibly presented conclusions range all the way from seeing close affinity to open warfare between the two. Since the experts are in disagreement on the matter, we will study the views of spokesmen for each main viewpoint. The various "compatibility" arguments, those which hold that no basic tension exists between the principles of liberal democracy and the tenets of orthodox Christianity, range from a general statement of compatibility to an insistence on inseparability. We will begin with the former.

A study of this issue by a Rockefeller panel presents some stimulating conclusions. The members do not claim that there are no basic ideological problems; rather, they argue that conflict can be avoided by means of ideological compartmentalization and official neutrality. They write,

> In a democracy the state must be neutral with regard to religion, philosophy, or science. . . . In short, cohesion is achieved in a democratic society in the first instance by carefully removing certain questions from the sphere of politics, by separating the things that are Caesar's from the things that are God's.[4]

This response, a typical one, assumes a willingness on the part of "true believers" to accept the neutrality of government. Herein lies the source of the difficulty. Reinhold Niebuhr has suggested a

---

[3] For a concise and closely reasoned analysis of liberal democracy, see C. W. Cassinelli, *The Politics of Freedom, An Analysis of the Modern Democratic State* (Seattle: University of Washington Press, 1961).

[4] Rockefeller Brothers Fund Panel, *The Power of the Democratic Idea*, Special Studies Project Report VI (Garden City: Doubleday, 1960), p. 18.

similar type of reconciliation between religious authoritarianism and a pluralistic democracy,[5] but on occasion he goes much farther, as for example, his classic comment that "man's capacity for justice makes democracy possible; but man's inclination to injustice makes democracy necessary."[6]

Another way to view this matter is to stress not a general compatibility but an agreement on specific emphases. The liberal belief in the moral worth and inherent dignity of every person is a case in point. J. Salwyn Schapiro has well said, "The fundamental postulate of liberalism has been the moral worth, the absolute value, and the essential dignity of the human personality."[7] This notion is parallel to the orthodox Christian view that every person has an eternal soul whose value is infinitely greater than the value associated with an abstract state. In his discussion of American democracy, Barbu reflects a similar theme.

> The makers of American democracy fought the old regime in the name of the law of God which they read in their consciences. ... "The rights of man" have the same character of sacredness as the voice of God. The supreme respect for human personality lying at the basis of British democracy is rooted in the Christian conception of human life.[8]

In both orthodox Christianity and liberal democracy, there is a respect for man which is not related to any status, but fundamentally to man's humanity.

Similarly, orthodox Christianity shares with liberal democracy a deep concern for the welfare of fellowmen. Man is believed to be his brother's keeper. The orthodox Christian is reluctant to rationalize this inequity as mere fate. He sees himself as a servant of an all-loving God, and hence cannot remain aloof and indifferent. Call

---

[5] Reinhold Niebuhr, *The Children of Light and The Children of Darkness* (New York: Scribners, 1944), 1960 edition, p. 134.

[6] *Ibid.*, p. 134.

[7] Schapiro, *op. cit.*, p. 9.

[8] Zevedei Barbu, *Democracy and Dictatorship* (New York: Grove, 1956), p. 62. It should be noted that many of the writers who analyze the relationship between Christianity and liberal democracy tend to ignore the Greek, more particularly the Athenian, model. An exception is Peter Viereck, *Conservatism Revisited* (New York: Collier Books, 1962), p. 46. "Accepting slavery as we accept the use of machines, the Athenian democracy was incomplete. More loving and universal, Christianity was founded on respect for the infinite preciousness of every single individual soul. This Christian respect is what inspires political democracy as well as economic justice and must therefore precede both."

it Christian charity or social welfare, there is a basic concurrence
here.

There are other points of similarity. Equality, especially of opportunity, is a valued tenet of liberal democracy; similarly, orthodox
Christianity believes that all men are equal before God, and that
every man should be given the opportunity to make a personal commitment of faith. In much of Christianity, there is thus a strong
egalitarian undercurrent. Also, both Christianity and liberal democracy stress individual responsibility. The man who is his brother's
keeper is also his own keeper. The concept of divine sonship is related to the tenets of individual dignity and ethical responsibility.
Then, too, the emphasis placed on individual participation, in both
conversion and Christian service, is highly conducive to the democratic method. Lastly, the orthodox Christian insistence on the
duality of human life, the transcendental and the immanent, has
perhaps lent plausibility and strength to the liberal democratic
distinction between individual, private values, and public, general
values. The emphasis here is on the actual concept of duality itself — the idea of a dynamic balance. Barbara Ward's comment,
although written to describe the overall effect of the emergence of
Christianity in an earlier age, is relevant today: "Few deny the
historical role of Christianity in creating a double order of reality
and a division of power out of which the possibility of freedom has
grown."[9]

On the next level of argument, Christianity is presented as
being not only compatible but also as constituting a significant
source of liberal democracy, as either a reinforcing factor or as a
necessary precondition. Obviously referring to Christianity, Niebuhr states, "The concept of 'the value and dignity of the individual' . . . is finally meaningful only in a religious dimension,"[10] which
is saying more than that the two creeds share a common emphasis.
In similar fashion, Russell J. Clinchy attributes certain liberal democratic values to Christian faith: "the liberal views man with a
sense of optimism and affirmation, not because of a romantic con-

---

[9] Barbara Ward, *Faith and Freedom* (Garden City: Doubleday, 1958), pp.
266f. See also Barker, *op. cit.*, especially "The Impact of Christianity,"
pp. 7-13.

[10] Niebuhr, *The Irony of American History (op. cit.)*, p. 62. Cf. The Rockefeller Panel, *op. cit.*, p. v, "Democracy is a powerful idea because it draws
much of its strength from religions that posit the sanctity of the individual
and the brotherhood of man."

ception of human nature, but through a profound faith in God."[11] Other writers emphasize that orthodox Christianity satisfies the need for ideals in an officially neutral state, and that it is a necessary antidote to the uncertainty, rootlessness, and moral laxity allegedly traceable to an overemphasis on secularization.

The ultimate level of argument along this line is that the two creeds, liberal democracy and orthodox Christianity, are basically inseparable. Charles Lowry's statement illustrates this view: "Since the whole development of man and history out of which the doctrine of basic natural rights came was the offspring and issue of Christianity, we can assume that there is no question of contradiction as between democracy and Christ."[12] He continues, "Democracy is a doctrine of man. . . . It is faith in the value of the individual human person. This faith, as we have seen, did not just happen. It is Biblical and Christian in origin."[13] What is his evidence? "It has arisen in no other culture or religious tradition." Moreover, "The crisis in which it finds itself today is in large part expressive of the decline and decay in the West as a whole of vital Christian faith."[14] Turning to the contemporary American scene, he concludes, "American democracy is an offspring of which the great mother Christianity need not be ashamed."[15]

In some of her writings, Barbara Ward, the noted Catholic scholar, echoes similar views, although she defines Christianity in a different way than evangelicals Carnell or Lowry do. She writes, "Even the most doubtful must confront the fact that totalitarian government in its extreme form has returned when the waning of religion left the altars of the soul empty and turned men back to the oldest gods of all — the idols of the tribe."[16] Put in its simplest form, this view states that totalitarianism, or at least Far Rightism or Far Leftism, enters when Christianity leaves. The fact that the reference is to Christianity in general makes it no less applicable to

---

[11] Russell J. Clinchy, *Faith and Freedom* (New York: Macmillan, 1947), p. 39. Clinchy represents the position of liberal Christian theology which Hargis, as a fundamentalist, rejects. Cf. the statement by Buckley, *op. cit.*, p. 144. "The point remains: the claims that are made in behalf of democracy, the showpiece of the Liberal ideology are illusory, for the attributes imputed to it are wholly extrinsic to democracy itself."

[12] Charles W. Lowry, *op. cit.*, p. 129.

[13] *Ibid.*, p. 99. See also the following pages.

[14] *Ibid.*; the two quotations are from pp. 105 and 106.

[15] *Ibid.*, p. 106. See also Carl Cohen, ed., *Communism, Fascism, and Democracy* (New York: Random House, 1962), pp. 427f.

[16] Ward, *op. cit.*, p. 267.

the orthodox interpretation. As the present writer sees it, however, the evidence is not conclusive. Major religions, even certain branches of Christianity, have been just as dominant in societies which glorified the "tribe" as in those which did not. Intolerance and persecution characterized both Luther and his equally zealous Roman Catholic foes, and the Thirty Years' War was not fought by infidels or agnostics. Professor Ward's admonition that Western man recover his faith in God is perhaps a timely one, but the further exhortation that this recovery is necessary in order to safeguard Western freedom is not entirely logical.[17]

Finally, as a last authority on this point, we bring the perceptive Frenchman of the last century, Alexis de Tocqueville, perhaps the most outspoken of all, for he is convinced that in general "men cannot do without dogmatic belief"[18] and that "Christianity must be maintained at any cost in the bosom of modern democracies...."[19] Thus he would seem to concur with Hargis's thesis that the official nurture of Christianity ought to be the concern of a democratic governmental system.[20]

Tocqueville gives several reasons for holding this view. First, he believes that a common religious belief is a prerequisite for peace and stability in any society, but especially, and increasingly so, as political domination is relaxed and a society becomes more democratic. He asks, "How is it possible that society should escape destruction if the moral tie is not strengthened in proportion as the political tie is relaxed?" He continues, "And what can be done with a people who are their own masters if they are not submissive to the Deity?"[21] For him there can be no equivocation on the view that "fixed ideas about God and human nature are indispensable to the daily practice of men's lives...."[22] Thus, assuming the necessity of a common ideological bond, he concludes:

> General ideas respecting God and human nature are therefore the ideas above all others which it is most suitable to withdraw from the habitual action of private judgment and in which there is most to gain and least to lose by recognizing a principle of authority.[23]

[17] *Ibid.*, Chapter 20.
[18] Tocqueville, *op. cit.*, Vol. 2, p. 21.
[19] *Ibid.*, p. 156.
[20] *Ibid.*, pp. 9f.
[21] Tocqueville, *op. cit.*, Vol. 1, p. 318.
[22] *Ibid.*, Vol. 2, p. 22.
[23] *Ibid.*

The second basic justification in Tocqueville's argument involves the individual. Tocqueville argues that the possession of a dogmatic creed — (doctrinaire Christianity is what he has in mind) — is essential for a meaningful existence. "If I now consider man in his isolated capacity," he writes, "I find that dogmatic belief is no less indispensable to him in order to live alone than it is to enable him to cooperate with his fellows. If man were forced to demonstrate for himself all the truths of which he makes daily use, his task would never end."[24] He believes that "when there is no longer any principle of authority in religion any more than in politics, men are speedily frightened at this aspect of unbounded independence."[25] It is interesting to note that, while Hargis and the French writer obviously disagree on the nature of true Christianity, there is considerable agreement in their stand on the basic church-state relationship.[26] It is also significant that more than a century separates the two individuals.

Having completed the survey of the various views expressing basic compatibility between liberal democracy and orthodox Christianity, we turn to an analysis of those expressing significant conflict. Some writers see important tensions only in certain areas, others see serious conflicts involving the ideologies as wholes, and others perceive a fundamental incompatibility.

Presenting various perspectives on this issue, Dexter Perkins lists the following facets of liberal democracy as areas of specific problems: a spirit of optimism concerning the future of mankind, a belief that governmental power can remedy social evils, and a faith in progress.[27] Barbu alludes to another factor, namely, the preeminence of things religious over things secular. He says, "The democratic significance of secularization consists in the fact that this process has resulted in the diminution of the religious aspect of life, thus making possible a balance between these two dimensions...."[28] For many an orthodox Christian, balance is not the goal; he views

---

[24] *Ibid.*, Vol. 2, p. 9.

[25] *Ibid.*, p. 23. On the same page he continues, "For my own part, I doubt whether man can ever support at the same time complete religious independence and entire political freedom. And I am inclined to think that if faith be wanting in him, he must be subject; and if he be free, he must believe."

[26] Cf. Hargis's pamphlets cited previously, *If Our Foundations Be Destroyed*, and *America, Let's Get Back to God*.

[27] Dexter Perkins, *The American Way* (Ithaca: Cornell University Press, 1957), pp. 30f.

[28] Barbu, *op. cit.*, pp. 30f.

this life mainly as a preparation for the next, and for him the tenets of Christianity take precedence in any conflict with liberal democracy.

A further, but related, point of tension involves the great importance which orthodox Christianity attaches to the supremacy of faith over reason, even when reason is conditioned by a general pro-Christian emphasis. Barbu states,

> Secularization was necessary up to the point at which Euro-
> pean man gained the conviction that he could follow from an
> inner impulse the pattern of reasons and moral life instilled into
> him by centuries of Christian civilization. This is the real func-
> tion of the so-called modern conscience which forms the nucleus
> of the democratic personality.[29]

Niebuhr infers that to the extent that Christianity emphasizes moral pessimism in politics, totalitarianism is encouraged.[30] Schapiro points to another point of tension by stressing that liberalism is just as concerned about freedom of non-belief as of belief, on the ground that truth is revealed through diversity.[31] Pluralism has far-reaching significance.[32] Democracy rests on heterogeneity; the individual needs to play many roles, and no single role should be permitted to dominate the others. The same equality which characterizes the individual's roles must also characterize the group with which he identifies. The democratic way of life does not flourish in a cultural climate dominated by a single value or a single interest group. A one-idea state is incompatible with democracy, as Professor Barker explains.

> The core of democracy is choice, and not something chosen;
> choice among a number of ideas, and choice, too, of the scheme
> on which those ideas are eventually composed. Democracy is in-
> compatible with any form of one-idea State, because its essence

---

[29] *Ibid.*, p. 63.

[30] Niebuhr, *The Children of Light and The Children of Darkness (op. cit.),* p. viii. See also Barbu, *op. cit.,* p. 4.

[31] Schapiro, *op. cit.,* p. 12. Note also his statement on the previous page. "Liberals came to the deep conviction that all opinions, even erroneous ones, should have freedom of expression.... Furthermore, in the conflict between opinions even error serves a useful purpose in that it stimulates truth to clarify and fortify itself."

[32] Niebuhr, *The Children of Light and The Children of Darkness (op. cit.),* p. 122. Zevedei Barbu, *op. cit.,* p. 53, argues that democracy cannot be defined in terms of a specific ideology. A thought-provoking challenge that "liberal democracy" be considered an ideology is Bernard Williams's "Democracy and Ideology," *Political Science Quarterly,* Vol. 32 (October-December), 1961, pp. 374-384.

is hospitality to a plurality of ideas, and because its method (which is also its essence) consists in holding together a number of different ideas with a view to comparison and composition of their difference. The democratic criticism of the one-idea State is not a criticism of its object (which may also be the object of the democratic State, or at any rate part of its object): it is a criticism of its whole process of life.[33]

Another specific item of tension includes the liberal democratic emphasis on change, instability, and dynamism. The orthodox Christian desires to maintain a "proper" status quo and stability. Since he sees society as composed mainly of "unbelievers," he "knows" that the moral tone of society is not likely to improve significantly, regardless of what the government does. His main hope is that more individuals will be converted. There are some orthodox Christians who clearly share a concern for social welfare, but many do not. At best, the latter hope for a return to a period of high moral values which ostensibly existed a generation or two ago. Their moral ideal lies in the past, not in the future. In their view the only type of dynamism present in "unsaved" society is an increased craving for worldly goods, a greater pursuit of sensual indulgences, and a generally more sophisticated sinfulness.

A further cause of friction involves different views of power and authority. Liberal democracy emphasizes the relativity of all power and authority. Power is contingent and qualified. Whereas the orthodox Christian sees an omnipotent Father-God at the apex of the entire human power structure, the liberal democrat vests final authority in the mass of citizens. He is convinced that ultimately, on most issues, the majority will make the right decisions. The orthodox Christian disagrees; in his eyes the masses tend to

---

33 Barker, *op. cit.*, p. 207; see also A. F. Carrillo de Albornoz, *The Basis of Religious Liberty* (New York: Association, 1963); Franklin Hamlin Littell, "The Basis of Religious Liberty in Christian Belief," *A Journal of Church and State*, Vol. 6 (Spring, 1964); Frank H. Knight, "Liberalism and Christianity" in F. H. Knight and Thornton W. Merriam, *The Economic Order and Religion* (New York: Harper & Brothers, 1945); William Lee Miller, "The Principles of Religious Liberty," *A Journal of Church and State*, Vol. 6 (Winter, 1964); James Hastings Nichols, *Democracy and the Churches* (Philadelphia: Westminster, 1951); J. H. Randall, Jr., "The Churches and the Liberal Tradition," *Annals of the American Academy of Political and Social Sciences* (March, 1948); Samuel A. Stouffer, *Communism, Conformity, and Civil Liberties* (New York: Doubleday, 1955); John Wild, *Human Freedom and Social Order*, (Durham, N.C.: Duke University Press, 1959); Arthur Summerland Pigott Woodhouse, *Puritanism and Liberty* (London: Dent, 1938).

be wrong. He finds evidence for this conclusion in the majority's persistent error of rejecting personal salvation.

Generally speaking, liberal democrats posit the central notion that "society can safely be founded on" the "self-directing power of personality."[34] In the opinion of many orthodox Christians, it is precisely the unbeliever's personality which has been perverted by the sinister workings of Satan. Fallen man does not know his own best interests and ought not to be the final arbiter on moral issues.

Moreover, a basic tension results when all confidence is placed in rationality.[35] Orthodox Christians can never place complete trust in reason, so the argument goes, because they do not accept the premise that the problems of life can be solved by the normal exercise of the mind. They question the assumption that an individual can formulate solutions for all basic issues. The antidote to social problems, according to this view, lies not in more and better training of the mind, but in replacing a "sinful heart" with a new value system whose source is super-human, divine. Most orthodox Christians also reject the notion that what the individual cannot achieve by himself, he can, and probably will, attain in cooperation with others. Is the low-level ethic of a group going to be raised merely by the involvement of more people with the same outlook on life?[36]

The above argument is, of course, not entirely unassailable. The history of government in general, and democratic government in particular, illustrates that man can and does cooperate to achieve that which the lone individual cannot achieve and that society does succeed in curbing, even preventing, excessive deviation from general norms. But this fact does not disprove the claim that liberal democracy and orthodox Christianity do, in fact, part company on the question of human nature and its potential. While the latter proclaims the universal depravity and innate wickedness of mankind, the former affirms the human potential for, if not the inevitability of, endless improvement and perhaps even ultimate perfectibility. The one claims that only divine assistance can produce improvement, the other holds that "the human being is perfectible and social progress predictable, and that the instrument for ef-

---

[34] L. T. Hobhouse, *Liberalism* (New York: Holt, 1913), p. 123.

[35] See, for example, Stouffer, *op. cit.*, esp. pp. 140-155, and Wild, *op. cit.*, esp. Chapter 2, "Christianity, Myth, and Rationalism."

[36] In *Moral Man and Immoral Society* (New York: Scribners, 1960), Reinhold Niebuhr takes the argument even further by insisting that the morality of a group is inevitably and necessarily lower than that of the individuals composing it.

fecting the two is reason."[37] Stated in its extreme form, the difference is that the one holds that fallen man is inherently corrupt,
the other that man is still largely ignorant.

Liberal democracy has accepted as a central belief the liberal
doctrine of intellectual freedom. The human mind is to be trusted;
the more latitude permitted, the greater the likelihood that error
will be recognized. For this emphasis there is a logical reason.

The stress placed by liberalism on intellectual freedom derives from the conviction that man is essentially a rational creature
— not indeed that he is always reasonable, but that he has the
faculty of being so. Liberals in general have believed in the
existence of objective truth, discoverable through reason according
to the scientific method of research, experiment, and verification.[38]
Orthodox Christianity, on the other hand, is not so much concerned
with a wide variety of choice as with the rightness of the choice
made. It is not concerned with the latitude of the area to be in-
vestigated, because it is convinced that it has already discovered
the direction of ultimate truth and virtue.

Stated somewhat differently, liberal democracy insists that
there must be respect for every view; that ideas must compete —
and the best, hopefully, survive — in the public marketplace of
values. Tolerance, for its own sake, is the highest good.[39] Dogmatic
Christianity, however, holds that on all major value questions about
man, God, and history, there is only one acceptable view. The criterion of the "rightness" of any explanation is not efficacy or majority opinion, however strong that majority might be, but agreement with divinely revealed, supposedly timeless, "truth."

Liberal democracy also believes that the solution of societal
problems requires compromise. As Niebuhr has said, "democracy is
a method of finding proximate solutions for insoluble problems."[40]

---

[37] Buckley, *op. cit.*, p. 23.

[38] Schapiro, *op. cit.*, pp. 11-12.

[39] Tolerance requires a flexibility of mind and an awareness of ideological
limitations — both run against the grain of fundamentalism and to a lesser
extent also of orthodoxy. For a concise analysis of the necessity of both
toleration and pluralism for liberal democracy, see Reinhold Niebuhr, "A
Note on Pluralism," in John Cogley, ed., *Religion in America, Original
Essays on Religion in a Free Society* (Cleveland: Meridian Books, 1962).

[40] Niebuhr, *The Children of Light and The Children of Darkness (op. cit.)*,
p. 118. Cf. Schapiro, *op. cit.*, p. 9. "As a philosophy liberalism does not fall
into the category of a closed system of thought, with fixed, unchanging
dogmas. Rather, it may be characterized as an attitude of mind toward life
and life's problems that stresses the values of freedom for individuals, for
minorities, and for nations."

But compromise is incompatible with a full commitment to a total ideology, especially if that ideology encompasses abstract theology.[41] Instead of compromise and gradual ideological relocation, the committed convert to orthodox, as well as fundamentalist, Christianity tends to stress sudden and total transformation. The American tradition of successful revolution serves to enhance this inclination.

Although perhaps less so than their fundamentalist cousins, orthodox Christians also tend to see ideological opponents as total enemies. This reaction is derived from the assumption, held by all believers in a "total" creed, that there is not a larger, more comprehensive ideological framework within which their own belief system functions as one of several respectable alternatives. Thus there is an inherent antipathy to such concepts as "loyal opposition" and "divided loyalty." For orthodox Christians God is both central and dominant; for liberal democrats God, whatever else He may be, is made subjective and compartmentalized. Related to this is the tendency of some religious "ideologues" to subordinate means to ends, at least concerning ultimate, other-worldly values. In contrast, liberal democracy stresses method more than specific content.

The last category of perspective holds that the two "Weltanschauungen" are basically incompatible. For example, Jesuit John Murray states that "religious pluralism is against the will of God."[42] Fellow Catholics Ryan and Boland are even more specific in their claim that "no state is justified in supporting error or in according error the same recognition as truth. . . ."[43] The Protestant Andrew Lytle puts the extreme orthodox position even more strongly:

> Liberal democracy is part of the Christian drama, but it represents the devil. Liberty and fraternity are Christian words. . . . But equality exists nowhere in nature or society, nor indeed in the promise of afterlife. It is a word of false illusions, which is the devil's strategy.[44]

This quotation reflects in an extreme form the view of many ortho-

---

[41] "Christian-Americanism" fuses religious and political values but includes more of the former and is therefore properly seen as a total ideology.

[42] John C. Murray, *We Hold These Truths* (New York: Sheed and Ward, 1960), p. 23.

[43] J. A. Ryan and F. J. Boland, *Catholic Principles of Politics* (New York: Macmillan, n.d.), p. 314.

[44] Andrew Lytle, "The Quality of the South," *National Review*, Vol. 5 (March 8, 1958), pp. 236f. Note also Niebuhr, *The Children of Light and The Children of Darkness (op. cit.)*, p. xii. "A consistent pessimism in regard to man's rational capacity for justice invariably leads to absolutistic political theories."

dox Christians that equality of opportunity is important only in the spiritual realm, and that pressure for socio-economic equality is un-Christian in that it violates the hierarchical social structure ordained by God.

Among the many analysts describing this third view are such diverse writers as the noted Presbyterian minister, William Lee Miller, and Professor Paul Tillich. Miller states that, although serious problems always arise in attempting to mix the dogma of religion with the relativism of politics, the situation becomes especially difficult when "believers" give political participation high priority.

> But if religion can have bad effects when it ignores the political arena, it can have even worse effects when it pays attention to it! Here come the crusaders, their banners emblazoned with "religion," God on their side, a claim of absolute superiority over their opponents on their lips, and an unwillingness to understand or compromise with the other, infidel side in their hearts.

> Religion extended into politics often lends its note of absoluteness to what are actually the very relative matters of politics.[45]

Tillich states:

> I want to ask the question whether religion may endanger a free society. I think there are forces in religion which always have and always will resist the development of a free society. Four of these can be named: a religious conservatism, a religious authoritarianism, a religious intolerance, and a religious transcendentalism.[46]

The type of Christian ideology expounded by Hargis exhibits all four of these traits. They are inherent in the faith, and become crucial when the distinction between individualistic religion and societal politics disappears.

We have now completed this brief survey of the various types of answers to our initial question, whether an inherent tension exists between orthodox Christianity and liberal democracy. Significantly, the great majority of the writers mentioned see at least some important problems and serious tensions. This conclusion probably reflects the views of political scientists in general, and the present writer shares this view. Basic differences over such matters as the role of reason, the nature of man, the place of religion, the principle of compromise, the vision of progress, and the role

---

[45] William Lee Miller, *The Protestant and Politics* (Philadelphia: Westminster, 1958), p. 28.

[46] Paul Tillich, "Freedom and the Ultimate Concern," in John Cogley, ed., *Religion in America* (Cleveland: Meridian, 1962), pp. 272-286. The quotation is from page 274.

of error cannot be fully eliminated. Many "true believers" do not push their views to logical conclusions. They apply one ethic to their personal religious life and another one to society as a whole. Their zeal is restrained by an awareness of their finiteness; sophistication blunts their fervor. They tend to be pragmatic on the question of the role of pragmatism itself, and this tendency constitutes their ideological salvation. But for the orthodox Christian who strives to practice his religious creed consistently and lets it determine his thought patterns, there are some serious difficulties. The values shared by both orthodox Christianity and liberal democracy have little significance for him. Niebuhr's point, that "it must be admitted that toleration in religion could probably not have been achieved in any modern democratic society had there not been a considerable decay of traditional religious loyalties,"[47] is well taken.

Support for the principles of religious democracy "requires something more than a religious devotion to ideals. It requires religious humility."[48] But, as is clear from history, and logical in theory, ideological humility is anathema to adherents of any religious system providing "total" answers, especially if they are under attack. This fact constitutes the essence of the dilemma. Although he admits that the dilemma is a basic one, Niebuhr appears to be reluctant to accept the full implications. He claims to see a way out.

> The solution requires a very high form of religious commitment. It demands that each religion, or each version of a single faith, seek to proclaim its highest insights while yet preserving an humble and contrite recognition of the fact that all actual expressions of religious faith are subject to historical contingency and relativity.[49]

Appealing as this solution may be in theory, it rests on a degree of sophistication, a maturity of insight, and an awareness of one's own frailty which is not to be expected from more than a small fraction of mankind. It begs the question by asking believers in a total creed to agree that the creed is both total and relative, and asks them to do this because reason requires it.

The thesis which logic and evidence seem to support, then, is not that orthodox Christianity in itself produces Far Rightism, but that a constant state of tension develops when orthodox Christianity and liberal democracy coexist in a society, or within an in-

---

[47] Niebuhr, *The Children of Light and The Children of Darkness (op. cit.)*, p. 130.
[48] *Ibid.*, p. 151.
[49] *Ibid.*, p. 134.

dividual, and that when the religious creed is threatened by a rival creed, such as Communism, it stiffens its stance, extends its scope, and usurps part of the realm of liberal democratic voluntarism and pluralism. The intensity of the reaction seems to be roughly proportionate to the intensity and duration of the threat. Furthermore, if the threat comes from external sources, the reaction tends to be more widespread and more permanent. If the threat is internal as well as external, the likelihood of a belligerent defensiveness increases. If the "enemy" threatens both the religious and the political creeds and has domestic as well as foreign components, and if the issue at stake is all-out victory, and if the outcome of the "battle" hangs in the balances, then the reaction will be all the more extreme. Orthodox Christianity thus presented is not an immediate precipitant of Far Rightism, but ultimately it contributes, by virtue of some of its emphases, at least some basic tensions. That the tension at present is a deep and frustrating one for many people is evidenced by the nature and intensity of the public debate on the Becker amendment.[50]

The general conclusion bears repetition; since the majority of orthodox Christians have not embraced Far Rightism as a political creed, the most one can say is that it is a conducive, not a precipitant, factor. The search for the efficient cause leads to an analysis of Christian fundamentalism.

---

[50] See Anson Phelps Stokes, *Church and State in the United States* (New York: Harper, 1950), Vol. 2, pp. 344-349.

10. THE SIGNIFICANCE OF CHRISTIAN FUNDAMENTALISM

MOST OF THE STUDIES OF THE FAR RIGHT CURRENTLY AVAILABLE emphasize sociological and psychological factors, with whole theories being built on one or both, but give very little attention to the significance of fundamentalism. The joint occurrence of the two has frequently been noted but, generally speaking, the nature of the relationship has not been analyzed. Frequently one finds a superficial designation of the two as being equally unrespectable and having an appeal only for the irrational. Granted, fundamentalism may be irrational, but it is hardly more so than many other religious orientations, both primitive and highly developed. Moreover, is the quality, much less the significance, of a religious outlook to be determined by the degree of its rationality? Acceptance of reincarnation, transubstantiation, and justification, as well as belief in Nirvana, purgatory, heaven, and hell, are matters of faith, not of reason.

The central argument in this chapter is that a basic and logical relationship — but not a one-to-one correlation — exists between Christian fundamentalism and the political Far Right. That is not to say that fundamentalism constitutes a definite prerequisite, but rather, that it is a major precipitant. Accordingly, an analysis of fundamentalism becomes essential. As the tenets and orientation of fundamentalism are presented below, it will soon become evident that to a large degree the phenomenon of the Far Right can be explained as a more or less consistent (but not intrinsically rational) transfer of the categories of Christian fundamentalism to the realm of politics. In this connection one should remember that the movement is still thriving and still important. As a critic recently put it, "Fundamentalism, when noticed at all by our popular journals, is

128

usually patronized as a colorful fragment of an older, vanishing way of life. But the truth is that fundamentalism is a growing socio-religious force in America."[1]

What do we understand by the term fundamentalism? The label was taken from the title of a twelve-volume series published in 1909.[2] This publication became the classic presentation of a particular reaction against allegedly "liberal" tendencies, such as the "Social Gospel," which spread rapidly among American Christendom in the turbulent decades following the Civil War and reached a peak at the turn of the century.[3] For decades this twelve-volume

[1] David Danzig, "The Radical Right and the Rise of the Fundamentalist Minority," *Commentary*, Vol. 33 (April, 1962), p. 292. Cf. the statement by Murray S. Stedman, *Religion and Politics in America* (New York: Harcourt, Brace and World, 1964), p. 13, "Extreme right-wing politics and extreme right-wing religion find much in common, and often the latter merely serves as a smoke screen to hide the former from exposure." While this may be true of some extremists, it is not true of Hargis. He does not seek to "smoke screen" any of his views; moreover, he does not make a basic distinction between right-wing politics and right-wing religion. Stedman's statement is probably an apt description of Gerald L. K. Smith, whom Hargis terms a "phony." See Adams, *op. cit.*, p. 195. See also Louis Cassels, "The Rightist Crisis in Our Churches," *Look*, Vol. 26 (April 24, 1962).

[2] A currently available edition is *The Fundamentals, A Testimony to the Truth*, 12 vols. (Los Angeles: Biola, 1917). For an analysis of fundamentalism, see Louis Gasper, *The Fundamentalist Movement* (The Hague: Mouton, 1963). For a perceptive discussion of the weaknesses in fundamentalism in relationship to society, see Carl F. H. Henry, *The Uneasy Conscience of Modern Fundamentalism* (Grand Rapids: Eerdmans, 1947). See also Henry's later work, *Aspects of Christian Social Ethics* (Grand Rapids: Eerdmans, 1964). For an account of the intellectual development of fundamentalism, consult Stewart G. Cole, *The History of Fundamentalism* (Hamden, Conn.: Shoe String Press, 1954); H. Richard Niebuhr, *Christ and Culture* (New York: Harper and Row, 1956), especially p. 102; and Daniel B. Stevick, *Beyond Fundamentalism* (Richmond, Va.: Knox, 1964). A book very disparaging of fundamentalism is Sidney E. Mead, *The Lively Experiment, The Shaping of Christianity in America* (New York: Harper and Row, 1963). The author says that the group was "utterly bankrupt" in intelligence and imagination.

[3] For an informative analysis of the "Social Gospel," see C. H. Hopkins, *The Rise of the Social Gospel in American Protestantism* (New Haven: Yale University Press, 1950), and Chapter X of Winthrop Hudson, *The Great Tradition of the American Churches* (New York: Harper and Row, 1953). For another viewpoint, see Anson Phelps Stokes and Leo Pfeffer, *Church and State in the United States* (New York: Harper, 1964), pp. 299-303. Walter Rauschenbusch, well-known apologist for the "Social Gospel," has said, "My sole desire has been to summon the Christian passion for justice and the Christian powers of love and mercy to do their share in redeeming our social order from its inherent wrongs." Cited in *ibid.*, p. 301. For a

series greatly influenced many of the Protestant denominations. The important point for our purposes, however, is not the technical theological disputation, but the nature of the fundamentalist orientation and its socio-political impact.

"Militant fundamentalism," writes Herbert Schneider, "is a twentieth-century movement of protest and unrest; it is apocalyptic, prophetic, critical of modern life and apprehensive of the future."[4] Additional traits of fundamentalism include an uncritical emphasis on biblical literalism, an acceptance of Scripture as the highest authority in all areas of life, a deep suspicion of rationalism and higher education, especially as opposed to indoctrination, and intolerance.[5] As generally defined, and as employed here, fundamentalism does not include the pietistic, Anabaptist, or pacifistic groups, such as Moravians, Amish, Mennonites, and most of the Quakers who, while emphasizing biblical literalism, nevertheless differ basically in that they place major emphasis on "the separated life," political non-involvement, or conscientious objection.

Since the thought patterns of fundamentalists are basically homogeneous, one may justifiably speak in terms of "the fundamentalist mind." Hofstadter deals with several facets of this concept, especially as it relates to the contemporary flowering of the Far Right. The statement presented below deals largely with the psychological and sociological rather than the theological aspects.

The fundamentalist mind has had the bitter experience of being routed in the field of morals and censorship, on evolution and prohibition, and it finds itself increasingly submerged in a world in which the great and respectable media of mass communication violate its sensibilities and otherwise ignore it. In a modern, experimental, and "sophisticated" society, it has been elbowed aside and made a figure of fun, and even much of the religious "revival" of our time is genteel and soft-spoken in a way that could never have satisfied the old-fashioned fundamentalist zeal. But in politics, the secularized fundamentalism of our time has found a new kind of force and a new punitive capacity. The political climate of the post-war era has given the fundamentalist type powerful new allies among other one-hundred percenters:

succinct presentation of Rauschenbusch's views, see his *Christianity and the Social Crisis* (New York: Macmillan, 1907). Other major works by Rauschenbusch include: *A Theology for the Social Gospel* (New York: Abingdon, 1917), and *Christianizing the Social Order* (New York: Macmillan, 1912).

[4] Herbert W. Schneider, *Religion in 20th Century America* (New York: Atheneum, 1964), p. 16.

[5] Stedman, *op. cit.*, pp. 129f. See also Roy, *op. cit.*, pp. 214f.

rich men, some of them still loyal to a fundamentalist upbringing, stung by the income tax and still militant against the social reforms of the New Deal; isolationist groups and militant nationalists; Catholic fundamentalists, ready for the first time to unite with their former persecutors on the issue of "Godless Communism"; and Southern reactionaries newly animated by the fight over desegregation.[6]

Certain central facets of fundamentalism seem to transfer readily to the political order, with far-reaching results. A simplistic dualism is a case in point. The fundamentalist sees two categories, righteousness and evil, and nothing in between.[7] Hargis, for example, writes, "Let me challenge you with this thought. God hates a coward. This is no time to be fearful. We have a choice before us. We can be American or Communist."[8] The theological source of this rigid dualism seems to be a literal application of a number of statements of Scripture, of which perhaps the most widely cited is Revelation 3:15-16, "I know thy works, that thou art neither cold nor hot: I would thou wert cold or hot. So then because thou art lukewarm, and neither cold nor hot, I will spew thee out of my mouth." Given this emphasis and an uncritical orientation, it is hardly surprising that many fundamentalists look upon the world, including the political sphere, not as an arena in which a given ideology seeks to come to terms with opposing forces, but as a battleground between absolute good and absolute evil. In contrast to the mature political mind which stresses procedures and institutions at least as much as particular values, the fundamentalist mind begins with a revealed definition of an absolute right and employs those methods which are believed to facilitate its realization. Note the tone of the following statement by the Reverend Mr. Carl McIntire, one of Hargis's crusading colleagues.

Whenever issues are drawn between two opposing sides there always are those who desire compromise and a middle course

---

[6] Richard Hofstadter, *Anti-Intellectualism in American Life* (New York: Knopf, 1963), p. 134.

[7] Commenting on the Far Right, as well as the Far Left, Harry and Bonaro Overstreet have argued that adherents "want to change the character of our society by splitting it down the middle into mutually warring camps." *The Strange Tactics of Extremism* (New York: Norton, 1964), p. 13. This may be a correct evaluation of the Far Left, but it does not fit the fundamentalist Far Right. These people are firmly convinced that the split already exists; it was not and is not their doing. Their goal is to have it recognized and "properly understood," and then to have the battle carried to the enemy. To this end they stress the dissemination of "facts" and the need for militancy.

[8] Hargis, *The Far Left (op. cit.),* p. 284.

for the sake of unity and immediate advantage. But where one of the sides in the conflict has hold of an eternal truth, as is the case with those of us who embrace the great doctrines of the historic Christian faith, to compromise in the slightest is to dishonor and destroy the faith. Truth cannot be compromised and continue to be truth.[9]

Carnell writes, "The mentality of fundamentalism is dominated by ideological thinking. Ideological thinking is rigid, intolerant, and doctrinaire; it sees principles everywhere, and all principles come in clear tones of black and white. It exempts itself," says this apologist for Christian orthodoxy, "from the limits that original sin places on history; it wages holy wars without acknowledging the elements of pride and personal interest that prompt the call to battle; it creates new evils while trying to correct old ones."[10]

Fundamentalist tendencies toward intolerance should not be interpreted as being mere reactionary malice. Tolerance comes easily for those who do not believe strongly in anything. They sacrifice nothing; they yield no ground in battle. But for a person who believes in absolutes, in the "knowable" distinction between true and false, and whose life centers on a religion which includes eternal rewards and punishments — for such a person full tolerance is impossible. If pressed by others he may grudgingly grant his opponent more or less equal liberties, but only as a privilege, not as a right, for he does not accept him as an equal. In his heart he knows his opponent to be in error.

Many fundamentalists, by virtue of authority allegedly derived from Scripture, speak readily on almost any subject. Carnell writes that the fundamentalist

> not only tells sinners to repent but he stands behind the sacred desk and pronounces on science, the United Nations, and the cause of immorality in France. He egregiously offends humility and truth, but he does not know enough about humility and truth to measure his offense. He adds to general insecurity by giving dangerously simple answers to bafflingly complex questions.[11]

This description fits many fundamentalists. The prerequisite of childlike faith for entrance into the Kingdom of Heaven is readily translated into the notion that native, divinely implanted abilities to judge moral and even political and scientific issues, are more

---

[9] Carl McIntire, *Servants of Apostasy* (Collingswood, New Jersey: Christian Beacon Press, 1955), p. 325.

[10] Edward John Carnell, *The Case for Orthodox Theology* (Philadelphia: Westminster, 1959), p. 114.

[11] *Ibid.*, pp. 122f.; cf. p. 120 for a discussion of "The Negative Ethic."

reliable than the opinions of university-trained experts, whose claim to authority rests on mere human attainment. The testimony concerning the theory of evolution, as presented at the famous Scopes trial, is a case in point.

A related tendency is to take absolute stands on debatable issues, even if this means ignoring obvious facts. In the fundamentalist perspective, nothing of significance is debatable. Relativism is blasphemy. The fact that this attitude may involve sins of pride and pretense is conveniently ignored. Thus, the fundamentalist "uses the Word of God as an instrument of self-security but not self-criticism. This is the source of his zeal and the cause of his irony."[12]

Many critics have overlooked the significance of the concept of hate in fundamentalism. A good fundamentalist hates sin as much as God does. He despises sin and Satan with a righteous biblical authority. Did God not say, "Hate the evil and love the good"?[13] Why should a person suddenly change his categories when he shifts to the political realm? Why be tolerant of known evil? True, a righteous hatred may provoke a reaction of intense unrighteous hatred, but that is to be expected: it too is biblical. "Marvel not, my brethren, if the world hate you." "Blessed are they which are persecuted for righteousness' sake: for theirs is the kingdom of heaven. Blessed are ye, when men shall revile you and persecute you.... Rejoice and be exceeding glad: for great is your reward in heaven: for so persecuted they the prophets which were before you." And, "The servant is not greater than his lord. If they have persecuted me, they will also persecute you."[14] Heresy-hunting is transferred easily from the religious to the political arena, in part because it seems to be in keeping with what has been called "the fundamentalists' apocalyptic conception of the world as strictly divided into the saved and the damned." Unfortunately, this resistance to heresy "has readily lent itself to reactionary political uses." That fundamentalism of the cross has merged so easily, es-

---

[12] *Ibid.,* p. 125.

[13] Amos 5:15. Note also the following: Psalm 5:4-5, "For thou art not a God that hath pleasure in wickedness: neither shall evil dwell with thee. The foolish shall not stand in thy sight: thou hatest all workers of iniquity." Psalm 97:10, "Ye that love the Lord, hate evil...." See also Proverbs 8:13; Luke 14:26; and John 15:18. Cf. Eric Hoffer, *The True Believer* (New York: New American Library, 1951), Mentor edition, p. 85, "Hatred is the most accessible and comprehensive of all unifying agents."

[14] I John 3:13; Matthew 5:10-12; John 15:20.

pecially since World War II, with a rigid fundamentalism of the flag should cause no surprise, for Communism threatens both the cross and the flag, militarily as well as ideologically.

Several contemporary analysts constantly berate the Far Right for what is termed "the preaching of division and discord."[15] These critics appear not to realize that fundamentalism is built around the concepts of discord and division and that, legitimately or not, they can quote Scripture to corroborate their view. Christ told his disciples, "I came not to send peace, but a sword. For I am come to set a man at variance against his father, and the daughter against her mother, and the daughter in law against her mother in law. And a man's foes shall be they of his own household."[16] The exhortation of the Apostle Paul to the Corinthians echoes a similar tone. Believers must not only keep themselves pure, undefiled, and unspotted from the world. They must also sever all ties with those who fail to do so. "Be ye not unequally yoked together with unbelievers: for what fellowship hath righteousness with unrighteousness? and what communion hath light with darkness? .... Wherefore come out from among them, and be ye separate, saith the Lord. . . ."[17] This doctrine, as perceived by the fundamentalist, would logically seem to oppose a close association of fundamentalism with nationalism. However, as was shown earlier, many fundamentalists superficially evade this point by holding to two definitions of being Christian. Hence, Rightist literature abounds with simultaneous, inconsistent emphases on spiritual, individual conversion and nationalistic Christian-Americanism.

Concerning the transfer of the fundamentalist orientation to politics, the fundamentalist firmly believes that he is behaving quite consistently, as in a sense he indeed is. What the critic describes as rigid fanaticism, the believing fundamentalist perceives as a respectable, in fact praiseworthy, ideological consistency. What the critic terms a new reactionism is only a new depiction of old-line fundamentalism in a new situation.

The question of evil also is important for the fundamentalist. Hoffer's contention that the true believer requires an omnipresent devil might have been stated more correctly in another way, namely,

---

15 Roy, *op. cit.*, p. x. Cf. Milton Rokeach, *The Open and Closed Mind* (New York: Basic Books, 1960), who argues (p. 403) that there is always a positive correlation between closed belief systems and anxiety, and that anxiety readily precipitates divisiveness.

16 Matthew 10:34-36.

17 II Corinthians 6:15-17.

that childhood instruction in an omnipresent devil generates "true belief."[18] Nevertheless, for Hargis Communism is the real devil, and since for him Communism is itself a creation of the biblical devil, it cannot be hated too much; hence, Hargis's fanatic anti-Communism. The biblical statements about the omnipresence of Satan and his great power as "Prince of this World"[19] make the omnipresence of the Communist conspiracy fully plausible; indeed, they can even be taken as "proof." This type of reasoning is the major source of the Far Right's characteristic sense of impending disaster.

One result of applying the conspiratorial view of the world to politics is that the devoted fundamentalist, like his Marxist adversary, readily jumps to unjustified conclusions, and sees definite relationships where none exist. For him the possible is thus translated into the probable, and the probable into the actual. Furthermore, verses describing Satan as an angel of light[20] make it easy for the committed, and especially the committed and naive, to identify socialism and political liberalism with cunningly disguised Communism. Thus Hargis can say, employing the very words of Scripture, "The strategy and tactics of Communism are shrewd, the very 'wiles of the devil.' "[21] And the secretary of a fundamentalist organization can report to that organization's convention that, "We are confronted with satanic forces — the numerous socialistic projects including socialized medicine, urban renewal and deficit spending — which will surely lead us to communism unless we follow God's infallible word and stress the rights of the individual rather than society."[22]

The equation of Communism with sin and Satan means that all political discussion takes on great moral fervor. Politics becomes a crusade and agitation a Christian duty, with patriotism exalted as proof of mature spirituality. The emotional fanaticism of Nazi Germany and the religious wars of Islam are other illustrations of a similar orientation.

As indicated in the quotation cited previously, fundamentalists do not hesitate to claim biblical support for conservative and ultra-conservative stands on various social issues and reform generally.

18 Hoffer, op. cit., p. 115.
19 John 16:11; John 14:30; and John 12:31.
20 II Corinthians 11:14 and II Timothy 2:26.
21 Hargis, Communism, The Total Lie! (op. cit.), p. 30.
22 Schneidler, op. cit., p. 75. For an analysis of this orientation, see Timothy L. Smith, Revivalism and Social Reform (Nashville: Abingdon, 1957).

In the main they reject social security and all similar welfare programs. Most would agree with Congressman August Johnson's denunciation of what he called "salvation by appropriation," and with one leading fundamentalist spokesman who said,

> Jesus Christ was not interested in lobbying before Pilate, Agrippa, or Caesar's government for betterment of social, economic, or political conditions.... He left his followers no legacy in the form of material comforts and a high standard of living. He left them only a cross and an eventual crown, to be obtained through persecution and martyrdom.[23]

Commenting on this outlook, a contemporary Anabaptist critic has said that what fundamentalism demands is "the preaching of the Gospel of personal redemption, looking to the coming of the Kingdom, and trusting God in His own way to supply any necessary additions. For these additions social action [is] unnecessary and uncalled for."[24] Similarly, Professor Perkins observes that,

> If one is preoccupied with the blessed hope of the world to come, if one regards one's state on this earth as transitory, preliminary to something far better, then it is easy to be patient under the slings and arrows of outrageous fortune and to feel that the amelioration of the human lot is of secondary importance to the worship of God and the observance of religious forms.[25]

He might have added that it is particularly "easy to be patient" if the "slings and arrows of outrageous fortune" affect others only. Most fundamentalists are quick to react to any infringement on their incomes or any injustice when they are the ones affected. Most Caucasian fundamentalists would likely do much more than contemplate the life to come, should they suddenly discover that they were being underpaid simply because of their race, religion, or any other unjust reason.

In keeping with the downgrading of social action to remedy social ills, fundamentalists emphasize the virtue of individualism. Harking back, at least by inference, to a self-regulating natural law and to certain biblical passages,[26] fundamentalists stress individual initiative and the related virtues of frugality, thrift, and self-reliance. (This emphasis is one of the reasons why fundamentalists often prosper economically.) Since the individual is more important than

---

23 Quoted in Ellsworth and Harris, *op. cit.*, p. 14.

24 Guy F. Hershberger, *The Way of the Cross in Human Relations* (Scottdale, Pa.: Herald, 1958), p. 132.

25 Dexter Perkins, *op. cit.*, p. 6.

26 Psalm 138:8; Proverbs 31:31; and II Thessalonians 3:10, "if any would not work, neither should he eat."

the state, or even society, it logically follows that there must not be any superior authority for shaping and directing wants. Every individual is a divinely created sovereign — "in the image of God made He man"[27] — capable of ascertaining his own wants and satisfying them in the open market place, and endowed with an inalienable right to exercise his free will. Any governmental tampering with God-given rights is considered to be morally wrong because it prevents the individual from developing his full potential. Each person shapes his own destiny. True, not all will necessarily succeed, but whatever a person's achievement, it is his own responsibility.[28]

The fundamentalist "Weltanschauung," then, is similar in many respects to the political creed of the Far Right. A closely related question concerns the extent to which Christian fundamentalism is antithetical to the liberal democratic value system. The discussion in Chapter 9 has indicated the nature of the complex relationship between liberal democracy and orthodox Christianity in general. Our concern at this point is with the peculiarly fundamentalist emphases.

In certain respects, such as the constant stress placed on the priesthood of all believers, the significance of each individual's conscience, the notion that every believer is his own final authority, and the ensuing theological and organizational pluralism, fundamentalism fosters liberal democracy. But the bulk of the influence is on the other side. Fundamentalism sees society as composed of two ultimately irreconcilable camps, a conception which denies the liberal democratic principle of the basic unity of society. Furthermore, as Ernest Barker has convincingly shown, the liberal democratic creed requires a belief in the basic distinction between the sacred and the secular, the one being ultimately personal and internal, the other quite properly public and governmental.[29] Here, too, the fundamentalist takes a different view. According to his dogma, the distinction is an artificial one, and in his attempt to eliminate it he weakens the body politic. Not only does he limit freedom for others by seeking to foist his views on an unwilling society, but he also creates a frustrating dilemma for himself by claiming broad freedoms and rights which he is not willing to grant his ideological adversaries.

---

27 Genesis 1:27.
28 See Harvey C. Bunke, *The Liberal Dilemma* (Englewood Cliffs: Prentice-Hall, 1964), pp. 52f.
29 Barker, *op. cit.*, pp. 42f.

Another dimension of this relationship involves fundamental-ism's status in society. Permanent minorities rarely become defenders of majority rule, and fundamentalism is no exception. A commit-ment to democracy requires a belief that on ultimate questions the majority can determine what is right. But fundamentalists (who constitute only a small minority) are convinced that the majority has been perpetually wrong on the most important of all value judg-ments, the one involving the issue of fundamentalism itself. Con-sequently, fundamentalists are predisposed from the outset not to accept majority rule, at least not on vital issues.

Not all observers are fully agreed on the relationship between fundamentalism and Far Rightism as set forth above. Murray Sted-man, for example, contends that "there is no apparent dictate in the inner logic of fundamentalism that would necessarily predispose its followers to political authoritarianism...."[30] The available evi-dence, however, seems to point in the opposite direction and to justify the assertion that the widespread alliance of fundamentalism and Far Rightism is more than coincidental.[31]

What does one finally make of the significance of funda-mentalism? How can one explain the fact that some fundamentalists are militant "Far Righters" while others seem to be unperturbed and politically inactive, even in the face of the global Communist threat? The explanation seems to be that the former have incau-tiously introduced political data into their creed, and have decided that socio-political agitation constitutes part of evangelism. They seem also to have misconstrued the doctrine of intolerance. These fundamentalists correctly assert that throughout the New Testament there is a recurring theme of intolerance, but they overlook the fact that it is always a spiritual intolerance, always directly related to crucial Christian doctrine. They forget that the weapons of Chris-tians, be they liberal or fundamentalist, should be only spiritual. Fundamentalism evolves into Hargis-type authoritarian nationalism when it ignores the fact that only a voluntary acquiescence in Christian dogma is meaningful, and when it overlooks the crucial fact that moral freedom, which according to fundamentalism itself is a divine gift to mankind, necessarily includes the right to err.

---

[30] Stedman, op. cit., p. 129.
[31] See the relevant chapters in Gasper, op. cit.

11. SOURCES OF "HARGISISM"

In the preceding chapters we saw that orthodox Christianity is not fully compatible with an unqualified liberal democratic value system, and that Christian fundamentalism is conducive to the development of a Far Rightist outlook. But that fact does not explain the recent upsurge of Far Rightism in general and religious Far Rightism in particular. It is to this question that we now turn our attention.

A rather frequent type of explanation stresses psychological factors. Roy V. Peel states, "Particular persons become WACKA-COBI because they have psycho-physiological constitutions that impel them to behave as they do."[1] Daniel Bell asserts, "In short, the radical right, having a diffused sense of fear, needs to find some story or explanation to explain, or justify, that fear. One can deny the external reality, and build up the internal threat, through such psychological mechanisms."[2] The present writer believes that it is not so much a matter of fear resulting in the need for an explanation, but rather, a given belief in an explanation, or theory, which generates the fear. It may be comforting to think that we are more normal than (or at least psychologically different from) those who are in fundamental disagreement with us, but this explanation is inadequate.

One must be careful to avoid the reductivist fallacy of assigning all significance in the problems considered to personality fac-

---

[1] Roy V. Peel, "The Wackacobi: Extremists of Our Own Times," *Western Political Quarterly*, Vol. 16 (September, 1963), p. 586. The "WA" represents the supporters of Congressman Walter and General Walker; the "CACO" the "Christian Anti-Communists," with the "K" thrown in to represent the Ku Klux Klan; and the "BI" refers to the members and supporters of the John Birch Society.

[2] Bell, "The Dispossessed," *op. cit.*, pp. 14f.

tors. Equally, one must avoid the temptation to 'psychologize' problems to such an extent as to strip them of their significance as genuine political or philosophical problems.[3]

With reference to intolerance and bigotry, Rokeach has demonstrated that all belief systems, regardless of the degree to which they are open or closed, are independent of personality.[4] To try to explain Rightist views by talking about a Fascist personality scale is inadequate if not erroneous.[5] On the question of personality and opinions in general, several authorities have pointed out that the whole phenomenon of opinion formation is extremely complex, and that they have been unable to establish any strong correlation between a person's opinions and his personality.[6] This fact does not mean that no correlation whatsoever exists between support of conservative or other doctrines and certain personality patterns. But it does mean that the nature of the connection and the reasons for it are not adequately known.[7] Also, the correlation tested, particularly in the studies done by Adorno and his associates,[8] covers only certain traits, not the Far Right as a whole. In short, the study of personality is helpful, but it does not provide the key to understanding Hargis or the thousands who support him. Regional, chronological, and other variations force us to concentrate more on situational factors; and, even if we agree that personality constitutes a significant determinant, we must recognize that it is not something "innate" or "racial," but is itself conditioned largely by early social environment.[9]

Before proceeding further we should answer the question whether Christian Crusade is more than Billy James Hargis; whether if we could explain him, we would have explained everything. The answer must be emphatically negative, for although Hargis

---

[3] Herbert McCloskey, "Conservatism and Personality," *American Political Science Review*, Vol. 52 (March, 1958), p. 44.

[4] Rokeach, *The Open and Closed Mind (op. cit.)*, p. 395.

[5] Milton Rokeach, "Political and Religious Dogmatism: An Alternative to the Authoritarian Personality," *Psychological Monographs*, Vol. 70 (1956). See also T. W. Adorno, et al., *The Authoritarian Personality* (New York: Harper, 1950), and Richard Christie and Marie Jahoda, eds., *Studies in the Scope and Method of 'The Authoritarian Personality'* (Glencoe: The Free Press, 1954). The latter includes a devastating analysis of the methodology employed by Adorno, et al.

[6] Brewster M. Smith, Jerome S. Bruner, and Robert W. White, *Opinions and Personality* (New York: Wiley, 1956).

[7] McCloskey, *op. cit.*, p. 38.

[8] Adorno, *op. cit.*

[9] *Ibid.*, p. 6.

dominates the entire movement, it could continue without him. There would be another name and another face (the Reverend Mr. David Nobel is his closest associate), but the crusade would carry on.

> No matter how vital we think the role of leadership in the rise of a mass movement, there is no doubt that the leader cannot create conditions which make the rise of a movement possible. ... There has to be ... an intense dissatisfaction with things as they are, before movement and leader can make their appearance.[10]

Hargis in many ways may resemble the late Senator Joseph Mc-Carthy, his hero and friend, but he is not the one-man swashbuckler that McCarthy was. He represents a movement which is more than his own personal empire.[11] Thus, if we want to understand it we will have to go beyond personality analysis.

A second line of explanation stresses sociological and socio-economic factors. This approach quickly leads to a long list of theories. Harold Proshansky and Richard Evans stress economic dislocation and shifts in the economic hierarchy during times of prosperity.[12] Evidence to support this thesis is at best inconclusive. Bell at one point emphasizes dispossession in general and argues that dispossessed social groups invariably seek targets on which to vent their resentments, and thus extremism and professional anti-Communism emerge.[13] Mark Chesler and Richard Schmuck point to feelings of personal ineffectiveness, and isolation, and a loss of status in a rapidly changing society.[14] Hofstadter asserts that what holds the Far Right together is "status motivation" and the desire for identity. His key concept is "status anxiety," which he relates to an assumed nagging doubt held by these people as to whether they are truly Americans.[15] Sherwin concludes that, "basically, they are frustrated and frightened.... A deep inferiority claims them all; in some the lack of identity is so aching that only in clinging to

---

10 Hoffer, op. cit., p. 103.

11 Ibid., pp. 105f. See also Gabriel Almond, The American People and Foreign Policy (New York: Praeger, 1960), Chapter 3, and esp. p. 52.

12 Proshansky and Evans, "The 'Radical Right': A Threat to the Behavioral Sciences," in Journal of Social Issues (op. cit.), p. 88. See also Richard Hofstadter, The American Political Tradition (New York: Random House, 1948), p. vi.

13 Bell, op. cit., p. 3.

14 Richard Schmuck and Mark Chesler, "On Super Patriotism," Journal of Social Issues, Vol. 19 (April, 1963), pp. 23f.

15 Richard Hofstadter, "The Pseudo-Conservative Revolt," in Bell, op. cit., p. 9. "The cement that holds them together is the status motivation and the desire for an identity."

a group of their compeers can they find a semblance of selfhood."[16]

Each of these socio-economic arguments has some validity, but for each one there is also contradictory evidence. Admittedly, there has been economic dislocation, but is it any greater now than it was 15 or 20 years ago? And how can this theory account for the dedicated leadership provided by H. L. Hunt, Robert Welch, and the other wealthy elite? And why has Far Rightism affected the dislocated only in certain regions? The theory of general dispossession and a sense of being threatened accounts for some of the reaction, but not at the grass roots level. The common folk, and especially fundamentalists such as Hargis, are no more dispossessed than they ever were and probably less so now, at least in financial terms, than ever before. They may have frustrations, but not on that count. The concept of "status anxiety" is helpful, especially as it relates to those who have recently attained new wealth, but in itself it is insufficient. Many questions remain. Personality dynamics and broad social and economic changes do not supply adequate answers.

A third type of analysis stresses frustration. Bell writes, "Today the politics of the radical right is the politics of frustration — the sour impotence of those who find themselves unable to understand, let alone command, the complex mass society that is the polity today."[17] Hoffer says that "frustration of itself, without any proselytizing from the outside, can generate most of the peculiar characteristics of the true believer...."[18] Clearly, frustration abounds and is significant, especially as it relates to fear. Ernest Kris and Nathan Leites in their "privatization" thesis point out that the new ingredient in the present frustration is that a sense of incompetence results, not in overt criticism, but in "projective distrust," that over a period of time this suppression of frustration within the individual causes him to hate what he cannot understand or master, and that if "appropriate education on a vast enough scale and at a rapid enough rate is not provided for, the distrust and privatization of the masses may be-

---

16 Sherwin, op. cit., p. 227. Cf. Hoffer, op. cit., p. 53, "There is perhaps no more reliable indicator of a society's ripeness for a mass movement than the prevalence of unrelieved boredom."

17 Bell, op. cit., p. 42.

18 Hoffer, op. cit., p. 10. Lipset, "The Sources of the 'Radical Right,'" in Bell, op. cit., p. 370, has written, "Political extremists are capitalizing on our doubts and fears, but it is the situation which creates these doubts and fears, rather than the extremists, that is mainly responsible for the lack of resistance by the political moderate." The evidence supports this conclusion.

come a fertile soil for totalitarian management."[19] That a powerful
United States is less the master of its own fate than was a weaker
United States in an earlier day, is frustrating to many people, particularly those who do not realize that total security and defense are
no longer attainable. For a nation which has traditionally subordi-
nated political issues to individual pursuits, and which is generally
inexperienced in peace-time foreign affairs, let alone world leadership, the current situation is very confusing, frustrating, and even
frightening.[20]

Clearly, Communism is the major precipitant of this frustration
and fear. It is new, and it seems to be everywhere. Its apparent in-
eluctability has produced a widespread sense of anxiety. The very
nature of Communism itself, its elusiveness, its imprecise theoretical
boundaries, its mysteriousness, its incomprehensibility, its "foreign-
ness," and the newness of its methods have combined to put its
opponents on the defensive. The confrontation involves a new kind
of war: no battle line, no definite campaign, no overall plan, and no
clear-cut victory in sight! Everybody feels that something must be
done, but few can say what should be! Thus the climate is ripe for
extremism.[21]

The post-World War II revelations about Communist espionage
as well as the actual international crises played a vital role in the
development of this fear and frustration. The early spy trials provided the first shock. Igor Gouzenko in Canada, Allan Nunn May

---

[19] Ernest Kris and Nathan Leites, "Trends in Twentieth Century Propaganda," in *Psychoanalysis and the Social Sciences* (New York: International
Universities Press, 1947), pp. 393f. See also Almond, *op. cit.*, p. 240, "The
evidence suggests that among the poor and ignorant of the cities and
countryside there are widespread feelings of powerlessness, of resentment, and
bitterness, which produce a certain susceptibility to activist movements —
whether they take the form of radical utopianism or reactionary nationalism."

[20] For a discussion of the frustrations of the military in the Cold War, see
Morris Janowitz, *The Professional Soldier* (Glencoe: The Free Press, 1960);
also, J. V. Murphy, "The Education of a Defense Secretary," *Fortune* (May,
1962). Burlingame stresses ignorance as a key factor. "The primary cause
of the American climate of fear is ignorance. In certain directions our education is dangerously defective.... Most prevalent among patriotic societies is
ignorance of the nature of communism." Burlingame, *op. cit.*, p. 91. The
present writer must disagree with the last statement.

[21] Barbu has noted that "when an attitude or a habit is formed under conditions of stress it tends to be rigid.... Many religious beliefs are emotional
systems built up under conditions of stress, fear and insecurity. This is the
principal reason why individuals holding such beliefs are intolerant...."
Democracy and Dictatorship (*op. cit.*), p. 101.

and Klaus Fuchs in Britain, and in the United States, Harry Gold, Morten Sobel, Julius and Ethel Rosenberg, as well as the Whitaker Chambers disclosures, all had a great impact.

In the Korean War the enemy revealed his true nature, methods, and aims, and managed to checkmate the United States. The war was not lost, but neither was it won — there must be a culprit. Much of the blame was placed upon the United Nations and the Democratic Party. Finding a scapegoat, especially a domestic one who had implicated himself in the "disaster," was intellectually and emotionally more satisfying than to admit that the risks necessary for total victory had become prohibitively great. But if the Korean War "exposed" Washington, it also provided the critics with heroes, MacArthur, McCarthy, Syngman Rhee, and Chiang Kai-shek, to name only the major ones. Rightists could now crystallize around actual persons. They could recognize one another and see the strength of their own numbers. Thereafter it was hardly a question of whether there would be a new Far Right, but a question of who would lead it, how powerful it would become, and how it would be organized. The activists among the frustrated were ready to act, and they did.

But why is Hargis-type Rightism limited almost entirely to the United States? Perhaps it is correct to say that the United States sprouted more Rightism, and more Far Rightists, simply because more Americans, compared to Britishers, Frenchmen, or Canadians, project morality into foreign affairs, promote ideological crusades, and actually possess more of an ideological commitment. Let us remember that fundamentalism was, and still is, largely an American phenomenon, and that no other democratic nation has developed a notion paralleling the concepts of Americanism and un-Americanism. No other nation seems to have infused its patriotism and nationalism with so much moral righteousness, and none has been quite as ready to label a purely power-political venture as an "ideological crusade." The importance of the general orientation of an entire society can hardly be over-stressed.

> Attitudes and opinions toward foreign policy questions are not only to be understood as responses to objective problems and situations, but as conditioned by culturally imposed qualities of character. These largely unconscious patterns of reaction and behavior strongly influence the perception, selection, and evaluation of political reality.[22]

[22] Almond, *op. cit.*, p. 29.

Those who were most fearful, mainly because they read more ideological significance into the Communist threat than others did, led the way in the burgeoning of the Far Right. At first they were mainly the hard-core Americanists, the true believers in the creed of Americanism. They were not necessarily isolationists, racists, or bigots. They were not un-American, at least not in motivation; indeed, in their own eyes they were more American than anyone else. They were jingoistic and exceptionally uncritical of themselves, for they were the totally committed, and the totally committed do not see things in shades of greys. These dedicated Americanists of the mid-fifties saw the enemy as a "total enemy." There was in their view no mere misunderstanding which might be eliminated by discussion, and no basis of negotiation with the Kremlin. There was only a need to act. and to act fast, because for the first time America itself was threatened with total destruction.

Increasingly, Christian fundamentalists joined the cause. They might have joined in greater numbers earlier, but many fundamentalists were (and still are) reluctant to get "mixed up" in politics, for that sounded too much like getting involved in the "Social Gospel."[23] It took some time for them to conclude that Communism was a special case.

In many ways, these fundamentalists were the natural allies of their Americanist compatriots. Indeed, some had been "pro-Americanists" all along. They also saw things in blacks and whites and stressed total, unquestioning commitment to an ideology. Despite their somewhat delayed reaction, fundamentalist-Americanists soon became the most uncompromising crusaders, because Communism posed an even greater threat to them than to the more secular Americanists. For them, Communism, by virtue of its record and its own declaration, was both a religious and a political threat. Being zealously religious themselves, these fundamentalists soon came to see Communism as the new religion which it is, and they recognized its potential. Because elected leaders were slow in recognizing the "truth," or even discounted it altogether and insisted on reminding everyone that Soviet Russia had been a vital wartime

---

[23] For a discussion of the theory of the Social Gospel, see Shailer Mathews, *The Social Gospel* (Philadelphia: Griffith and Howland, 1910); Harry F. Ward, *Social Creed of the Churches* (New York: Eaton & Mains, 1912); Harry F. Ward, *Social Evangelism* (New York: Missionary Education Movement of the United States and Canada, 1915). For a discussion of the fundamentalist resistance it evoked, see Stewart G. Cole, *The History of Fundamentalism* (Hamden, Conn.: Shoe String Press, 1931).

ally, the faithful were forced to shout even louder. And shout and organize they did.

Among that smaller group of activated fundamentalists which believed that Communism was the biblical Antichrist and the United Nations the incipient world government, the reaction was strongest of all. The enemy, as perceived by these people, was "atheistic, Satanic, and devilish" in all his ways. Whom was he fighting? "Godly, free, capitalist, civilized, honest, Christian America." And who among government leaders was taking up the cudgel against the wily Goliath? One lone Senator by the name of McCarthy. He alone seemed to realize the seriousness of the situation. True believers swarmed to the cause. When McCarthy's star faded, members of this religious Far Right were ready to take over the movement; they were more than ready, they were anxious.

They reasoned that the enemy must be met "head-on"! There was no room for compromise or for leaders who claimed to see some "bad" and some "good" on both sides. "He who is not with me is against me" — away with the naive, the weak, and the faint-hearted! Away with the compromisers, the appeasers, and those who "lost China"! The more the official leaders hesitated and talked, the more the Rightists clamored and agitated. Time, as they saw it, was swiftly running out.

The naiveté of the above view is obvious, but one must admit that the entire Rightist reaction makes considerable sense when seen from the Rightist perspective. The threat was, and is, very real. Traditional values were under great attack, and if America did not preserve them, who would? The salvation of the entire free world depended on America, and this belief, in the light of Communist victories, was still more cause to redouble efforts.

In this connection, the significance of the Cold War's bipolar nature should not be overlooked. As leaders of the free world, Americans presumably had a greater responsibility than anyone else. Lesser nations might be permitted a mistake or two, but not the United States. Other free nations knew that standing behind them, ready to lend support if invited, was the mighty United States. But Americans must realize that behind them there stood no greater ally.

Because of this situation, and because of their inexperience of such crises, some Americans panicked quickly. The tradition of a democratized foreign policy accentuated these tendencies and also broadened their effect. All these factors help to explain why Far

Rightism has had more influence in the United States than in any other democratic country.

International crises came quickly after the McCarthy era, and each served to strengthen the Far Right by aggravating their fears and frustrations. First came the French loss of Indochina, then the crushed Hungarian rebellion, and a year later the beeping Sputniks. The Sputnik crisis was especially humiliating, because it indicated that the Soviet Union had trumped the United States at its own game — that of always, and boastfully, being first in technological innovation. And it was embarrassing to realize how wrong Americans had been in estimating the scientific achievements of "those clumsy Russian peasants." Of course, Washington was again blamed for America's failures. The fact that it was under a Republican administration made the situation all the more galling.

The Cuban crisis was next; first came the frightening revelation that Castro was a Communist, then the humiliating Bay of Pigs fiasco. Cuba had always been important to the Far Right, especially to the Americanist groups who regarded it as the showcase of American magnanimity and benevolence — the answer to exploitative European imperialism. But now came this humiliation, this blasphemy against the Monroe Doctrine!

The Cuban affair, more than anything else, crystallized the Far Right into a strong, united movement. It "proved" what a number of Far Right leaders had been saying all along, that Washington was full of Reds, "comsymps," "comrats," fellow-travellers, dupes, duds, and "pinko eggheads."[24] As international Communism appeared to tighten its grip on the island outpost in the West, Far Right organizations sprouted across the land. By the close of 1961 the Far Right was for the first time a cohesive and significant national movement, a force to be reckoned with.

Domestic political developments during this period were of great significance. In the early 1950's, as the Truman era was drawing to a close, the conservative and potentially Far Rightist minority was becoming increasingly desperate. Most supporters were Republicans who rejoiced in the resounding Eisenhower victory, for it gave them new hope. But Eisenhower disappointed and in a sense trapped them. As Bell has put it, "eight years of moderation proved more frustrating than twenty years of opposition."[25] Dissatisfaction in-

---

[24] Hargis, *Weekly Crusader*, Vol. 3 (February 8, 1963), pp. 2-3. See also Fletcher Knebel, "Who's On the Far Right?," *Look*, Vol. 26 (March 13, 1962), pp. 21f.

[25] Bell, *op. cit.*, p. 3.

creased with continued deficit spending, growing federal power, "extravagant" foreign aid, reluctance to be firm with Cuba's Castro, and the repeated attempts to accommodate the Soviet Union. The historic Supreme Court decision on segregation, of May 17, 1954, led by a Republican Chief Justice and handed down while a Republican occupied the White House, dealt a stinging blow, and together with McCarthy's demise helped to alienate many erstwhile supporters of Eisenhower's "Modern Republicanism."

From this developed a basic polarization of the Republican Party. Moderates and the Far Right, despite superficial unity, parted company on basic questions of ideology. The extent of this split over a ten-year span became evident at the 1964 Republican convention in San Francisco; its ultimate significance is not yet clear. Illustrative of Far Right feeling toward Eisenhower is this statement by Hargis.

> Eisenhower, desirous of acceptance by both political parties, like his predecessors and successors, refused to take a second look at Communism internally.... He was no greater a foe to Communism internally than those before him or after him. Being a military man, he should have known better.[26]

As the Eisenhower era waned, those Rightists who had become vocal, especially over Cuba, were joined by others, and became increasingly restless.[27] They looked around for a hero. Goldwater fitted the role even then, but since he was not widely known they placed their trust in former vice-president Richard M. Nixon. Not only did he lose, but he lost to a liberal, an Easterner, a Catholic, a Harvard man, and an admirer of the New Deal. Meanwhile, Cuba seemed to be stabilizing itself as a Communist country. The stage was set for a great Rightist reaction and it came. The John Birch Society, Hargis, Schwartz, and McIntire became household words almost overnight.

Our listing of the causes of the recrudescence of the Far Right is still not complete. A frustrated feeling of Manifest Destiny is another significant contributing factor. Boorstin states, "The concept of destiny has been an ever deepening current in American thought. Conviction that America has a mission to mankind was perhaps never stronger than today."[28] Bell adds, "American achievement and masculine optimism created a buoyant sense of progress, almost

---

26 Hargis, Communism, The Total Lie! (op. cit.), p. 12.

27 For a discussion of this point, see Arthur Schlesinger, Jr., "The Threat of the Radical Right," New York Times Magazine (June 17, 1962), esp. p. 10.

28 Boorstin, op. cit., p. 163.

omnipotence. America had never been defeated. America was getting bigger and better. America was always first."[29] The concept of destiny on a continent was extended to the whole world; and then, suddenly, even while America was still getting stronger, something went awry. A nation that had always been able to point to an "obvious" Manifest Destiny now found that the destiny had lost its manifestness. The disruption in American thought, experience, and aspirations — and in self-confidence — left people frustrated and confused. The traditional American emphasis on action, on talking tough and getting things done, could no longer be put into practice. This was especially true of the American policy in Vietnam after 1966. The frustration of a mission necessitated the uncovering of a culprit; the Far Right claimed to have found culprits everywhere. Indiscriminately, the entire "Left" was indicted and denounced.

Another factor contributing to the expansion of the Far Right was the lackluster nature of much of the anti-Communism emanating from the majority liberal camp. Liberals, conservatives, and Rightists such as Hargis have all commented on this point. Vicreck has written, "Nationalist demagogy, whether McCarthy style or John Birch style, would never have become such a nuisance if liberal intellectuals and New Dealers had earlier made themselves the controlling spearhead of American anti-Communism with the same fervor they showed when spearheading anti-fascism."[30] Gabriel Almond expresses similar sentiments, especially in relation to foreign policy issues,[31] and Harvey Schecter wrote, perhaps somewhat too sharply, "The real tragedy of the American anti-communist movement lies . . . in the fact that American liberals, who know the Communists best . . . have been silent on the question of communism."[32] Schecter continues, "Liberals have failed their own movement and the whole community by their failure to educate the American public in a sane and sober manner about the true character of the Communist conspiracy."[33]

[29] Bell, *op. cit.*, pp. 17f.

[30] Peter Viereck, "The Philosophical 'New Conservative,'" in Bell, *op. cit.*, p. 194.

[31] Almond, *op. cit.*, p. xxxvi. "How can one reconcile the deterioration of American foreign policy in the last decade with these favorable trends in public opinion about foreign policy? The only conclusion we can draw is that the elite responsible for the formulation and conduct of foreign policy have failed. . . ."

[32] Harvey B. Schecter, "The Liberals Have Helped the Radical Right," *New York Times Magazine* (April, 1962), p. 13. See also pp. 93-96.

[33] *Ibid.*, p. 96.

The shortcoming cannot be ignored. Many liberals appeared to be almost naive in their acceptance at face value of Communist statements, both domestic and foreign, and often seemed to adopt a double standard. The slightest hint of fascism evoked a volley of denunciation, while Communism was politely not criticized.[34] Many liberals seemed to resent being called anti-Communist, and by this reluctance allowed the term to take on an even more extremist connotation. As Schecter has put it, "Just as the Birch-minded are inclined to see Communists everywhere, some liberals are inclined to see Communists nowhere."[35]

As usual, Hargis is blunt when discussing liberals and their "unwillingness" to oppose Communism. Since he has already dismissed them completely, all that remains to be done is to "expose" them fully. Of all Hargis's descriptions of the alleged liberal double standard, one of the most interesting involves some Russian peasants from the Siberian hinterland. Reportedly, a band of fundamentalist Christians, six men, twelve women, and fourteen children, walked under cover of darkness some 2,100 miles to the American embassy in Moscow, where they sought political asylum. According to Hargis, "Our representatives in Moscow held them three hours and forty-five minutes until the Russian police arrived to arrest them and whisk them away, probably to be shot."[36] For him, this incident provides another "proof" of liberal "hypocrisy": "The liberals seem united in their defense of the poor, persecuted religious minority in South Viet Nam, the Buddhists, but showed no similar concern for the persecuted Christians in the Soviet Union who came to our Moscow Embassy seeking refuge and were denied it."[37]

A further significant causal factor is the inherent inadequacy of pragmatism, which is still the dominant philosophical outlook in America.[38] The widespread absence of fixed values, despite the tendency to see everything in ideological terms, leaves a gap which in a period of stress may be filled by extremist dogma. Many Americans have suddenly realized that they have no personal ideological

---

[34] Buckley, op. cit., pp. 26f. See also Hargis, Weekly Crusader, Vol. 3 (October 11, 1963), pp. 1f.

[35] Schecter, op. cit., p. 13.

[36] Hargis, Weekly Crusader, Vol. 3 (October 11, 1963), p. 4.

[37] Ibid.

[38] Ernest Van den Haag, "Communism, Democracy and Religion," National Review, Vol. 5 (March 22, 1958), pp. 275f. "Democracy as such is not a fit antagonist of Communism, for it has not total vision. Religion has, however, and assaults upon it are self-indulgent and extravagant. . . ."

moorings and have taken refuge in the structures, ideological and organizational, which their Americanist and Christian fundamentalist compatriots have already built. Faced with a choice between pragmatism and ultra-Americanism, thousands opted for the one most satisfying emotionally. A feeble bulwark against the ideological claims and pretensions of Communism, pragmatism has proven to be an equally ineffective antidote to the extremist counteraction. Thus, to a large degree, fear, frustration, and the need for faith have robbed pragmatism of both its appeal and its moderating influence, in the present ideological confrontation.

The last causal factor is the appeal of Far Rightism in a society which lacks meaningful ideologies. Historically, a rigid Protestantism served this purpose, but increasing urbanization, sophistication, prosperity, and commitment to scientism have eroded its foundation. The traditional emphasis on selflessness and other-worldliness has, for many people, an aura of unreality in a prosperous and success-crazed twentieth century America. The new religious Far Rightism constitutes the kind of ideology for which many Americans have been searching.

In this new approach, militant Americanism, undergirded by capitalist materialism, has been ideologically fused with "God's plan of Salvation." Troublesome tensions between selfless Christian love and capitalist profits, and the moral problems of nationalism and militarism have been conveniently ignored. The true believer can now succeed in both worlds, the material and the spiritual.

In summary, we see that no single factor has by itself led to the burgeoning of Far Rightism, although certain causes have been more significant than others. But the occurrence in one country and at one time of fundamentalism, world leadership, the nuclear factor, the Communist threat, a thwarted Manifest Destiny, and disappointing national leadership, has produced a novel situation in history, and has provided the major source of "Hargisism"; therein lies its complexity, and therein its strength.

PART THREE

HARGIS AND THE AMERICAN SCENE

"Political intolerance has always been an endemic part of the American political process."
Seymour Lipset, in Daniel Bell, ed., The Radical Right, p. 446.

"Extremism is not new in the United States. Side by side with our democratic traditions has run a persistent mistrust of democracy."
Mark Sherwin, The Extremists, p. 225.

"In the United States, religion is ... mingled with all the habits of the nation and all the feelings of patriotism, whence it derives a peculiar force."
Alexis de Tocqueville, Democracy in America, Henry Reeve Translation, Vol. II, p. 6.

12. THE CONSERVATIVE TRADITION IN AMERICA

THIS AND THE SUBSEQUENT TWO CHAPTERS WILL ANALYZE THE widespread view that Hargis and the Far Right are totally outside of the American tradition. The present chapter seeks to determine whether the conservative element in "Hargisism" is largely within the continuing tradition of conservatism in America. Chapter 13 explores the notion that Hargis is largely consistent with the traditional American attempt to fuse Christianity, or at least a part thereof, with nationalism. Chapter 14 will delineate the history of extremism in America and relate it to Hargis and the contemporary scene.

First we need to analyze the notion that there is no conservative tradition. In his classic essay, Louis Hartz writes, "The ironic flaw in American liberalism lies in the fact that we have never had a real conservative tradition."[1] This "absence of opposing principles" reflects "the fact that beneath its political heroics the nation was of the 'same mind' on the liberal formula. . . ."[2] Schapiro concurs; "America was born a liberal nation," all "the founders of America were liberals. . . ."[3] "Liberalism has been on the march in America since the day of the Declaration of Independence."[4] Admittedly, liberalism has had a long and vigorous tradition in America, but it is not the only political tradition that America has experienced.

---

[1] Louis Hartz, *The Liberal Tradition in America* (New York: Harcourt, Brace and World, 1955), p. 57. For another statement of this view, see Ralph de Toledano, *Lament For A Generation* (New York: Farrar, Straus, and Cudahy, 1959).

[2] Hartz, *op. cit.*, p. 141.

[3] Schapiro, *op. cit.*, p. 77.

[4] *Ibid.*, p. 87. See also Carl L. Becker, *The Declaration of Independence, A Study of the History of Political Ideas* (New York: Harcourt, Brace, 1922).

Hartz, and others, fail both to allow for the possibility that a tradition can persist without being intellectualized, and to recognize the shifts in meanings of the major terms. The term "liberal" has not entirely reversed its meaning, but its connotation has altered markedly. Most of what the founders meant by the term is now subsumed under the concept "conservative," the preeminence of virtually unrestricted individualism being a case in point. The liberals in early America placed their major emphasis on what is now called "negative freedom." For them, the basic function of government, aside from defense and security, was to eliminate such evils as religious persecution, governmental arbitrariness, and unfair taxation. It was not until the 1890's, or even later, that the "positive freedom" views of T. H. Green and his associates became prominent in America. And only in the last few decades has the liberal camp in America fully accepted the belief that government should help the individual achieve the liberty and freedom which are his in theory. It was this democratization of freedom, particularly the economic aspects, which drove a wedge between the notions of liberty and privilege, and which made liberalism appear to be the enemy of conservatism. Prior to this attempt to actualize the theoretical, that segment of America which was Burkean in outlook had no quarrel with the theoretical tenets of liberalism.

Moreover, the implied definition of liberalism which Hartz uses is much too inclusive. He includes an orientation which he refers to as the "irrational" and "Americanist" mood. Thus he concedes that "the Bolshevik Revolution transformed irrational 'Americanism' into pure hysteria."[5] The reference seems to be to a traditional nativism and at least mild intolerance. On other occasions, he speaks of a "colossal liberal absolutism"[6] and of "dogmatic liberalism" as constituting part of the American tradition.[7] All of this authoritarianism is posited as part of the liberal tradition! Hartz has included too much and has thus begged the question. To lump all of these phenomena into one category, and to call them all by one name, blurs basic differences.

Hartz emphasizes a single factor, the absence of feudalism,[8] as the cause of the lack in the United States of both a genuine revolutionary tradition and a tradition of reaction. (By inference, reaction is very nearly equated with conservatism.) The result, as Hartz sees

[5] Hartz, op. cit., pp. 208f.
[6] Ibid., p. 285.
[7] Ibid., p. 9.
[8] Ibid., pp. 20f.

it, is a "natural liberalism," "the universality of the liberal idea."[9] Hartz fails to see that feudalism as a set of values, as well as the ideological reaction to it, can be present despite the absence of actual feudalistic institutions. He glosses over the fact that feudal institutions per se had already declined or even disappeared in England before the Pilgrims sailed for the New World. He also underrates the feudalistic nature of various American endeavors, especially Southern plantations. And for many immigrants, the American Way and the desire to identify with it were in themselves a reaction against feudal values.[10] Thus, the American tradition, properly seen, is not fully separated from feudalism and the conflicts it engendered, but is actually a part of these conflicts. Since Hartz's explanation is inadequate, we turn to other writers.

Introducing his perceptive analysis of the colonial period, Leonard Labaree states, "Only by taking note of the conservative side of colonial thought and action, as well as the liberal, can we arrive at a true estimate of the whole."[11] He is not alone in cautioning us to look beyond liberalism. In his popular commentary, Dean Smith emphasizes that conservative influences played a major part in the founding of America, the forging of the Constitution, and the building of the country.[12] And Jasper Shannon contends that "conservatism has played a significant role in the development of American politics notwithstanding the revolutionary tradition in the

---

[9] *Ibid.*, pp. 5f. Hartz also argues that where there is a feudal tradition there is a socialist-leftist tradition. The situation in Quebec seems not to bear him out on this point. Feudalism in Canada was limited almost entirely to Quebec, yet the socialist-leftist movements have the greatest followings in Ontario and British Columbia. Socialism is virtually non-existent in Quebec. Hartz also states (p. 309), "Can a people 'born equal' ever understand peoples elsewhere that have to become so?," to which one can respond by asking, To what extent was this equality real and to what extent merely theoretical?

[10] Many nineteenth century immigrants came from strongly feudalistic traditions; can one assume that this was so much less significant for America than the historical fact of feudalism for other countries?

[11] Leonard Labaree, *Conservatism in Early American History* (Ithaca, New York: Cornell University Press, 1959), p. vii. Note also Labaree's comments on page 2, "Even within the limits of the property qualifications, the male inhabitants were far from equal in their ability to exercise actual political power. There was, in fact, in almost every colony a definite ruling class." "The colonial ruling class was unquestionably one of the most important forces of conservatism in the colonies."

[12] Dean Smith, *op. cit.;* see especially Part Two.

United States."[13] These judgments are well taken. The early settlers came here, in the words of John Adams, not because they desired anything new but because they wished to conserve their faith and freedom. Even later, when they declared their independence from Britain, it was not because of a quarrel over new demands but because they did not want to give up established rights.[14]

At the very center of early American conservatism, one finds an insistence on limited government and sanctity of property, a reluctance to change the status quo, a belief in a hierarchical class structure (under God), a disinclination to emphasize equality, even equality of opportunity, and a general identification of civil rights with property rights. Distrust of the masses and a notion of divine right, for aristocracy if not for monarchy, rounded out the view.[15]

The Revolution was not fought in the name of some abstract doctrine of "Rights of Man" or to gain any additional liberties, or for the tenets of liberalism per se. The Declaration of Causes of Taking Up Arms, July 6, 1775, clearly stated that fighting was being undertaken "in defence of the freedom . . . which we ever enjoyed till the late violation of it."[16] Critics sometimes mistakenly attribute to the men of '76 ideas and doctrines which were first advocated by Jackson in 1828. Dignity of the individual, the supreme contribution of eighteenth and nineteenth century liberalism, has played a major role in American history, but it has not had the field to itself. Labaree suggests that we "need to remind ourselves only that property quali-

---

[13] Jasper Shannon, "Conservatism," *Annals*, Vol. 344 (November, 1962), p. 13. Shannon suggests that, lacking a crown and nobility, American conservatives have stressed private property and the Constitution.

[14] Dean Smith, *op. cit.*, p. 57.

[15] In his *Conservatism (op. cit.)*, Viereck states (p. 15) that "the two earmarks of the temperamental conservative" are "a distrust of human nature, rootlessness, and untested innovations" and "a trust in unbroken historical continuity and in some traditional framework to tame human nature." This, plus the discussion in earlier chapters, will constitute our working definition. See also the definition in Beck, *op. cit.* An interesting attempt at a full definition is the recent compilation of thirteen articles by several well-known writers, including Frank S. Meyer, Russell Kirk, Willmoore Kendall, and William Buckley. The work, edited by Meyer, is, *What Is Conservatism?* (New York: Holt, Rinehart and Winston, 1964). *The Anthology of Conservative Writing in the United States* (Chicago: Regnery, 1962), edited by A. G. Heinsohn, Jr., is more "Rightist." Some of the better-known contributors include Tom Anderson, Dan Smoot, and Admiral Ben Moreell. For an earlier analysis, see Ralph Gabriel, *The Course of American Democratic Thought*, 3 vols. (New York: Harcourt, Brace, 1927-1930).

[16] Boorstin, *op. cit.*, p. 72.

fications for the right to vote existed everywhere at the time of the Revolution"[17] in order to realize the conservative coloration of early American political thought.

Just as the Revolution was largely conservative in orientation, so also "the framers of the constitution were motivated by a desire to create stability and security, especially the security of property."[18] Perkins asserts even more emphatically, "It was conservatives who framed the Constitution of the United States,"[19] and J. Allen Smith in 1907 castigated the Founding Fathers for what he thought to be an undemocratic ultra-conservatism.[20] Hofstadter speaks of the "antagonism, long latent, between the philosophy of the Constitution and the [later] philosophy of American democracy"[21] and of the irony that "the constitution which Americans venerate so deeply, is based upon a political theory that at one crucial point stands in direct antithesis to the main stream of [recent] American democratic faith." "Modern American folklore assumes that democracy and liberty are all but identical," and "that democracy is necessary to liberty." The Founding Fathers, on the other hand, "thought that the liberty with which they were most concerned was menaced by democracy. In their minds liberty was linked not to democracy but to property."[22] "It was the opponents of the Constitution who were most active in demanding such vital liberties as freedom of religion, freedom of speech and press, jury trial, due process, and protection from 'unreasonable searches and seizures.' "[23]

The Federalist, in Nos. 9, 49, 50, 62, 68, 71, 73, 78, and 81, reveals the staunch conservatism of the Founding Fathers. Although much is spoken of liberty, this term had a more limited meaning at that time. Leonard Levey, for example, claims that Jefferson was not the civil libertarian he has usually been presented as being.[24] In a letter to John Adams, the venerated Jefferson stated, "I will have to agree with you that there is a natural aristocracy among men. The

---

[17] Labaree, *op. cit.*, p. 1. Note also the view of R. B. Perry, *op. cit.*, p. 123; the American Revolution was "not a crusade undertaken in behalf of a creed formulated in advance."

[18] Shannon, *op. cit.*, p. 15.

[19] Perkins, *op. cit.*, p. 19.

[20] J. Allen Smith, *The Spirit of American Government* (New York: Macmillan, 1911). See also the various writings of Charles A. Beard.

[21] Hofstadter, "Pseudo-Conservatism Revisited," in Bell, *op. cit.*, p. 15.

[22] *Ibid.*, p. 10.

[23] *Ibid.*, p. 11.

[24] Leonard Levey, *Jefferson and Civil Liberties* (Cambridge: Harvard University Press, 1964).

grounds of this are virtue and talent"; he added, this "natural aristocracy I consider the most precious gift of nature, for the instruction, the trusts, the government of society. . . ."[25] Viereck writes that
"the extraordinary conservatism of America's founding fathers is
today often ignored," and that "liberals discuss it with pained embarrassment as a family skeleton."[26]

"The relative stability and continued growth of American
society" after 1787 "owes much to the influence" of early conservative leaders.[27] A conservative emphasis has persisted, sometimes
weaker, sometimes stronger, sometimes on the defensive, sometimes
on the offensive, but always alive.[28] The belief in "givenness," the
reluctance to change, and the reverence, at least formally, for an
authoritarian Christian creed are still largely with us. Burns comments in similar fashion: "This fundamental conservatism seems to
underlie the major portion of American history, and is both a consequence and an ingredient of the national idea of mission."[29]

In addition to the "idea of mission," there are many other
policies and laws which cannot be properly explained if one allows
only for liberalism. The Alien and Sedition Acts, for example, form
part of the continuing American tradition of conservation and status
quo, an attempt to thwart change and coerce consensus. The tradition continues in an unbroken thread from colonial times to the 1940
Smith Act, and to the most recent flag-waving demonstrations against
any relaxation in American immigration laws and any further implementation of the liberal creed in the area of civil rights. The whole
issue goes beyond the problem of altered definitions of conservatism
and liberalism, for most of the values now espoused by Hargis have
been advocated and defended, under one name or another, by a
vocal and frequently influential segment of the American public,
from the earliest colonial days through our own time.

There is very little in America's "conservative" past, as the
term was described above, with which Hargis would disagree. Of
course, if we substitute definitions, it can also be said that many of
the values espoused by Hargis have their roots in early American
liberalism, and that Hargis is seeking to conserve or reestablish an

---

[25] Dean Smith, op. cit., p. 67.
[26] Viereck, Conservatism Revisited (op. cit.), p. 42. See also Burns, op. cit.,
pp. 95-101.
[27] Labaree, op. cit., pp. 169f.
[28] Viereck, Conservatism (op. cit.), pp. 87-108.
[29] Edward Burns, The American Idea of Mission (New Brunswick, New
Jersey: Rutgers University Press, 1957), p. ix.

early form of liberalism. He supports an emphasis on negative free-dom and lack of economic restrictions, such as was preached and widely practiced in the nineteenth century; whether this view be called liberal or conservative is of little consequence.[30]

---

[30] Victor Ferkiss, "Political and Intellectual Origins of American Radical-ism, Right and Left," *Annals*, Vol. 344 (November, 1962), p. 8: "Intellect-ually, this theory [i.e. Far Rightism] stems from adherence to the values of nineteenth-century laissez-faire liberalism. . . ."

13. THE CHRISTIAN TRADITION IN AMERICA

CHAPTER 2 DEALT WITH HARGIS'S VIEW OF EARLY AMERICA. IN THE present chapter we wish to probe the actual extent of Christian emphasis in American political history and to determine the degree to which Hargis continues that historical emphasis.

In the introduction to his informative volume, Thomas Hall writes that "the story of that tradition [i.e. American], especially upon its religious side, has been so misread or neglected that whole chapters of North American history are even now crying for rewriting."[1] His major charge is that much error has been read into

---

[1] Thomas Cumming Hall, *The Religious Background of American Culture* (Boston: Little, Brown, 1930), p. vii. Other useful accounts of religion in America are: John Courtney Murray, *op. cit.*; "Religion in American Society," *The Annals*, Vol. 332 (November, 1960); Gerhard Lenski, *The Religious Factor* (Garden City: Doubleday, 1961); Martin Marty, *The New Shape of American Religion* (New York: Harper, 1959); Clifton E. Olmstead, *Religion in America, Past and Present* (Englewood Cliffs: Prentice-Hall, 1961); John P. Roche, *The Quest for the Dream — The Development of Civil Rights and Human Relations in Modern America* (New York: Macmillan, 1963); James Smith and Leland Jamieson, eds., *Religion in American Life*, 4 Vols. (Princeton: Princeton University Press, 1961); William L. Sperry, *Religion in America* (New York: Macmillan, 1946); Winthrop S. Hudson, *The Great Tradition of the American Churches* (New York: Harper & Row, 1963); Milton Yinger, *Religion in the Struggle for Power* (Durham, N.C.: Duke University Press, 1946); Anson Phelps Stokes and Leo Pfeffer, *Church and State in the United States*, revised one-volume edition (New York: Harper and Row, 1964); and W. W. Sweet, *Story of Religion in America*, second revised edition (New York: Harper and Brothers, 1950); Burns, *op. cit.*, Chapter 8, has a concise account of the historical inter-relationship of religion and politics. See also H. Richard Niebuhr, *The Kingdom of God in America* (New York: Harper and Brothers, 1937), and Littell, *From State Church to Pluralism (op. cit.)*.

this period by ill-informed, myth-making generations, and that a reevaluation of America's religious background is necessary.

The Mayflower Compact, at the very beginning of American history, reveals the intentions of the Pilgrims — "to advance the cause of Christ," and "to serve God." These people had adopted a deviant Christian creed, but they had not rejected the Old World doctrine of the role of faith or the place of the Christian creed in society. To a large extent, they transmitted the Old World absolutist traditions to the New World. Littell notes, "The first settlements in North America simply transplanted the religious concepts and practices of Europe, modifying them only when frontier conditions required. . . . For over half of our history American church life was modeled on European lines."[2] Greene agrees; "the general idea of a Christian society for whose maintenance and protection against subversion, the state as well as the church was responsible," was transplanted intact by the early colonists from England.[3] He continues, "In short, what early Puritans wished was the reformation of the Church of England, directed by men like themselves. They had no objection to a national church so reformed and had no idea of dispensing with the coercive power of the state."[4] Woodhouse concludes that early American Puritanism was "a determined and varied effort to erect the holy community."[5]

Prior to the American Revolution, nearly all the American

[2] Littell, From State Church to Pluralism (op. cit.), pp. 4-5. See also Merle Curti, The Growth of American Thought, second edition (New York: Harper and Brothers, 1951), pp. 50-78.

[3] Greene, op. cit., p. 21.

[4] Ibid., p. 19. Cf. Cousins, op. cit., p. 10, "There was also strong spiritual content in the confidence of the American founders in the capacity of man to govern his own affairs. . . ." Note also R. B. Perry, Puritanism and Democracy (New York: Vanguard, 1944), p. 191, "Emphasis on the sovereignty of God disposed Puritans to the acceptance of a theocratic state which derived its sanction from above. The idea of election, according to which only a favored few, chosen for reasons known only to God, could hope for salvation, accustomed a Puritan community to the idea of privilege, and hardened the hearts of the elite to the plight of the unfortunate." Analyzing the dilemma of Puritanism seeming to advocate both democracy and Christian conformity, Hudson states, "The apparent conflict between their zeal for liberty and their concern for reform was resolved for them by their firm trust in the efficacy of discussion and the power of persuasion. To achieve and preserve the Christian character of society, they relied on the power of a godly public opinion created by the preaching of the Word." Hudson, op. cit., p. 44. See also pp. 45f.

[5] Woodhouse, op. cit., p. 37.

colonies were characterized by the existence of established churches. Generally speaking, Congregationalism in New England, Anglicanism in the South, and Quakerism, Presbyterianism, etc., in the Middle Colonies all enjoyed official status. In all of New England and in many other regions the dominant church was able to enforce its will. A heavy pro-Protestant bias prevailed everywhere.[6] To the extent that there was any concept of religious equality, it was to be applied only within the narrow limits of rigid Protestant Christianity. This state of affairs remained basically unchanged until the coming of the Revolution. As late as 1775 nine out of the thirteen colonies still had a publicly supported state church.

With the outbreak of fighting the situation changed somewhat. "The inconsistency of religious discrimination with the natural-rights doctrines of freedom ... came to be increasingly felt by thoughtful persons. . . ."[7] The shift, however, was only a partial one. Those who instigated the Revolution insisted that they were God-fearing men and were not about to renounce what they took to be their right and duty.[8] Indeed, virtually all of the national leaders during and immediately after the Revolution described themselves as Christians.[9] Even Jefferson asserted, "I am a REAL CHRISTIAN, that is to say, a disciple of the doctrines of Jesus. . . ."[10] George Washington insisted that public religion and public worship were essential to morale in both civil and military life; in holding this view he reflected the opinions of the vast majority of the public.[11] The practice, initiated by Washington, of presidential identification with and official endorsement of Christianity persisted throughout the nineteenth century and into the twentieth. Each president, either at his inauguration or elsewhere, publicly identified himself with Christianity, and until recently with Protestantism specifically. Anything else would hardly have been tolerated. The heated arguments

6 Stedman, op. cit., p. 36. Cf. Shannon, op. cit., p. 16: The "fundamental premises in the American tradition ... although advanced by the liberals in the seventeenth and eighteenth centuries ... were children of both theology and practical experience. Governments were regarded as inherently evil. Were it not for the evil nature of man, government would not exist at all." The basic similarity to Hargis's view is obvious.

7 Greene, op. cit., p. 76.

8 Ward, op. cit., p. 131.

9 See Cousins, op. cit.

10 Saul K. Padover, ed., Jefferson On Democracy (New York: Penguin, 1946), p. 122.

11 Stokes and Pfeffer, op. cit., pp. 35 and 37f. This volume constitutes perhaps the best study of church-state relations in America.

on religion during the presidential campaigns of 1928 and 1960 indicate the persistence of this feeling even in modern times. At least nominal Christianity appears still to be a necessary qualification for the presidency.

The doctrine of separation of church and state, one of the great American contributions to political theory and practice and the major feature of American church-state relations, can also be reinterpreted. Pfeffer writes, "Church-state separation in the United States has historically very little European secularism about it"; the basic American concern has been and still "is one of religious freedom in favor of the churches and not against them."[12] Littell claims that the doctrine is only a myth. "Even Thomas Jefferson (1743-1826), who coined the famous and often misused phrase on the 'wall of separation,' no more believed in separating religion from public life than did his Federalist opponents in New England."[13] Much depends on how one defines the concept. If it is defined to mean a state structure neutral on all questions involving religion, which appears to be the contemporary definition, then separation has never been complete. But if we accept the definition offered by Hargis,[14] that the state shall be officially Christian and support (Protestant) Christian values without giving special preeminence to any one denomination, it is correct to say that the doctrine has been adhered to by national governments ever since the nation was founded. Because Protestant Christianity has always been the dominant faith in American society, it is not surprising that a strong, even if not always official, pro-Protestant bias has been evident in law and in practice. Various court rulings have given firm legal

----

[12] *Ibid.*, p. 523. See also the editorial, "The Christian State," in *A Journal of Church and State*, Vol. 6 (Autumn, 1964), pp. 277-284, and Bryce, *op. cit.*, Vol. I, p. 778, "No political party, no class in the community has any hostility either to Christianity or to any particular Christian body."

[13] Littell, *From State Church to Pluralism* (*op. cit.*), p. 13. Note also his statement on page 100, "religious liberty and a 'wall of separation' are not identical and — in fact — we have had neither." Washington said, "Whatever may be conceded to the influence of refined education on minds of peculiar structure, reason and experience both forbid us to expect that national morality can prevail in exclusion of religious principle." Cited in *Christian Crusade*, Vol. 15 (August, 1963), p. 21.

[14] *Communist America . . . Must It Be?* (*op. cit.*), p. 32, "let it be remembered that separation of Church and State simply means that there will be no official church in the U. S. but that all may be free to worship God, according to dictates of their conscience."

status to this situation.[15] The general fusion of political and religious holidays in America, the use of officially adopted Christian
slogans, as well as the use of Christian prayer at governmental
ceremonies illustrate an over-riding, although formalistic, Christian
orientation.[16]

Furthermore, much pro-Christian prejudice and legal differentiation continued at the state level long after Article VI of the Constitution and the First Amendment had established a formal tolerance at the national level. Tax support for the established churches
was practiced in Connecticut until 1818 and in Massachusetts until 1833.[17] Non-monetary preferential treatment persisted well into
this century and still persists in some states.

Private endorsement of the idea of a fused church-state has not
been lacking. Outstanding figures such as George Bancroft (1800-
1891), Ralph Waldo Emerson (1803-1882), and Walt Whitman
(1819-1892), to name but a few, rejected any thought of a secular
state.[18] The perceptive Austrian traveller of the 1830's, Francis
Grund, reported that the Faith was widely and publicly revered by
great and small.

> It is to religion they [i.e. leaders in society] have recourse whenever
> they wish to impress the popular feeling with anything relative to
> their country; and it is religion which assists them in all their
> national undertakings. The Americans look upon religion as a
> promoter of civil and political liberty; and have, therefore, trans-
> ferred to it a large portion of the affection which they cherish for
> the institutions of their country.... Religion presides over their
> councils, aids in the execution of the laws, and adds to the dignity
> of the judges. Whatever is calculated to diminish its influence and
> practice, has a tendency to weaken the government....[19]

On another occasion Grund wrote,

> The religious habits of the Americans form not only the basis
> of their private and public morals, but have become so thoroughly
> interwoven with their whole course of legislation, that it would be
> impossible to change them without affecting the very essence of
> their government.[20]

---

[15] See Greene, *op. cit.*, especially page 133, and Stokes and Pfeffer, *op.
cit.*, pp. 111f.

[16] *Ibid.*, pp. 232-243.

[17] Probst, *op. cit.*, p. 223. See also Perkins, *op. cit.*, p. 44.

[18] Probst, *op. cit.*, Part V and Part IX.

[19] *Ibid.*, pp. 232-243.

[20] *Ibid.*, p. 241. On the degree to which Christianity permeated American
society see Bryce, *op. cit.*, Vol. II, pp. 763-786.

As one reflects on this discussion of past practice, it becomes clear that Hargis, when arguing for government identification with Protestant Christianity, is not really proposing an innovation, but is pleading for a return to traditional values and practices.

It will be recalled that the idea of an "American mission," a variation on the broader theme of Manifest Destiny,[21] is very important for Hargis. Does he deviate in this emphasis or is he simply perpetuating and reemphasizing traditional views on this count as well? Evidence fully supports Burns' contention that "one of the principal clues to knowledge of America is the sense of mission which has run like a golden thread through most of her history." A sense of mission is widespread among the nations of the world, but it has been exceptionally powerful in the United States. "To a greater extent than most other peoples, Americans have conceived of their nation as ordained in some extraordinary way to accomplish great things in the world."[22] A swaggering nationalism, which Hargis exemplifies, is no new thing in America; myths of superior national morality arose early and are still widely accepted and perpetuated.[23]

Both before and after the Revolution, assertions of national uniqueness have been common, particularly as related to a national mission to foreign countries. In 1765, John Adams saw America as God's grand design to emancipate mankind. Thomas Paine regarded it as part of God's great plan to have the settlement of America associated with the Reformation.[24] Richard M. Johnson, Vice-President under Martin Van Buren, pushed the idea of religious uniqueness to its limit when he said, "With the exception of the United States, the whole human race consisting, it is supposed, of eight hundred millions of rational human beings, is in

---

21 For a stimulating discussion of this concept, see Albert K. Weinberg, *Manifest Destiny* (Chicago: Quadrangle Books, 1963). He says the term was an "expansionist slogan, expressed a dogma of supreme self-assurance and ambition — that America's incorporation of all adjacent lands was the virtually inevitable fulfillment of a moral mission delegated to the nation by Providence itself" (pp. 1f.). See also Burns, *op. cit.*, Chapter 2.

22 Burns, *op. cit.*, p. vii. Niebuhr observes, "From the earliest days of its history to the present moment, there is a deep layer of Messianic consciousness in the mind of America." *The Irony of American History* (*op. cit.*), p. 69.

23 Hargis, *Christian Crusade*, Vol. 15 (October, 1963), p. 10. See this for Hargis's views.

24 Burns, *op. cit.*, p. 11. See also Dennis Brogan, *The American Character* (New York: Vintage Books, 1956), especially p. x.

religious bondage."[25] Ralph Waldo Emerson and John C. Calhoun spoke similarly.[26] The early decades of independence saw Americans spending much time rationalizing their idea of national mission and its effect on other peoples.

But, as Reinhold Niebuhr notes, "The illusions of a unique innocency were not confined to our earliest years."[27] Nor were these illusions isolated and sporadic. It is easy to forget that when William A. Scott wrote the following in 1848 he represented more than a fringe element: "God has a great design for this continent — for our generation. As the Jews of Old — as the Apostles — as the Reformers — as our fathers of 1776 — so are we, as a race and as a nation, a peculiar people and called to a high and glorious destiny."[28] President William McKinley's justification for the Spanish-American War, especially the action in the Philippines, ran along the same lines.[29] Few criticized him or raised their voices in disagreement, let alone protest. In our own century, Senator Albert Beveridge, discussing God's special role in American colonialism, proclaimed:

> He has marked the American people as His chosen nation to finally lead in the regeneration of the world. This is the divine mission of America, and it holds for us all the profit, all the

---

[25] Cited in Probst, op. cit., pp. 250f.

[26] Weinberg, op. cit., p. 17.

[27] See Niebuhr, The Irony of American History (op. cit.), p. 28. Cf. his statement in The Children of Light and the Children of Darkness (op. cit.), p. ix, that Americans "are still inclined to pretend that our power is exercised by a peculiarly virtuous nation."

[28] See Kohn, op. cit., p. 124.

[29] Ibid., pp. 190f. Before the outbreak of hostilities President McKinley reported to Congress as follows: "If it shall hereafter appear to be a duty imposed by our obligations to ourselves, to civilization and humanity to intervene with force, it shall be done without fault on our part and only because the necessity for such action will be so clear as to command the support and the approval of the civilized world.... I speak not of forcible annexation for that cannot be thought of. That by our code of morals would be criminal aggression." Later, in explaining how he arrived at his policy, he said, "I walked the floor of the White House night after night until midnight; and I am not ashamed to tell you gentlemen that I went on my knees and prayed to Almighty God for light and guidance more than one night. And one night it came to me this way — that there was nothing left for us to do but to take them all, and to educate the Filipinos and uplight and civilize and Christianize them, and by God's grace to do the best we could by them, as our fellowmen for whom Christ also died. And then I went to bed and went to sleep and slept soundly." Quoted in Robert F. Davidson, Philosophies Men Live By (New York: Holt, Rinehart and Winston, 1952), pp. 429 and 430.

glory, all the happiness possible to man. We are trustees of the world's progress, guardians of its righteous peace. The judgment of the Master is upon us: "Ye have been faithful over a few things; I will make you ruler over many things."[30]

As indicated previously, a special variation of messianic nationalism consists of casting America in the role of a modern Israel.[31] Washington and Jefferson used the image frequently.[32] Jefferson observed that divine Providence "led our forefathers, as Israel of old, out of their native land and planted them in a country flowing with all the necessaries and comforts of life."[33] In 1785, he suggested that "the seal of the United States should represent the children of Israel led by a pillar of light...." In his inaugural address in 1805 he repeated the same theme.[34] Even members of the academic elite endorsed this Hebraic nationalism. No less a figure than Professor Ezra Stiles, president of Yale University, described mid-nineteenth century United States as "God's American Israel."[35] The consolidation of national unity gave the doctrine of the Promised Land a further impetus.[36]

It is this general line of thinking about national messianism and American Israelism, in a somewhat modified form, which Hargis is propagating today. He is correct when he insists that he is saying nothing new in his basic doctrines of Christian-Americanism. Hargis is repeating views which were fully respectable, even popular,

---

[30] Quoted in Urban Whitaker, ed., *Nationalism and National Progress* (San Francisco: Chandler, 1961), pp. 18f. Cf. Burns, *op. cit.,* p. 187, "Ideas of race superiority in the United States have shown a tenacity almost unmatched by that of any other doctrine. From colonial times until well into the twentieth century there has never been a period when men of influence and prominence could not be found in substantial numbers arrayed on the side of ethnological prejudice." In Chapter 9 Burns describes the American disposition for crusading wars.

[31] Niebuhr, *The Irony of American History (op. cit.),* p. 24. "Whether, as in the case of the New England theocrats, our forefathers thought of our 'experiment' as primarily the creation of a new and purer church, or, as in the case of Jefferson and his coterie, they thought primarily of a political community, they believed in either case that we had been called out by God to create a new humanity. We were God's 'American Israel.' "

[32] *Ibid.,* p. 70.

[33] *Ibid.,* p. 46.

[34] Cited in Weinberg, *op. cit.,* pp. 39f.

[35] Niebuhr, *The Irony of American History (op. cit.),* p. 25.

[36] Stedman, *op. cit.,* p. 38; also pp. 46f. See also Kohn, *op. cit.,* p. 16. Tocqueville noted that "religious zeal is perpetually warmed in the United States by the fires of patriotism." *Op. cit.,* Vol. I, p. 317.

until well into the present century.[37] If Hargis's pro-Christian emphasis can properly be seen as being deviant or even reactionary, it is not because he has introduced strange or alien ideas, but because the perspective of the majority of Americans has changed markedly in recent decades. In a situation in which the majority have "fallen from the faith" the "true believers," the defenders of traditionalism and the status quo, take on the aura of reactionism.

Just as the specifics of Hargis's creed of Christian-Americanism are no innovation, so also, as we have seen, and as Hargis has insisted, has a more diffused but strong pro-Christian "Weltanschauung" long been widespread in America. "Our colonial background, our formative years as a nation, and the greater part of our national history are all stamped with a distinctively Protestant style of thinking and feeling. . . . There is no understanding of American national character without reference to Protestantism."[38] Events of the last fifteen years further substantiate this view. Congress has decided that the United States is in fact "a nation under God," proof of which — "In God We Trust" — is to be imprinted on all currency. Congress has also included the words "under God" in the pledge of allegiance (1954), and has officially declared "In God We Trust" to be the nation's motto (1956).

Although Hargis is correct in these several claims, he is correct only in a technical sense. America has been Christian, but not in the sense in which he, as a fundamentalist, uses the term. Well before the time of the Revolution, the Christianity which characterized America as a state was largely external and formalistic. Littell argues that "the idea that the American people were once Christian [i.e. at the time of the Revolution] and have subsequently declined is false, and the historical perspective involved is unsound. America has never been a Christian nation except in the

---

[37] Niebuhr, *The Irony of American History (op. cit.)*, p. 36. See also page 4.

[38] Rene de Visme Williamson, "Conservatism and Liberalism in American Protestantism," in *The Annals*, Vol. 344 (November, 1962), p. 77. Note also the following: In a letter to E. E. Thompson in March, 1927, Calvin Coolidge wrote, "The foundations of our society and our government rest so much on the teachings of the Bible, it would be difficult to support them if faith in these teachings should cease to be practically universal in our country." Cited in *Christian Crusade*, Vol. 15 (August, 1963), p. 26.

At his first inaugural, Lincoln stated, "Intelligence, patriotism, Christianity, and a firm reliance on Him who has never yet forsaken this favorite land are still competent to adjust in the best way all our present difficulty." Cited in *Christian Crusade*, Vol. 15 (August, 1963), p. 21. See also Hofstadter, *The American Political Tradition* (New York: Random House, 1948).

nominal sense."[39] Statistics support his claim. Once church membership was made voluntary it dropped drastically, only to build up gradually to the present all-time high.[40] However, much of present membership in itself reflects not a commitment to any rigorous creed. There may be inscriptions on coins, ritualistic incantations, even legal designations, but all of this paraphernalia is a far cry from the personal, salvational, and spiritual Christianity espoused by the early Pilgrims and by fundamentalists in our own time. It seems curious that Hargis, who is so quick to condemn the lack of fundamentalist views in the large Christian denominations, should nevertheless heap praise on a diluted and tribally oriented religiosity in the nation as a whole.[41]

A final point concerns the question of Christianity and its relationship to the formal constitution. Hargis asserts that modern governmental leaders, particularly in the executive and judicial branches, have subverted the intent of the founders. Admittedly, the contemporary Supreme Court has handed down some rulings which would have shocked their counterparts a century ago, but that does not necessarily mean that the present justices have misinterpreted either the Constitution or public opinion.

What has happened, this writer suggests, is that the propensity for secularism which flowed logically from the American Constitution, or at least was latent in it all along, eventually became a reality, for several reasons; of these, commercial development, industrialization, urbanization, growth of scientism, and increasing academic sophistication were of major importance. In any event,

---

[39] Littell, *From State Church to Pluralism* (*op. cit.*), p. x.

[40] *Ibid.*, p. 32. Here are his statistics on church membership in the United States:

1776 . .	5%	1900 . .	35.7 %
1800 . .	6.9%	1926 . .	50 + %
1850 . .	15.5%	1960 . .	69 %

Henry Steele Commager has observed, "By every test but that of influence the church had never been stronger than it was at the opening of the twentieth century, and its strength increased steadily. Everyone was a Christian, and almost everyone joined some church, though few for reasons that would have earned them admission to Jonathan Edwards' Northampton congregation.... Never before had the church been materially more powerful or spiritually less effective." *The American Mind* (New Haven: Yale University Press, 1959), pp. 166f. See also Benson Y. Landis, "Trends in Church Membership in the United States," in *The Annals*, Vol. 332 (November, 1960), pp. 1-8.

[41] See, for example, his pamphlet *The National Council of Churches Indicts Itself.*

a gradual but fundamental change in the political orientation of the majority occurred, and "as time went on ... the main stream of American political conviction deviated more and more from the anti-democratic position of the Constitution makers."[42]

This fundamental change, which consists largely of a secularization of the political value-system, has now reached an advanced stage. It is now evident that a constitution functions quite differently when administered by zealous Puritans and orthodox Protestants than it does when secular rationality has become influential. The argument can perhaps be put another way by saying that the pro-Christian conventions and interpretations which were initially superimposed on a predominantly liberal, and potentially democratic and secular, constitution and political system have been shaken loose by a logical, if not inevitable, maturation and development.[43]

ADDENDUM TO CHAPTER 13

Reference has already been made to a number of the observations by that prescient and authoritative Frenchman, Alexis de Tocqueville, but since he said so much, and said it so early in the American experience,[44] and since his statements tend to support much of Hargis's depiction of early America, he deserves this special mention. Various of his comments are relevant to each of the chapters in this section.

"On my arrival in the United States," writes Tocqueville, "the religious aspect of the country was the first thing that struck my attention; and the longer I stayed there, the more I perceived the great political consequences resulting from this new state of things."[45] It is evident that "in the United States, religion is ... mingled with

---

[42] Hofstadter, *The American Political Tradition* (*op. cit.*), pp. 14f. The statement continues, "Yet, curiously, their general satisfaction with the Constitution together with their growing nationalism made Americans deeply reverent of the founding generation, with the result that as it grew stronger, this deviation was increasingly overlooked."

[43] See Edward Earle, ed., *The Federalist* (New York: Modern Library, 1937), p. xvii. The same general development, of course, occurred in the area of civil rights. In 1787 it seemed quite consistent to count Negroes as 3/5 of a person each for purposes of taxation and representation, and to deny them the vote completely, while at the same time proclaiming "that all men are created equal, that they are endowed by their Creator with certain unalienable Rights...."

[44] Tocqueville was in the United States in the 1830's.

[45] Tocqueville, *op. cit.*, Vol. I, p. 319.

all the habits of the nation and all the feelings of patriotism, whence it derives a peculiar force."[46]

The Frenchman saw primarily desirable, but also some undesirable, results stem from this fact. "Thus, while the law permits the Americans to do," more or less, "what they please, religion prevents them from conceiving, and forbids them to commit, what is rash or unjust."[47] But he also believed that, "if America has not as yet had any great writers, the reason is" that "there can be no literary genius without freedom of opinion, and freedom of opinion does not exist in America."[48] That he believed Christianity to be the culprit, despite his seemingly contradictory statement that it is a necessity,[49] is evident from the following:

> In the United States Christian sects are infinitely diversified and perpetually modified; but Christianity itself is an established and irresistible fact, which no one undertakes either to attack or to defend. The Americans, having admitted the principal doctrines of the Christian religion without inquiry, are obliged to accept in like manner a great number of moral truths originating in it and connected with it. Hence the activity of individual analysis is restrained within narrow limits. . . .[50]

The magnitude of the grip of Christianity which Tocqueville perceived is described thus:

> Among the Anglo-Americans some profess the doctrines of Christianity from a sincere belief in them, and others do the same because they fear to be suspected of unbelief. Christianity, therefore, reigns without obstacle, by universal consent; the consequence is, as I have before observed, that every principle of the moral world is fixed and determinate.[51]

Specifically, on the question of the relationship of Christianity and American government, Tocqueville said: "Religion in America takes no direct part in the government of society, but it must be regarded as the first of their political institutions. . . ."[52] He believed

---

[46] *Ibid.*, Vol. II, p. 6.

[47] *Ibid.*, Vol. I, p. 316.

[48] *Ibid.*, Vol. I, p. 275.

[49] See again *ibid.*, Vol. II, pp. 9f., and especially p. 156, "Christianity must be maintained at any cost in the bosom of modern democracies. . . ."

[50] *Ibid.*, Vol. II, p. 7.

[51] *Ibid.*, Vol. I, p. 315. On page 317, he relates that a court witness declared he did not believe in the existence of God and that the judge therefore refused to admit his evidence, saying the witness had lost the court's confidence. The press, relates de Tocqueville, reported the incident without any comment.

[52] *Ibid.*, Vol. I, p. 316.

religion to be a major underpinning of the political order: "I have
endeavored to point out . . . the causes to which maintenance of the
political institutions of the Americans is attributable, and religion
appeared to be one of the most prominent among them."[53] He continued, "The Americans show by their practice that they feel the
high necessity of imparting morality to democratic communities by
means of religion."[54]

Perhaps the most significant comment of all is the one which
Tocqueville made to his peers upon his return to Paris.

> Sirs, I went at your bidding; I ascended the mountains; I
> went into the valleys; I visited their commercial markets and
> their emporiums of trade; I entered their legislative halls and
> their judicial courts. I searched everywhere in vain until I entered
> the church. It was there, Sirs, as I listened to the soul-elevating
> and soul-equalizing Gospel of Christ as it fell from Sabbath to
> Sabbath upon the waiting multitudes, that I learned why America
> is great and free, and France is slave.[55]

---

[53] *Ibid.*, Vol. II, p. 152.
[54] *Ibid.*, Vol. II, pp. 152f. In Vol. I, p. 276, Tocqueville states, "I
attribute the small number of distinguished men in the political life to the
ever increasing despotism of the majority in the United States." It should be
emphasized here that Tocqueville used the term "democracy" in a special
way. He stressed equality, especially formal equality of condition, and not
freedom of toleration.
[55] Quoted in *Christian Crusade*, Vol. 15 (August, 1963), p. 26.

14. THE EXTREMIST TRADITION IN AMERICA

In addition to the conservative and Christian traditions surveyed in the previous chapters, it is necessary for us to review a third American tradition, that of intolerant extremism or bigotry, in order to determine where the contemporary Far Right in general, and Hargis in particular, fit into American life.

Seymour Lipset has written, "Political intolerance has always been an endemic part of the American political process."[1] Janson and Eismann state, "The seeds of reaction are deep in the furrows of American history."[2] Sherwin asserts, "Extremism is not new in the United States. Side by side with our democratic traditions has run a persistent mistrust of democracy."[3] Shannon adduces specific examples to show that "intolerance is no stranger to American experience."[4] These men, all experts, make serious charges which require examination.

Relevant material, including both primary and secondary sources, is plentiful[5] and reveals liberalism and much toleration, especially in later years, but also intolerance, bigotry, prejudice, and persecution. Both tendencies took firm root in colonial America. The "Pilgrims and Puritans," says Littell, "intended to establish a theocracy," a revival of Calvin's Geneva experiment. The "attempt was made to organize all of social life under the lordship of Jesus

---

1 Lipset, "Three Decades of the Radical Right," in Bell, op. cit., p. 446.
2 Janson and Eismann, op. cit., p. 11.
3 Sherwin, op. cit., p. 225.
4 Shannon, op. cit., p. 23.
5 See Myers, op. cit. See also Greene, op. cit., pp. 23-46; Roy, op. cit.; and Alice Felt Tyler's Freedom's Ferment (New York: Harper and Brothers, 1962).

Christ. ...."[6] The ideological basis for the system was ruthlessly logical and intolerant, and the leaders did it justice. "Religious liberty, though implicit in their style of thinking about the church, was not their aim," Littell continues; "they sought liberty for themselves, not for all. The Mayflower Compact ... was radical Puritan and democratic in implication but not in intent."[7]

Was there then no religious freedom in colonial America? There was liberty of sorts, certainly, but only within specific bounds. Some deviation was allowed on lesser issues, but in most of the colonies conformity on cardinal doctrines was required. As R. B. Perry says, "A society of Puritan believers was essentially intolerant. Ideas derived from authority were untroubled by doubt and imposed without qualms."[8] In early America, Protestants, including all the various sects, and also Catholics, sought to suppress each other, and both desired and worked for the suppression and punishment of free-thinkers.[9]

The general result of this single-mindedness was widespread oppression. Myers concludes that the general spirit in all of the American colonies, but especially in New England, "was one of rampant persecution."[10] Cousins concurs,

> There was hardly a form of persecution in the Old World which was not transplanted to the New. The Bill of Rights came into being not so much as a reaction to the oppressions of Europe as the specific means for preventing the human indignities and abuses of freedom experienced here in colonial America.[11]

The evidence supports Cousins. Suppression was taken for granted.[12] Religious liberty as we understand the term was not present in the Puritan era. Waller claims that this widespread "Puritan myth" needs to be scuttled once and for all,[13] and Muller suggests that "everybody except one hundred per cent patriots knows that the

---

[6] Littell, *From State Church to Pluralism* (*op. cit.*), p. 5.

[7] *Ibid.*, p. 6.

[8] R. B. Perry, *op. cit.*, p. 191.

[9] Labaree, *op. cit.*, p. 70.

[10] Myers, *op. cit.*, p. 4.

[11] Cousins, *op. cit.*, p. 10. See also Tocqueville, *op. cit.*, Vol. I, pp. 39f.

[12] Greene, *op. cit.*, p. 46. "Generally speaking, in colonial America it was the accepted duty of the state to foster not merely religion in general, or Christianity in general, but a particular form of Christian faith and polity. Furthermore, the acceptance of this responsibility usually involved the suppression, if not always of dissenting opinions, at least of public worship other than that by law established."

[13] Waller, *op. cit.*

Puritans came to Massachusetts seeking freedom only for themselves, and soon proved that they were as intolerant as any Christians had ever been."[14] Probst agrees and adds, "In the early years of this Puritan society there was no religious toleration, and the struggle for religious freedom was incessant and arduous before toleration prevailed."[15]

Admittedly, specific experiments in religious liberty were tried, especially by Lord Baltimore in Maryland, Roger Williams in Rhode Island, and William Penn in Pennsylvania, but they resulted in only a relative liberty. Observance of Sunday was rigidly enforced even in Pennsylvania, and all atheists, Catholics, and Jews were denied full citizenship privileges.[16] In Maryland, there was a legal provision for a death penalty for all who denied the doctrine of the Trinity, and in Rhode Island Jews were mistreated and after 1762 were denied citizenship entirely.[17] Even this relative freedom existed only in a few areas. "Not Roger Williams and William Penn dominated the colonial churches, but John Endicott and Sir William Berkeley."[18] On the eve of the Revolution the situation in some regions became so critical that the English Privy Council felt compelled to intervene on behalf of imprisoned dissenters.[19] Interestingly enough, public sympathy even in England did not generally side with the persecuted minorities. No less a man than the enlightened John Locke, the philosophical father of various English reforms as well as of the American Constitution, concluded his memorable *Letter Concerning Toleration* with the statement: "Lastly, Those are not at all to be tolerated who deny the being of God. ... The taking away of God, though but even in thought, dissolves all."[20]

After the Revolution, the situation improved markedly, but

---

[14] Herbert J. Muller, *Religion and Freedom in the Modern World* (Chicago: University of Chicago Press, 1963), p. 68.

[15] Probst, *op. cit.*, pp. 222f.

[16] Burns, *op. cit.*, p. 30. On the same page we also read, "Not even the benevolent William Penn would accord full privileges to atheists, Catholics, and Jews." See also Littell, *op. cit.*, p. 12.

[17] Greene, *op. cit.*, pp. 51-58.

[18] Littell, *op. cit.*, p. 4.

[19] Greene, *op. cit.*, p. 69.

[20] Schapiro, *op. cit.*, p. 106. Note the comment of Myers, *op. cit.*, p. 42. "If a particular law was transient, soon to be wiped out, it would now convey no special significance. But when we find a series of laws, all to the same end and extending over large stretches of time, then we can accept them as a sure depiction of the processes of that time."

much suppression and even persecution remained. Many of the early constitutions emphasized the "inalienable right" of all men to worship God as they wished, but did not guarantee the right not to worship God. Many denied civil rights to all who did not acknowledge "the being of a God." In most of the states "religious equality was not . . . secured"; Jews and atheists were still at a severe disadvantage, even in business relationships. Not surprisingly, "most of the states had religious tests for the holding of public office."[21] In 1787, only three states, Pennsylvania, Delaware, and Maryland, gave Catholics the right to vote.[22] Even physical persecution persisted. For example, in 1792, in Fairfield County, South Carolina, a number of persons reputed to be witches were tried; four were found guilty, were beaten, and had the soles of their feet burned off over a fire. Numerous acts of terror took place, such as the burning of New York's St. Mary's Catholic Church in 1832 and the ransacking of the Ursuline Convent in Charlestown, Mass., a few years later.[23] Other similar incidents occurred, two as late as 1928.[24]

The formation of political parties in the last century helped to crystallize the tradition of intolerance and bigotry. The "Native American" party, which was "anti" many things but especially anti-foreign, had already developed an impressive following by 1835. The party was then endorsed by Samuel Morse, the great inventor, who in that same year published his vitriolic, anti-Catholic and anti-foreign diatribe, *Foreign Conspiracy Against the Liberties of the United States*. The reaction was particularly vehement in those sections of the country which had received the millions of Irish and other Catholic immigrants who had fled Europe after the Napoleonic Wars.

After a temporary decline, extremism again blossomed forth in the 1850's, in the nativist, anti-foreign Know-Nothings, who in the 1854 elections captured forty seats in the New York legislature, won the governorship and all but two seats in the Massachusetts legislature, and elected nine of Indiana's eleven Congressmen. In 1855 they won governorships in Rhode Island, New Hampshire, Connecticut, California, and Kentucky. In the thirty-

---

21 Greene, *op. cit.*, p. 81.

22 Myers, *op. cit.*, p. 111. For religious discrimination that survived till our age see Greene, *op. cit.*, pp. 94f. and Myers, *op. cit.*, pp. 104f.

23 Roy, *op. cit.*, p. 144.

24 Myers, *op. cit.*, p. 39. Cf. Exodus 22:18: "Thou shalt not suffer a witch to live."

fourth Congress they had five representatives in the Senate and forty-three in the House.[25] The movement reached its zenith in 1856, when the Know-Nothing presidential candidate, Millard Fillmore, polled almost one-fourth of the total popular vote for president.[26] They won important offices in various parts of the country and took virtually all of the important posts in six Southern states.[27]

Following the Civil War, a large number of nativist organizations sprang into being. Several of these merged in 1887 to form the highly intolerant and anti-foreign American Protective Association, which enjoyed widespread popularity for many years. The new century brought new leaders and new associations, of which the most important was the notorious Ku Klux Klan. Even at the height of prosperity in the 1920's, the Klan grew steadily and hooded Klansmen dominated political life in Indiana, Maine, Colorado, Oklahoma, Texas, Oregon, Arkansas, Ohio and California. The estimated membership of the secret order at that time was four to four-and-a-half million.[28]

Many of the extremist elements enjoyed great notoriety during the Great Depression. Among the lesser known but still significant enterprises one finds the following: National Gentile League, American Rangers, Militant Christian Patriots of Los Angeles, America Awake, and the Silver Shirt Legion. A full listing would fill several pages. The general mood of these groups was anti-foreign, anti-Catholic, anti-Semitic, and anti-"modernism." While many of them paraded a religious veneer of one form or another, none identified itself with fundamentalism to the extent that Hargis has done. Perhaps the most popular of all extremist spokesmen in the 1930's was that highly controversial Roman Catholic priest, Father Coughlin, whose radio audiences were estimated at more than 19 million. Coughlin began his "ministry" in 1926, but did not achieve national fame until 1936, when he turned against President Frank-

---

25 These statistics are cited in William B. Hesseltine, *Third Party Movements in the United States* (New York: Van Nostrand, 1962), pp. 24-30. See also W. Darrell Overdyke, *The Know Nothing Party in the South* (Baton Rouge: Louisiana State University Press, 1950).

26 Lipset, "Sources of the 'Radical Right,'" in Bell, *op. cit.*, pp. 310. See also Charles McKenzie, *Party Government in the United States* (New York: Ronald Press, 1938), p. 194.

27 For a fuller account see Stokes and Pfeffer, *op. cit.*, pp. 235f., and McKenzie, *op. cit.*

28 See Lipset, *op. cit.*; and Hofstadter, "The Pseudo-Conservative Revolt," in Bell, *op. cit.*, p. 82.

lin Roosevelt and the New Deal. He agitated against Jews, against banking institutions, against public relief and, of course, against Communism. Millions, both Catholics and Protestants, deeply admired him, and contributed heavily. His 1938 income, despite the continuing poverty, approached the half-million mark. His weekly magazine, *Social Justice,* was a voice to be reckoned with, and his general influence continued well into World War II.[29]

The foregoing evidence shows conclusively that bigotry, prejudice, and intolerance, including Main Street vigilantism, religious suppression, and witch-burning, have had a long tradition in America. Although this tradition is not central, it involves no minuscule fringe. This same phenomenon is still present in several types of American Protestantism, as indicated in briefs recently submitted to the courts on the public prayer cases, which advocated the use of the coercive arm of government to enforce church positions.

When, therefore, Hargis preaches a militant Christian-Americanism and when he exhibits extremist tendencies, he is well within an important American tradition. Indeed, the specific policies which he advocates are mild compared to those which were preached and practiced in earlier years. He does not ask for any violence or persecution, other than prosecution against known Communists, and whatever intolerance he manifests is a mere shadow of what was once respectable and even official. From witch-hunting, to "Klanism," to "Coughlinism," to "Hargisism," constitutes an overall tendency toward increasing tolerance and freedom.

Even in our time, Hargis represents a broader segment of American opinion than is generally supposed. Lipset has reviewed the extensive research which substantiates the contention that many, perhaps most, Americans do not endorse full toleration of unpopular views.[30] He concludes his survey by saying:

> The historical evidence . . . indicates that, as compared to the citizens of a number of other countries, especially Great Britain and Scandinavia, Americans are not a tolerant people. In addition to discriminating against ethnic and religious minorities, each war and most prewar situations have been characterized by the denial of civil liberties to minorities. . . .[31]

In his comparison of Britain and the United States, Herbert Hyman arrives at a similar conclusion: "Many American surveys

---

[29] Myers, *op. cit.,* Chapter 33, especially pp. 444f.
[30] Lipset, *op. cit.,* pp. 316f.
[31] *Ibid.,* p. 316.

have shown that the public espoused general democratic values in the abstract, but did not apply them to particular concrete cases. ...."[32]

Many critics have denounced Hargis as being un-American, but such a judgment ignores the evidence summarized in the three previous chapters. If this category is to be invoked at all, Hargis must be categorized as more American than un-American. The Overstreets may have overstated the case somewhat, but there is much truth to their conclusion that the contemporary Far Right is quite properly seen as the "exaggeration of traits common among us in many gradations."[33]

An especially interesting question involves the relationship between Christian fundamentalism and Populism in the late nineteenth and early twentieth centuries. Certain areas in the United States, including much of the proverbial Bible Belt with its significant percentage of fundamentalists, gave Populism considerable support. Some scholars have argued that the post-World War II Far Right is in the tradition of American Populism.[34] They stress the similarity of views on conspiracy, the place of prejudice, the repudiation of trained leadership, a distrust of elites, the emphasis on native practical sense (conscience), and the extent of naive emotional fervor. But what they tend to overlook is that the pivotal notion in Populism was opposition to international financiers, bankers, railroad owners, etc., because of their alleged economic exploitation of the people. Populism was essentially an economic reaction, not a crusade for a total world view. It differed also from the Far Right in that it wanted more, not less, governmental intervention and regulation. And while Rightism shares with Populism an emphasis on mass participation, it substitutes a good bit of "Fuehrerprinzip" in place of Populist egalitarianism.[35]

---

[32] Herbert H. Hyman, "England and America: Climates of Tolerance and Intolerance," in Bell, *op. cit.,* p. 278. Note also his statement on page 275, "Yet this very same complex of objective events led in the United States to McCarthyism, but in England, despite even more compelling conditions, it did not. Obviously, there is much more to it than these objective conditions."

[33] Overstreets, *op. cit.,* p. 20.

[34] See, for example, Victor C. Ferkiss, "Ezra Pound and American Fascism," *Journal of Politics,* XVII (1955), pp. 173-198, and Richard Hofstadter, *The Age of Reform* (New York: Knopf, 1955).

[35] Note the conclusions of John D. Hicks, *The Populist Revolt,* second edition (Lincoln, Nebraska: University of Nebraska Press, 1961), p. 406. "The Populist philosophy thus boiled down finally to two fundamental propositions; one, that the government must restrain the selfish tendencies

A great difference exists in the nature of methods and organization. Populist movements developed mainly from the "bottom up," while most current Far Right groups are organized from the "top down." Current Rightist leaders are convinced that the nature of the enemy necessitates a tightly knit organization, even a secret one, while Populist leaders, aware of the economic power wielded by their supposed enemy, believed that their only hope lay in cooperative mass action. Assuming that many fundamentalists actually did endorse Populism, what might have motivated them? Perhaps the lack of an immediate and specific foreign threat permitted critics to concentrate on domestic issues, such as economic exploitation, political bossism, and the rapid secularization of society. And possibly a significant part of the explanation is simply that fundamentalists think and act one way when the question of personal income is concerned, and adopt another approach when issues are remote and are viewed ideologically. One is reminded of the French peasant who, in response to the accusation that he had his political heart in the left and his economic heart in the right, responded that this constituted a reasonable and consistent inconsistency. Ideological inconsistency may well be a major flaw in the fundamentalist "Weltanschauung." In any event, it is significant that virtually all of the current studies of Populism do not stress fundamentalism as a major determinant, and some ignore it altogether.[36]

---

of those who profited at the expense of the poor and the needy; the other, that the people, not the plutocrats, must control the government."

[36] See, for example, C. Vann Woodward, "The Populist Heritage and the Intellectual," in *American Scholar*, XXIX (Winter, 1959-1960), pp. 55-72, and Hicks, *op. cit.* The latter volume contains no discussion of the significance of fundamentalism or of any other religion in the development of Populism; the former argues that the Far Right is not in the Populist tradition. For an interesting study of a partially analogous situation, see D. B. Robertson, *The Religious Foundations of Leveller Democracy* (New York: Columbia University Press, 1951).

15. THE RELIGIOUS FAR RIGHT

Up to this point we have used the label "Far Right" in a general sense; and we now need to become more precise in our definition. The Far Right, as the term is used here, shades off on one side into mere conservatism (*Modern Age: A Conservative Review*, and the writings of Russell Kirk) and on the other into crass racism (Conde McGinley) and fascism (George Lincoln Rockwell). The unifying concept of the entire contemporary Far Right is an intense, active anti-Communism. The absoluteness of the Communist menace and the life-death struggle against it overshadow everything else. Evidence of the Red conspiracy is discerned on all sides. It is a Rightist's first duty to be always alert and to fight the conspiracy on all fronts. While the external enemy is not entirely overlooked, the major emphasis is invariably placed on the domestic threat. There is also a constant advocacy of direct action. A second common denominator is a full-blown individualism, with its corollary of opposition to "big government." Limited government is revered as the antithesis of a presumed socialist-Communist-internationalist conspiracy. This viewpoint is also generally identified with patriotism. Thirdly, a negativistic and at times pessimistic tone permeates the entire movement: negativistic, because the entire phenomenon is essentially a reaction to developments which Walter Lippmann has termed "acids of modernity"; pessimistic because, from the Rightest point of view, the visible response of key decision-makers to the ominous "truth" is usually very disheartening. And fourthly, Far Rightest groups are generally led by small-town evangelists, the *nouveau riche*, retired military personnel, or persons who have been involved in subversion professionally, for example, former FBI agents, undercover and counterespionage men, and ex-Communists. Additional traits include an emphasis on emotion rather than reason, a profound belief in sim-

183

plicity (there are no grays, only blacks and whites), a total commitment, and a readiness to attribute evil motives to all ideological opponents.

The term "Religious Far Right" refers to that section of the Far Right which closely identifies its politics with a Christian theology and which asserts that the religious and political components are necessarily related. Examples of the Religious Far Right include: Dr. Fred Schwartz of Christian Anti-Communism Crusade; Verne Kaub of the American Council of Christian Laymen; Carl McIntire of The Twentieth Century Reformation Hour; and, of course, Billy James Hargis of Christian Crusade. While the bulk of the Religious Far Right is Protestant, there is also a significant Roman Catholic segment. Some of the leading spokesmen of the John Birch Society are conservative Catholics. The largest fully Catholic Rightist movement is the Cardinal Mindszenty Foundation, which was founded in 1958 by Fr. Stephen Dunker, C.M. The Foundation claims to have 3,000 active "study groups" in 49 states. A recent Foundation-sponsored seminar in Houston, Texas, attracted some 4,000 people to the final session.[1] Examples of the Far Right without a marked Christian emphasis include: The Minutemen, The American Flag Association, For America, and the Daughters of the American Revolution. Some groups, such as the John Birch Society and We, the People!, seem to be borderline cases.[2]

Estimates of the size of the Far Right differ according to the various definitions and vantage points. The most generous figure is found in the statement by Dore Schary: "It has been estimated that some 20 percent of the American electorate can be grouped as Extremists on the Right Wing."[3] Events at the 1964 Republican National Convention lend some substantiation to that figure. Janson and Eismann estimated the overall membership of the active Far Right at more than a million in 1963.[4] Ellsworth and Harris, in their thorough review of Rightist publications, avoid citing a specific figure, but state that "the literature described does not proceed from a splinter group, but represents a large portion of

---

[1] For a discussion of Catholic Rightism, see Louis Cassels, "The Rightist Crisis in Our Churches," Look, Vol. 26 (April 24, 1962), pp. 40f.

[2] Concerning "We, the People!" Hargis states, "We, the People! is political. It gives me a chance to do something in the political area. But the Christian Crusade is strictly religious." Quoted in Adams, Nation (op. cit.), p. 194.

[3] Forster and Epstein, op. cit., p. xii.

[4] Janson and Eismann, op. cit., p. 7.

American opinion."[5] Commenting on the situation after the 1964 election, the Reverend Mr. Robert Moon, a well-known Methodist minister, writes that there are now more than 500 significant right-wing organizations in the United States and that during the last nine years they have been expanding at an average rate of 22 per-cent per year.[6] It is hardly on overstatement to label as significant a movement which airs 7000 radio and TV programs weekly[7] and has resources running into the tens of millions of dollars.[8]

Although the overall cause of the Far Right evokes intense emotional response from the faithful, there is no organizational unity. The right-wing political landscape includes a vast multitude of organizations. A comprehensive catalogue, *The First National Directory of Rightist Groups, Publications, and Some Individuals in the United States* (1962), has more than 2000 entries including 1492 separate organizations,[9] and even then, many of the primarily religious groups have been omitted.

Many of the thousands of listed undertakings are very small; several hundred, however, are truly national in scope. Of these, the following twelve are perhaps best known and most influential: Twentieth Century Reformation Hour (Carl McIntire); Christian Crusade (Billy James Hargis); Manion Forum (Dean Clarence Manion); John Birch Society (Robert Welch); Dan Smoot Reports (Dan Smoot); Christian Anti-Communism Crusade (Fred Schwartz); American Council of Christian Laymen (Verne Kaub); Christian Economics (Howard E. Kershner); The Conservative Society of America (Kent and Phoebe Courtney); Lifeline (H. L. Hunt); The Minutemen; and Christian Freedom Foundation.[10] These organizations are all major endeavors and all are still grow-ing. Their current combined membership probably exceeds 300,000.

---

[5] Ellsworth and Harris, *op. cit.*, p. 8.

[6] Robert Moon, *What's Wrong With The Far Right?* (Fresno, California: First Methodist Church, 1965), Introduction, first page.

[7] See *Group Research Report*, Vol. 3, No. 20 (October 29, 1964). This series of reports is published by Group Research, Inc., Washington, D.C. Moon, *op. cit.*, states that Hargis broadcasts over more than 400 radio stations, with a daily program on virtually all of them; that the Manion Forum has more than 300 and Carl McIntire's "Twentieth Century Reformation Hour" more than 600 (p. 1).

[8] Since most Rightists do not reveal their income, any total figure must be only a guess. Hargis is one of the few who publish audited financial statements.

[9] This catalogue is available from The Noontide Press, Sausalito, California.

[10] See the UPI release in the *New York Times,* September 23, 1964.

The total following, however, is much greater, and their financial resources surpass $20 million annually.[11] Each of these twelve enterprises is significant in its own right; together they constitute a formidable power complex.

While some writers view the Far Right as merely an unfortunate nuisance, an increasing number of responsible observers are disagreeing. David Danzig cautions, "Whoever has taken the radical right as amounting to nothing more than the fulminations of a few crackpots, or the temporary prominence of the lunatic fringe achieved mainly by publicity, would do well to ponder the matter further."[12] Similarly, Daniel Bell writes, "Today, the ideology of the right wing in America threatens the politics of American civility. Its commitment and its methods threaten to disrupt the 'fragile consensus' that underlies the American political system."[13] Ralph Roy stresses the effect on established religion as well as on politics: "The development of extreme right-wing groups under the banner of Protestantism poses a significant threat to the independence of the churches as well as to the future of democracy."[14] Forster and Epstein indicate their view in the title of their study, *Danger on the Right.* The National Council of Churches laments that the "Radical Right" has "moved from the fringes of American life into a prominent role."[15] It is significant that in the fall of 1964 a nationwide organization, The Council for Civic Responsibility, was established to counteract what its leaders termed the "half-truths" and "bigotry" of the Far Right.[16] As of November 9,

---

[11] Dean Smith, *Conservatism: A Guide to Its Past, Present and Future in American Politics* (New York: The Hearst Corporation, 1963), p. 30. See also Bell, *op. cit.,* pp. 250f.; *Journal of Social Issues,* Vol. 19 (April, 1963), pp. 4f.; and Ellsworth and Harris, *op. cit.,* pp. 2f. for useful surveys of the Far Right.

[12] David Danzig, "The Radical Right and the Rise of the Fundamentalist Minority," *Commentary,* Vol. 33 (April, 1962), p. 298.

[13] Daniel Bell, "The Dispossessed," *op. cit.,* p. 2.

[14] Roy, *op. cit.,* p. 285. See also F. J. Cook, "The Ultras: Aims, Affiliations, and Finances of the Radical Right," *The Nation,* Vol. 194 (June 30, 1962), pp. 565-606. Cook deals mainly with Fred Schwartz, in whom he sees a very real threat.

[15] National Council of Churches of Christ in America, *Information Service,* Vol. 43 (October 10, 1964), p. 1. See also Moon, *op. cit.,* Introduction. "The Far Right is a dangerous enemy of the church and of the democratic process. For a while some of us hoped it would not amount to much, but its impact and influence are now so great that it cannot be casually dismissed as ridiculous or insignificant."

[16] *Group Research Report (op. cit.),* p. 79, and UPI release of September 23, 1964.

1964, the CCR was releasing its daily rebuttal on more than a thousand stations.[17]

Part of the controversy surrounding the Far Right involves the question of conservatism. Is the contemporary Far Right basically a part of the current conservative revival?[18] One group of writers feels that it is. Dean Smith, adopting that approach, writes that although extremists "are ridiculed by Liberals and viewed with concern by more moderate Conservatives," they, "the Right Wing groups, represent still another evidence of the Conservative Revival."[19] Smith emphasizes, however, that despite the close interrelationship of the conservative revival with the burgeoning of the Far Right, significant tensions still exist. The majority of conservatives, while anxious not to alienate Far Right support, are nevertheless apprehensive about certain of "the radical approaches advocated by the Far Right."[20] He believes, for example, that "Conservatives, generally speaking, do not wish to see the United Nations fall, nor do they advocate United States withdrawal."[21]

Correspondent Alan Barth takes the opposing view. Discussing Hargis, Schwartz, and others, he writes: "They are commonly called 'Rightists' — a term which connotes conservatism. But in sober truth there is nothing conservative about them. They are much more in a rage to destroy than a fervor to conserve."[22] Westin agrees.[23] Peter Viereck suggests that the difference between the true conservative and the Far Rightist lies in the fact that the former conserves discriminately while the latter does so indiscriminately.[24]

This writer's view is that much of the Far Right, including Hargis, differs from the conservative mainstream primarily in de-

---

[17] *Ibid.* A banner headline in *Weekly Crusader,* Vol. 5 (March 5, 1965), informs readers that the Council for Civic Responsibility has ceased operations because of "lack of funds."

[18] The present writer answers in the affirmative. For a comment on this point, see Leonard Labaree, *Conservatism in Early American History* (Ithaca, New York: Cornell University Press, 1948), Great Seal Books edition, 1959, p. viii. Cf. Jasper Shannon, "Conservatism," in *Annals of the American Academy of Political and Social Science,* Vol. 344 (November, 1962), p. 14.

[19] Smith, *op. cit.,* p. 30.

[20] *Ibid.*

[21] *Ibid.,* p. 196.

[22] Alan Barth, *op. cit.,* p. 25.

[23] A. Westin, "The Deadly Parallels: Radical Right and Radical Left," *Harper's Magazine,* Vol. 224 (April, 1962), pp. 25-32.

[24] Peter Viereck, *Conservatism Revisited* (New York: Collier Books, 1962), p. 32.

gree of orthodoxy and intensity of presentation. Both movements speak for the privileged, not for the destitute, and accept an outlook which Boorstin has termed a belief in "givenness." Both see evil within persons as well as in masses, and usually prescribe Christian or other indoctrination as an antidote for evil. Both believe that American domestic policy during the past three decades has been much too socialistic and hence they vigorously denounce "big government." Both indicate an unyielding attachment to private property, a strong endorsement of social and economic inequality, a rejection of most state regulation of "private" economic pursuits, an acceptance of fervid nationalism, and a resistance to change, especially to rapid change. Finally, both agree that there has been too much softness and appeasement in reacting to the "Red Conspiracy." But concerning the reason for this shortcoming, the two differ, and this difference is a crucial one. Forster and Epstein are correct in suggesting that "the basic difference is that, unlike the Radical Right, the extreme Conservatives generally do not tend to ascribe the alleged socialism and softness to any sinister plot in high places, but rather to blindness, stupidity, and bungling. . . ."[25] Thus, a difference between the Far Right and the main body of conservatives, at least concerning the issues of Communism and the Cold War, relates not so much to goals, or even to methods, as to the question of the motivation of high government officials. But most Far Right leaders minimize this difference, and see themselves as conservatives of the truest and purest types possible. They use the term frequently to describe themselves and dislike prefixes such as neo, pseudo, or ultra.

It is not only on the question of motivation, however, that the contemporary Far Right is out of step with the conservative creed. The average Far Rightist is not content merely to denounce most governmental action, but also brushes off the existence of social problems themselves and fails to suggest alternative plans of action. The Rightist also differs from his conservative cousin by minimizing the notion of legitimate opposition and accepting a conspiratorial interpretation of history. He sees politics as the arena in which he grapples with ever-present conspirators. For the Religious Far Rightist the battle is an all-out religio-ideological struggle in which the only acceptable outcome is total victory.

In contrasting the Far Right with traditional conservatism, one should not overlook the reactionary tendencies prevalent in most

---

25 Forster and Epstein, *op. cit.*, p. xvi.

of the Far Right. The Far Rightist, as exemplified by Hargis, wants not only to conserve but also to overthrow — albeit only by legal means. He wants to conserve, but he does not want to conserve everything that the "liberals" have introduced, for then he would be contradicting his own values. What he would like to conserve is the type of society which supposedly existed before the promoters of big government began tampering with it. Accordingly, what the critic terms reactionism, the Far Rightist sees as respectable ideological consistency. Moreover, the Far Rightist might well argue that he is an orthodox conservative on the question of basic government institutions; his reactionism involves only specific legislation and later innovations in government practices.

Another question involves the extent to which Christian tenets bind the Far Right to conservatism. Hargis, in a discussion with this writer, suggested that he could not see how a "born again believer" could be anything but a conservative politically, and that insofar as such a person would be true to his "Christian calling," he would also identify with the Far Right. He is clearly convinced that conservatism is "the biblical Way." After all, does not the Word say, "My son, fear thou the Lord and the king; and meddle not with them that are given to change"?[26]

Of all the major conservative writers, perhaps the one closest to Hargis on this question is Peter Viereck. "Conservatism," he writes, "is usually associated with some traditional and established form of religion, whether as a credo to believe literally, or as a framework historically valuable."[27] He adds, "Conservatism, which is for politics what classicism is for literature, is in turn the political secularization of the doctrine of original sin."[28] Conservatives accept the Christian doctrine that "men are not born naturally free or good" and, "whether intentionally or unconsciously," they apply this doctrine to politics.[29]

---

26 Proverbs 24:21. For Hargis's views on conservatism, see Chapter 3. Significantly, the Bible also states, "He hath put down the mighty from their seats..." (Luke 1:52).

27 Peter Viereck, *Conservatism* (Princeton, New Jersey: Van Nostrand, 1956), p. 16. For additional comments on the interrelationship of conservatism and Christianity, see Dexter Perkins, *The American Way* (Ithaca, New York: Cornell University Press, 1959).

28 Viereck, *Conservatism Revisited (op. cit.),* p. 47.

29 Viereck, *Conservatism (op. cit.),* pp. 13f. For a theoretical discussion of the question, see Robert N. Beck, *The Meaning of Americanism* (New York: Philosophical Library, 1956). On page 135 Beck states, "Religion is at the core of conservative tenets, and the conservative is happiest when there is an institutionalized church in his society."

But there is another side to the picture. Hargis and other Far Right spokesmen have overlooked the many facets of Christian doctrine which lend support to political liberalism. Despite their insistence that Christianity is the major buttress of what they consider to be the only acceptable "Weltanschauung," they seem to have missed the biblical emphasis on social responsibility, universalism, and selflessness.

PART FOUR
HARGIS AND "HARGISISM"

"To identify any particular form of government with Christianity is a dangerous error: for it confounds the permanent with the transitory, the absolute with the contingent."
T. S. Eliot, The Idea of a Christian Society, *p.* 57.

"Every man has a right to his opinion, but no man has a right to be wrong in his facts."
Bernard Baruch

"God is not necessarily on our side; he is on the side of justice and concern for men."
M. Richard Shaull, Encounter With Revolution, *p.* 66.

16. EVALUATING HARGIS

In Chapter 8 we evaluated Hargis's political thought; we still need to evaluate the man and his work as a whole, and his effect on the American body politic and society in general.

First, Hargis has awakened a sense of fear. To the extent that this awakening results in a rational response to a real threat, he may have performed a valuable service. But as Barbara Ward has said, "Fear alone is a poor counsellor because it is essentially negative."[1] The Holy Bible, on which Hargis claims to base his entire orientation, is emphatic in asserting that "God hath not given us the spirit of fear, but of power and of love."[2]

Hargis's emphasis on fear is paralleled by a heavy dose of pessimism. The importance of this fact can hardly be exaggerated, for "pessimism is a paralyzing doctrine.... In declaring that the world is evil wholesale, it makes futile all efforts to discover the remedial causes of specific evils and thereby destroys at the root every attempt to make the world better and happier."[3] To be sure, Hargis's emphasis on pessimism regarding humanity and the world in general is balanced in part by a materialistic optimism; but his optimism, such as it is, is reserved almost entirely for "Christian-America."

On occasion Hargis has been described as a rabid racist, but this accusation is not founded in fact.[4] In only one early pamphlet,

---

1 Barbara Ward, *op. cit.*, p. 264.

2 II Timothy 1:7.

3 John Dewey, *Reconstruction in Philosophy* (New York: Holt, 1920), p. 178. See also the subsequent pages.

4 See Hargis's statement in *Weekly Crusader*, Vol. 2 (March 30, 1962), p. 2, where he says that the letter which he sent to some 100 groups inviting them to a Washington, D.C. unity conference included this sentence, "Organizations that are anti-Catholic, anti-Jew, anti-Protestant, anti-Negro are not welcome at this meeting."

"The Truth About Segregation," did he defend segregation, and that he has long since repudiated. In describing social unrest, he does at times show some segregationist tendencies, but segregation and integration are not major themes in his writings. His current view is that the problem "definitely has two sides," that forced integration is both unwise and unjustifiable, that one can take sides on the issue for reasons other than race hatred, that the issue of discrimination has been "extensively exaggerated," and that "nowhere in history has there been a case of a backward people of another race being uplifted so rapidly and so greatly benefited by the dominant race as has the American Negro."[5]

Hargis has also been described as an example of "The Authoritarian Personality."[6] Some psychologists argue "that there is a close correlation between a number of deep-rooted personality traits, and overt prejudice,"[7] that "personality may be regarded as a determinant of ideological preferences,"[8] and that this is the clue by which to recognize the "potentially fascistic individual." The claim is not convincing,[9] and in any event the thesis does not fit Hargis. No evidence has been found to indicate that the secret to understanding Hargis is to view his personality as being inherently authoritarian. Hargis is jovial and friendly and rarely makes any significant decision without consulting with numerous advisers. While it is true that there are indications of rigid conformity,

---

[5] *Weekly Crusader,* Vol. 3 (July 12, 1963); *Weekly Crusader,* Vol. 3 (July 19, 1963). See his pamphlet *Racial Strife . . . and America's Future* (Tulsa: Christian Crusade, n.d.).

[6] See, for example, Proshansky and Evans, *op. cit.*

[7] T. W. Adorno, et al., *The Authoritarian Personality* (New York: Harper, 1950), p. vi.

[8] *Ibid.,* p. 5. See also Chapter 6, "Ethnocentrism in Relation to Some Religious Attitudes and Practices."

[9] For a penetrating criticism of the research conducted by Adorno, et al., consult M. Rokeach, "Political and Religious Dogmatism: An Alternative to the Authoritarian Personality," *Psychological Monographs,* Vol. 70, No. 18, 1956. The Adorno volume tends to minimize the religious factor, stating, "Religion does not play such a decisive role within the frame of mind of most people as it once did; only rarely does it seem to account for their social attitudes and opinion" (p. 727). It should be remembered, however, that the sample was atypical. In fact, it was almost entirely non-religious, a point the researchers themselves admit. Undoubtedly the results would have been quite different if the interviewing had involved rural Kansans. All in all, the book tends to overemphasize the personality component and to minimize the situational factor.

stereotyped thinking, and intolerance of ambiguity,[10] all indications are that these relate primarily to his fundamentalist theology and do not stem from any deviant or abnormal personality structure. In short, his personality appears to be no more deviant or unusual than are those of millions of other people who consciously choose to believe in fundamentalism, Marxism, Islam or any other "total" creed. The above statement is made in spite of the specific assertions of several writers that the secret to understanding the man lies in assuming him to be mentally unbalanced.[11] No evidence whatsoever has been found by this writer which would justify such a conclusion.

In Chapter 15, it was suggested that to a degree "Hargisism" is reactionary. Unfortunately, the word "reactionary" has taken on a negative connotation not justified by the term itself. A reactionary is a person who favors a return to an older order. Technically, the designation is an amoral one, but critics have tended to overlook the fact that reactionism is not necessarily evil. They forget that the people who advocated the repeal of the Prohibition Amendment were thorough-going reactionaries, for they sought to recreate a social order which had been superseded by a new one. Simply to ignore or denounce Rightists because they are reactionaries begs the issue.

One of Hargis's most important shortcomings is that many of the real problems of our modern Western society always seem to fall outside of his conceptual analysis. He repeatedly stresses the significance of the individual, but even on those occasions when he does attempt to relate the individual to society he seems to by-pass the whole problem of power, both political and economic. This inadequacy is crucial, since the "proper" use and control of power is the central problem of civil government.

Hargis apparently fails to see that historically the "Christian" majority in America has largely failed to practice Christian ethics in its relations with the rest of society, and that this failure has produced much of the inequity and frustration which currently fill the land. Instead of advocating a remedy for this default, Hargis insists on blaming one culprit, "Leftism." Christianity, in his scheme, functions primarily as a buttress for a status quo society.

For Hargis, the basic question of man and society invariably boils down to an uncritical defense of American civilization. Since

---

10 For a useful discussion of various types of personalities, see Z. Barbu, *Democracy and Dictatorship* (New York: Grove, 1956), especially Chapter 8, "Democratic Personality."

11 See, for example, the inference in Peel, *op. cit.*

he draws his arguments almost entirely from his own social background, his conclusions are implicit in his premises. Unsettling extraneous evidence is rejected.

Hargis's response to the challenge of Communism is largely polemical. He sees an absolute conflict of system with system; incarnate virtue in battle with unmitigated evil. While the clash is a total one in his depiction, he nevertheless manages to avoid any genuine encounter with Communism itself. He fails to deal with the insights of Marxist dogma and to allow for its modification and adaptation in actual practice. His encounter turns out to be an undialectical rejection. Importantly, his absolute "NO" to Communism precludes much valid criticism of the West. This stance helps to explain why "most far-right action-programs are, in plain fact, gigantically irrelevant to the real threat of international communism...."[12]

Ultimately, Hargis's anti-Communism is out of joint with the Christian faith of which it claims to be a part, for in its positive assertions, it is frequently an idolatrous faith in a man-made culture. The result is that in this configuration, "the Christian remains bound not to Christ in the world, but to the world of Communist power and pretension, itself."[13] This shortcoming is crucial. Throughout the "free world" men are looking for a faith that will sustain them as they face the challenges of Communist ideology and the nuclear threat. They have had enough of frustration and fear, illusion and despair. Unfortunately, Hargis has not provided a viable new alternative.

It has become customary to label Rightists as "irresponsible."[14] Much depends on what one means by that term. If by "responsible" one means that "Hargisism" is a fully coherent scheme, that it is a workable system in present-day America, or that the conceptions

---

12 Overstreets, *op. cit.*, p. 15.

13 West, *op. cit.*, p. 77.

14 Cf. the following: Barbara Green, Kathryn Turner, Dante Germino, "Responsible and Irresponsible Right-Wing Groups: A Problem in Analysis," in *The Journal of Social Issues*, Vol. 19 (April, 1963), p. 3. "The responsible groups offer a policy alternative which they seek to advance through the existing political system. They are content to work through accepted political techniques." Although no specific evidence is cited, the authors imply that Hargis is irresponsible (p. 7); they also categorize Dan Smoot and the Courtneys as "irresponsible right-wingers" (p. 15), but cite no supporting evidence. Fred Schwartz's Christian Anti-Communism Crusade is termed "ambiguous" (p. 4). Cf. also Janson and Eismann, *op. cit.*, p. x, where these writers distinguish between the Far Right and "responsible conservatism."

on which it is based are sound, then "Hargisism" would have to be termed irresponsible. But if we mean that a person is sincere, that he appears to be honest, and that he advocates change only via legal means, then Hargis must be placed in the camp of responsibility.[15] One does find occasional statements implying resistance to authority, but they are not nearly as frequent or central in Hargis's writings as in the speeches and pamphlets of some recognized and respected contemporary civil rights leaders. The emphasis on "lawfulness," however, is not necessarily meant to imply high morality or to minimize naiveté, ignorance or faulty perception. The last-mentioned inadequacy deserves special comment. It would seem that of all Hargis's shortcomings, the most glaring is his faulty perception of the real world. It explains many of his erroneous and questionable conclusions, and much of his crusading fervor.

We have dealt at length with the negative aspects of "Hargisism," especially his anti-Communism. The positive features remain to be discussed. Hargis has pointed out the failure of Christian leftists such as John Macmurray, Harry F. Ward, Emil Fuchs, and Hewlett Johnson to grasp the true meaning of Soviet Communism,[16] and has vividly shown the way in which the Communist mind is warped and the extent to which it is dedicated to a new idolatry backed by power. He has illustrated the importance of distrusting promises and appearances, and has reminded us of the many promises broken by Communists. Hargis and his followers have forced the world to consider more carefully the fact of terror and oppres-

---

[15] Some examples of contemporary irresponsible Rightist groups are: The Silver Shirts of America, The Ku Klux Klan, The American Christian Nationalist Party, and The American Nazi Party. For a discussion of other similar groups, see Roy, *op. cit.* The Overstreets, *op. cit.*, in explaining their usage of "extremist," state that they "hold back from applying it to even ultra-conservative groups so long as their internal structure is democratic and so long as they do not demand conformity to one 'correct' view or try to prevent their members from reading what they want to read and thinking what they want to think" (p. 211). One wonders how the Overstreets would categorize the Roman Catholic Church and certain Protestant denominations which keep an "index" and whose internal structure and government can hardly be termed democratic.

[16] Some of the major attempts to reconcile Communism and Christianity include: John Macmurray, *Creative Society* (London, 1935), Hewlett Johnson, *The Soviet Power* (New York: International Publishers, 1940), Harry F. Ward, *The Soviet Spirit* (New York, 1945), Emil Fuchs, *Marxismus und Christentum* (Leipzig, 1953), and Josef Hromadka, *An der Schwelle des Dialogs zwischen Christen und Marxisten* (Frankfurt am Main: Stimme Verlag, 1964).

sion. They have warned us of the folly of writing off the fate of millions of men, as in Stalin's Russia, as an acceptable price for technical and social improvements.

John Stuart Mill once said that supposed error always served a purpose in society; not only might it contain some truth, but it would precipitate debate and force the majority to reevaluate its own position. Hargis illustrates what Mill described.

17. CONCLUSION

WE MAY CONCLUDE THAT HARGIS IS A BELIEVER WITH AN UNDER-standable creed fighting a very real foe. The fact that no country has ever gone Communist by the route he describes neither perturbs nor dissuades him. He carries on the battle, and he carries it on in good faith. He is an agitator and a rather effective one. However, he is as much a product of his times as a shaper of them, and cannot be understood apart from his times, his faith, and his country.

The responsible Far Right does not fit into any of our tra-ditional political categories; it is not fascist, democratic, liberal, anarchic, or totalitarian. Organizationally, it does not form an interest group, for its quarrel is not with any particular division of the spoils, but with the basic orientation and the currently domi-nant political values within the system. Nor is the Far Right a political party, for it is not sufficiently cohesive, organizationally, and it runs no candidates. Neither is it the Rightist equivalent of Marxism, for while it shares the desire to change political leaders, it does not advocate a restructuring of the institutional framework, nor does it endorse violence and terror. It strives for more, not less, nationalism, and disagrees almost completely with Marxism on the nature of the ultimate utopia. In short, the responsible Far Right defies easy categorization either ideologically or organiza-tionally. It might appropriately be termed a non-economic interest group with a program influencing virtually all of society. This combination of qualities is an innovation. However, while its claims and activities are widespread, it has, up to the present, achieved little, mainly because it is unwilling to make any compromises.

The answer to the question of whether Hargis fits into the American tradition is not an easy one. There are many traditions; some dominant at one time, some at another. Undoubtedly Hargis speaks for only a minority, but it is not necessarily a deviant minority on all counts. The crusaders for whom he speaks now find themselves described as reactionaries in part simply because they are in the minority. On the basic question, "What shall be the ends of society?" it is not Hargis and the Far Right but his critics who deviate most from traditional American norms. Crane Brinton has well said that "the United States is not much like early New England.... You are inevitably tempted to wonder what the Pilgrim Fathers would think of it all. Would they recognize their descendants, their successors? Or would they feel that this enormously successful America had gained a world but lost its own soul?"[1] Adorno and associates agree with Brinton and add, "Religion does not play such a decisive role within the frame of mind of most people as it once did; only rarely does it seem to account for their social attitudes and opinions."[2]

Obviously, Hargis does not represent all of the American tradition. He has ignored most of the liberal elements while stressing and preaching the "Christian" and the "conservative." He has overemphasized origins and destiny, peculiarity and superiority, and he has failed, intellectually, to escape from America in order to evaluate America and to perceive its dynamism.

What about the future? Will Hargis and the Far Right continue to expand, or is Richard Rovere right when he contends that "what evidence there is suggests that the [current Far Right] organizations are frantic efforts to prevent ultra-conservatism from dying out"?[3] This observer must disagree with Rovere. As long as the factors remain which produced the current Far Right, so long also will it persist and even grow. Not only are the problems of Communism, big government, modernity, and even the racial crisis greater than ever before, but with the passing of time the responsible Far Right is becoming increasingly more respectable. Senator Frank Church has observed that "we have already become accustomed to a level of political absurdity that would have seemed, a few

---

[1] Crane Brinton, *Ideas and Men; The Story of Western Thought,* Second Edition (Englewood Cliffs: Prentice-Hall, 1963), p. 127.

[2] Adorno, *op. cit.,* p. 727. See also Almond, *op. cit.,* p. 59: The "American has moved away from older moral and traditional norms without acquiring new bases of judgment. His toleration of difference therefore is unstable, and there is a substratum of ideological fundamentalism which frequently breaks through...."

[3] Richard Rovere, "Letter from Washington," *The New Yorker,* Vol. 38 (February 24, 1962), p. 119.

years ago, quite impossible,"[4] and that it is dangerous "to assume that the forces of irrationality and vituperation have been vanquished." And all of this does not take into account the tremendous frustration caused by massive American involvement in Vietnam.

Not only is the center-point moving to the right, but the political spectrum itself is broadening. In 1954 Goldwater was hardly taken seriously; in 1964, with extensive Far Right backing, he became the GOP presidential candidate, and was nominated by a delegation which reportedly included 100 members of the John Birch Society.[5] In 1954 Seymour Lipset wrote, "It is extremely doubtful that the radical right will grow beyond the peak of 1953-54."[6] Lipset was wrong. The Far Right has grown markedly and will likely continue to grow. Up to a point, its leaders view the election results of 1964 not as a defeat but encouragement. They feel that in a satiated society short on causes they are still the only movement with a meaningful and relevant cause. Senator Church cautions, "the real menace of extremism cannot be laughed away. It is, unfortunately, a fever that has not been overcome by the election results."[7] Hargis states,

> In the wake of the tragic events of November 3 [1964], and their fearful consequences on the course of human events in the years to come, Crusaders must most assuredly don their armor of Christian responsibility and face the rigors of the battle ahead. With the cross of Christ and the American Flag as our only standards, we must reconsecrate our efforts, regardless of the cost, to right the terrible wrong which has been done. . . .[8]

But, as he sees it, the situation has two sides: "Twenty-five million Americans voted for what is decent, for what is clean, for what has always been and always will be true Americanism."[9] True be-

---

[4] Frank Church, *Congressional Record*, 89th Congress, First Session, United States Senate, III (January 12, 1965), p. 554.

[5] Overstreets, *op. cit.*, p. 232.

[6] Lipset, "The Sources of the 'Radical Right,'" in Bell, *op. cit.*, p. 369. Interestingly, Barth, *op. cit.*, p. 132, predicted that the Rightists with "their darling" Barry Goldwater would fail to grasp control of the GOP at a national convention. San Francisco, 1964, of course, proved him to be wrong.

[7] Church, *op. cit.*, p. 554.

[8] Hargis, *Christian Crusade*, Vol. 16 (December, 1964), p. 5.

[9] *Ibid.*, p. 30. See also the article by Dr. Frederick Curtis Fowler in *Weekly Crusader*, Vol. 5 (November 20, 1964). Note his thesis: "Conservatism is back in the mainstream of the American life and thought — after having had the Democratic Party captured by the Extreme left-wing Fabian Socialists, and the Republican Party captured by the 'me-too' moderates. Conservatism is now back and young, tough, and aggressive. . . . It means to hold every advantage gained, and go on to final victory" (p. 8).

lievers are not easily dissuaded. The Crusade is not about to end. The cause of "right" must always be defended — win, lose, or draw. Ultimate victory is assured. In the meantime Billy James Hargis will beg and boast, preach and pray, and shout and sing; he will carry on in the battle for "conservatism and capitalism," for "God and Country."

The Far Right is still very much a minority movement — but as long as confusion, frustration, and incomprehension are widespread in American society, so long will the Far Right gain new supporters. And as it gains new supporters, the complexion of American politics will change even more, and become more ideological. The Far Right has injected a rigid doctrinaire ideology into a society that for a century or more has been politically non-ideological, and has stressed consensus, not opposition. Other groups in history also propagated a rigid political ideology, but they either lost their doctrine quickly, or they failed to become politically significant. The contemporary Far Right has maintained its rigidity while achieving political significance. Perhaps it is the Communist threat which makes the difference, perhaps it is something in the American character; in any event, the contemporary Far Right is both ideologically doctrinaire and politically significant.

If the impression which remains is that there is a significant threat in the current burgeoning of the Far Right, then this writer's judgment has shone through. Nevertheless, the threat does not lie so much in a conscious attempt to subvert democratic processes, at least not on the part of the law-abiding segment represented by Hargis. Rather, it lies in the distorted perceptions, the misleading simplifications, the thwarting of social progress by labeling all social action as Communist-inspired, and the dangerous practice of transplanting final, total answers, from the private, religious sphere to the public, political sphere. The threat lies, in part, in the failure to distinguish between the finality of ultimate, divine authority and the partial insight of the human purveyor. What Hargis denies, at least implicitly, is not the democratic process itself, but the frame of mind which strengthens it and may even be its crucial prerequisite. The fact that this stance results largely, perhaps even logically up to a point, from an honest commitment to a religious creed makes it no less portentous. [10]

But the threat comes not from one side only. A significant number of generally sophisticated and cautious scholars have ex-

10 Cf. the following: "The cardinal socio-psychological concepts of de-

hibited an amazing degree of carelessness when reacting to the Far Right. The very principles they claim to be defending have all too frequently been jettisoned in their own analyses. An even greater threat than that which the responsible Far Right now poses would not justify such academic slovenliness. What is sorely needed is more information, more analysis, more understanding, and more education; hopefully this monograph has helped to fill that gap.

---

mocracy are the concepts of individuality, critical mind, objectivity, and leisure." Barbu, *op. cit.*, p. 70. For a thorough discussion of the importance of a pro-democratic frame of mind as a prerequisite for liberal democracy, see T. V. Smith, *The Democratic Way of Life* (New York: The New American Library, 1951).

APPENDIX

CHRISTIAN ECHOES MINISTRY, INC.
TULSA, OKLAHOMA
STATEMENT OF INCOME & EXPENSE
JANUARY 1, 1964 TO DECEMBER 31, 1964.

Resources:

Christian Crusade Tours & Rallies —		
Offering for General Funds	106,977.99	
Offering for Radio Broadcasts	87,956.20	
Special Gifts & Contributions	184,966.90	
Christian Crusade Publications	126,582.98	
Monthly Newsletter Offerings	182,290.26	
Membership Fees & Pledges	75,920.92	
Christian Crusade Schools	12,608.20	
Christian Crusade Youth University	34,210.36	
Christian Crusade-Building Fund	12,827.00	
Miscellaneous Income	10,438.41	
Gross Receipts		834,779.22

deduct,

Religious Promotional Expenses:

Salaries & Wages (66 Employees)	144,285.01
Radio & Television Expense	221,370.02
Printing & Publications	141,884.44
Crusades (Auditorium Rental, Advertising, Etc.)	69,221.82
Convention & Leadership School Expense	5,883.28
Postage & Mailing Expense	51,008.15
Office Expenses	25,245.62
Freight & Transportation	6,885.08
Equipment Repair & Maintenance	3,377.37
Telephone Expense	7,222.48
Insurance Expense	13,913.63

205

Rent	13,901.33	
Parsonage Expense	4,350.97	
Legal & Accounting Departments	8,840.97	
Interest on Loans	4,770.20	
Depreciation	15,551.00	
Contributions	1,390.92	
Christian Crusade Youth University Expense	30,380.36	
Christian Crusade Building Reserve Fund	12,827.00	
Total Expense		782,309.65
Net Income — General Fund (Used to Reduce Past Indebtedness)		52,469.57

— KEN BLACKBURN
Public Accountant

CHRISTIAN ECHOES MINISTRY, INC.
TULSA, OKLAHOMA
STATEMENT OF INCOME & EXPENSE
JANUARY 1, 1965 TO DECEMBER 31, 1965

Contributions and Resources:

Christian Crusade Tours & Rallies —		
Offering for General Funds	122,547.96	
Offering for Radio Broadcasts	34,078.76	
Radio Contributions	54,460.83	
Special Gifts & Contributions	212,380.87	
Christian Crusade Publications	137,566.94	
Monthly Newsletter Offerings	204,084.76	
Membership Fees and Pledges	84,049.03	
Christian Crusade Schools	8,063.19	
Christian Crusade Youth University	40,123.90	
Miscellaneous Income	10,781.87	
Gross Receipts		908,138.11

DEDUCT

Expenses:

Salaries & Wages (76 Employees)	206,650.85
Radio & Television Expense	259,954.16
Printing & Publications	131,161.33
Crusades (Auditorium Rental, Advertising, etc.)	71,224.95
Leadership School Expense	9,868.10
Postage & Mailing Expense	62,593.77
Office Expenses	32,880.41
Freight & Transportation	6,320.14

Equipment Repair & Maintenance	3,934.35
Telephone Expense	10,208.78
Insurance Expense	13,949.87
Office Rent	12,431.50
Properties of Christian Crusade	4,180.51
Legal & Accounting Departments	7,176.27
Interest & Bank Charges	4,428.34
Depreciation	19,859.14
Charitable Contributions	1,383.75
Christian Crusade	
Youth University Expense	32,168.53
Miscellaneous Expense	1,054.39

Total Expense	891,429.14

Net Income — General Fund
(Used to Reduce Past Indebtedness)   16,708.97

In addition to the above, the total contributions and other income for the Church of the Christian Crusade, Inc., "Building Fund" were $211,605.68. These funds were spent in their entirety in the construction of the Cathedral of the Christian Crusade.

VERNON VAN HORN
Comptroller

BIBLIOGRAPHY

A. *MATERIAL BY HARGIS*

Some familiarity with the extensive writing by Hargis is essential to an understanding of the man and his movement.

1. Major books:

Billy James Hargis. *Communism, The Total Lie!* Tulsa: Christian Crusade, 1963.

Billy James Hargis. *Communist America... Must It Be?* Tulsa: Christian Crusade, 1960.

Billy James Hargis. *The Facts About Communism and Our Churches.* Tulsa: Christian Crusade, 1962.

Billy James Hargis. *The Far Left.* Tulsa: Christian Crusade, 1964.

2. Periodicals:

Much of Hargis's writing appears as editorials or feature articles in either his weekly or monthly magazines.

The Weekly Crusader, Tulsa: Christian Crusade.

Christian Crusade, Tulsa: Christian Crusade.

3. A representative selection of booklets and pamphlets, all published by Christian Crusade:

Unmasking The Deceiver, Martin Luther King, Jr.
Racial Strife and America's Future
Does Challenging the NCC Aid Communism?
The Ugly Truth About Drew Pearson
The Postal Propaganda Problem
"Counter Strategy for Counter Attack"
Brotherhood of Man... A Smoke Screen
Radicalism of the Left — Americans for Democratic Action
We Have Been Betrayed
"Christians, Is It Nothing to You?"
The Muzzling of General Walker
A Call to Action to Every Real American
The Communist Program To Subvert American Youth

How The Communists Influence American Elections
Communism and American Labor
Uncle Sam M.D.?
The United Nations, Destroying America By Degrees
Threats To Christian Education
This I Believe
American Socialism . . . Moving America Downhill
Mental Health
Should We Surrender to Castro or Smash Him?
What's Wrong With America?
UNESCO, The Snake in Our Schoolroom, We Put It There
Good Reasons for Fighting Communism
What's Wrong With Jesus?
If Our Foundations Be Destroyed
America — Let's Get Back TO GOD!
"Unto God's Glory"
Jesus Christ, God Wrapped in Human Flesh
Short Course in Bible Knowledge

B. BOOKS

A Summary of Resolutions of the National Council of Churches,
1950-1961. New York: National Council of the Churches of
Christ in the U. S. A., 1961.

Adorno, T. W., et. al. *The Authoritarian Personality.* New York:
Harper, 1950.

Agar, Herbert, et al. *The City of Man: A Declaration of World*
Democracy. New York: Viking, 1940.

Albornoz, A. F. Carrillo de. *The Basis of Religious Liberty.* New
York: Association, 1963.

Allen, Steve, et al. *Dialogues in Americanism.* Chicago: Regnery,
1964.

Allport, G. W. *The Nature of Prejudice.* New York: Doubleday,
1958.

Almond, Gabriel A. *The American People and Foreign Policy.*
New York: Praeger, 1960.

Bach, Marcus. *God and the Soviets.* New York: Crowell, 1958
(1961).

Baltzell, E. Digby. *The Protestant Establishment, Aristocracy and*
Caste in America. New York: Random House, 1964.

Barbu, Zevedei. *Democracy and Dictatorship.* New York: Grove,
1956.

Barker, Ernest. *Principles of Social and Political Theory.* New York:
Oxford University Press, 1961.

Beard, Charles H., and Mary R. Beard. *The American Spirit.* New
York: Collier Books, 1942 (1962).

Beck, Robert N. *The Meaning of Americanism.* New York: Philosophical Library, 1956.

Becker, Carl L. *The Declaration of Independence, A Study of the History of Political Ideas.* New York: Harcourt, Brace, 1922.

Bell, Daniel (ed.). *The Radical Right.* Garden City, New York: Doubleday, 1963, Anchor Paperback, 1964.

Bennett, John C. *Christian Ethics and Social Policy.* New York: Scribners, 1946.

Bennett, John C. *Christianity and Communism Today.* New York: Association, 1960.

Bennett, John C. *Christians and the State.* New York: Scribners, 1958.

Bennett, John C. *When Christians Make Political Decisions.* New York: Association, 1964.

Berger, Peter. *The Noise of Solemn Assemblies.* New York: Doubleday, n.d.

Beth, Loren P. *The American Theory of Church and State.* Gainsville: University of Florida Press, 1948.

Billington, Ray Allen. *The Protestant Crusade, 1800-1860: A Study in the Origins of American Nativism.* Chicago: Quadrangle, 1964.

Boorstin, Daniel J. *The Genius of American Politics.* Chicago: University of Chicago Press, 1953.

Brinton, Crane. *Ideas and Men; The Story of Western Thought,* Second Edition. Englewood Cliffs: Prentice-Hall, 1963.

Brogan, Dennis W. *The American Character.* New York: Vintage Books, 1956.

Bryce, James. *The American Commonwealth,* 2 vols. New York: Putnam, 1888 (Macmillan, 1910).

Buckley, William. *Up From Liberalism.* New York: Hillman Books, 1961.

Bunke, Harvey C. *The Liberal Dilemma.* Englewood Cliffs: Prentice-Hall, 1964.

Burlingame, Roger. *The Sixth Column.* Philadelphia: Lippincott, 1962.

Burns, Edward M. *The American Idea of Mission; Concepts of National Purpose and Destiny.* New Brunswick, New Jersey: Rutgers University Press, 1957.

Cain, Edward. *They'd Rather Be Right; Youth and the Conservative Movement.* New York: Macmillan, 1963.

Campbell, Paul, and Peter Howard. *America Needs an Ideology.* London: Frederick Muller, 1957.

Carnell, Edward John. *The Case for Orthodox Theology.* Philadelphia: Westminster, 1959.

Cassinelli, C. W. *The Politics of Freedom, An Analysis of the*

Modern Democratic State. Seattle: University of Washington Press, 1961.

Christie, Richard, and Marie Jahoda (eds.). *Studies in the Scope and Method of 'The Authoritarian Personality.'* Glencoe: Free Press, 1954.

Clinchy, Russell J. *Faith and Freedom*, New York: Macmillan, 1947.

Cobb, Sanford H. *The Rise of Religious Liberty in America*. New York: Macmillan, 1902.

Cogley, John (ed.). *Religion in America, Original Essays on Religion in a Free Society*. Cleveland: Meridian Books, 1962.

Cohen, Carl (ed.). *Communism, Fascism, and Democracy*. New York: Random House, 1962.

Cole, Stewart G. *The History of Fundamentalism*. Hamden, Conn.: Shoe String Press, 1931.

Commager, Henry Steele. *The American Mind (An Interpretation of American Thought and Character Since the 1880's)*. New Haven: Yale University Press, 1959 (1950).

Cousins, Norman. *"In God We Trust" (The Religious Beliefs and Ideas of the American Founding Fathers)*. New York: Harper & Brothers, 1958.

Cunningham, William. *Christianity and Politics*. New York: Houghton Mifflin, 1951.

Curti, Merle. *The Growth of American Thought*, Second Edition. New York: Harper & Brothers, 1951.

DeBoer, Cecil. *Responsible Protestantism*. Grand Rapids: Eerdmans, 1957.

DeKoster, Lester. *Communism and the Christian Faith*. Grand Rapids: Eerdmans, 1962.

Destler, Chester M. *American Radicalism, 1865-1901: Essays and Documents*. New York: Octagon, 1946.

Dodd, C. H. *Gospel and Law*. New York: Columbia University Press, 1951.

Drakeford, John W. *Red Blueprint For The World*. Grand Rapids: Eerdmans, 1962.

Dudman, Richard. *Men of the Far Right*. New York: Pyramid Books, 1962.

Eastman, Max. *Reflections on the Failure of Socialism*. New York: Grosset and Dunlap, 1955 (Universal Library Edition, 1962).

Eliot, T. S. *The Idea of a Christian Society*. London: Faber & Faber, 1939.

Ellsworth, Ralph E., and Sarah M. Harris. *The American Right Wing*. Washington, D. C.: Public Affairs Press, 1962.

Fletcher, Joseph F. (ed.). *Christianity and Property*. Philadelphia: Westminster, 1946.

Forster, Arnold, and Benjamin Epstein. *Danger on the Right.* New York: Random House, 1964.

Fuchs, Emil. *Marxismus und Christentum.* Leipzig, 1953.

The Fundamentals, A Testimony to the Truth, 12 vols. Los Angeles: Biola, 1917.

Furniss, Norman F. *The Fundamentalist Controversy.* Hamden, Conn.: Shoe String Press, 1954.

Gabriel, Ralph H. *The Course of American Democratic Thought,* 3 vols. New York: Ronald Press, 1956.

Gardner, E. C. *Biblical Faith and Social Ethics.* New York: Harper & Brothers, 1960.

Garvie, Alfred E. *The Christian Ideal for Human Society.* New York: Richard R. Smith, 1930.

Gasper, Louis. *The Fundamentalist Movement.* The Hague: Mouton, 1963.

Gettell, Raymond G. *History of American Political Thought.* New York: Appleton-Century, 1928.

Geyer, Alan F. *Piety and Politics.* Richmond: Knox, 1963.

Gilbreath, J. Earl. *Individual Worth in a Social Crisis.* New York: Fleming & Revell, 1938.

Gilson, Etienne. *Dogmatism and Tolerance.* New Brunswick, New Jersey: Rutgers University Press, 1952.

Goldwater, Barry. *The Conscience of a Conservative.* New York: MacFadden Books, 1960.

Gorman, William. "A Catholic View: Toward a More Perfect Union Regarding the American Civil Liberty of Religion," in *The Wall Between Church and State.* Dallin H. Oaks (ed.). Chicago: University of Chicago Press, 1963 (Phoenix Books edition).

Graham, George A. *Morality in American Politics.* New York: Random House, 1952.

Greene, Evarts B. *Religion and the State, The Making and Testing of an American Tradition.* Ithaca, New York: Cornell University Press, 1941 (Great Seal Books, 1959).

Greifer, Elisha (ed.). *Joseph De Maistre: On God and Society.* Chicago: Regnery, 1959.

Guerry, Emile. *The Popes and World Government.* Baltimore: Helicon, 1964.

Hall, Thomas Cumming. *The Religious Background of American Culture.* Boston: Little, Brown, 1930.

Hallowell, John H. *The Moral Foundation of Democracy.* Chicago: University of Chicago Press, 1954.

Hartz, Louis. *The Liberal Tradition in America.* New York: Harcourt, Brace and World, 1955.

Heinsohn, A. G., Jr. (ed.). *Anthology of Conservative Writing in the United States, 1932-1960.* Chicago: Regnery, 1962.

Henry, Carl F. H. *Aspects of Christian Social Ethics.* Grand Rapids: Eerdmans, 1964.

Henry, Carl F. H. *The Uneasy Conscience of Modern Fundamentalism.* Grand Rapids: Eerdmans, 1947.

Hershberger, Guy F. *War, Peace, and Nonresistance.* Scottdale, Pa.: Herald, 1953.

Hershberger, Guy F. *The Way of the Cross in Human Relations.* Scottdale, Pa.: Herald, 1958.

Hesseltine, William B. *Third Party Movements in the United States.* New York: Van Nostrand, 1962.

Hicks, John D. *The Populist Revolt,* Second Edition. Lincoln, Nebraska: University of Nebraska Press, 1961.

Hoffer, Eric. *The True Believer.* New York: New American Library, 1951.

Hofstadter, Richard. *The American Political Tradition.* New York: Random House, 1948.

Hofstadter, Richard. *Anti-Intellectualism in American Life.* New York: Knopf, 1963.

Hofstadter, Richard. "The Pseudo-Conservative Revolt," in *The Radical Right,* Daniel Bell (ed.). Garden City, New York: Doubleday, 1963.

Hofstadter, Richard. "Pseudo-Conservatism Revisited: A Postscript," in *The Radical Right,* Daniel Bell (ed.). Garden City, New York: Doubleday, 1963.

Hopkins, Charles H. *The Rise of the Social Gospel in American Protestantism.* New Haven: Yale University Press, 1940.

Horney, Karen. *The Neurotic Personality of Our Time.* New York: Norton, 1965.

Hromadka, Josef L. *An der Schwelle des Dialogs zwischen Christen und Marxisten.* Frankfurt am Main: Stimme Verlag, 1964.

Hudson, Winthrop. *The Great Tradition of the American Churches.* New York: Harper and Row, 1953.

Hutchison, John A. (ed.). *Christian Faith and Social Action.* New York: Scribners, 1953.

Hutchison, John A. *The Two Cities: A Study of God and Human Politics.* Garden City, New York: Doubleday, 1957.

Hyman, Herbert H. "England and America: Climates of Tolerance and Intolerance," in *The Radical Right,* Daniel Bell (ed.). Garden City, New York: Doubleday, 1963.

Janson, Donald, and Bernard Eismann. *The Far Right.* New York: McGraw-Hill, 1963.

Johnson, Hewlett. *The Soviet Power.* London, 1940.

Katz, Wilbur G. *Religion and American Constitutions.* Evanston: Northwestern University Press, 1964.

Kauper, Paul G. *Religion and the Constitution.* Baton Rouge: Louisiana State University Press, 1965.

Kay, Thomas O. *The Christian Answer to Communism.* Grand Rapids: Zondervan, 1961.

Kelley, Alden D. *Christianity and Political Responsibility.* Philadelphia: Westminster, 1961.

Kik, J. Marcellus. *Church and State: The Story of Two Kingdoms.* New York: Nelson, 1963.

Kirk, Russell. *The Conservative Mind, From Burke to Eliot,* Revised Edition. Chicago: Regnery, 1960.

Knight, Frank H. & Thornton W. Merriam. *The Economic Order and Religion.* New York: Harper & Brothers, 1945.

Kohn, Hans. *American Nationalism: An Interpretative Essay.* New York: Collier, 1957.

Kraus, C. Norman. *Dispensationalism in America, Its Rise and Development.* Richmond, Va.: Knox, 1958.

Labaree, Leonard. *Conservatism in Early American History.* Ithaca, New York: Cornell University Press, 1948 (Great Seal Books edition, 1959).

Latham, Earl (ed.). *The Meaning of McCarthyism.* Boston: Heath, 1965.

Lechler, Joseph. *The Two Sovereignties; A Study of the Relationship Between Church and State.* New York: Philosophical Library, 1952.

Lens, Sidney. *The Futile Crusade, Anti-Communism as American Credo.* Chicago: Quadrangle Books, 1964.

Lenski, Gerhard. *The Religious Factor.* Garden City: Doubleday, 1961.

Levey, Leonard. *Jefferson and Civil Liberties.* Cambridge: Harvard University Press, 1964.

Lipset, Seymour. "The Sources of the 'Radical Right,'" in *The Radical Right,* Daniel Bell (ed.). Garden City, New York: Doubleday, 1963.

Littell, Franklin H. *From State Church to Pluralism.* Garden City, New York: Doubleday, 1962.

Lowry, Charles W. *Communism and Christ.* New York: Morehouse-Gorham, 1953.

Luccock, Halford. *Christian Faith and Economic Change.* New York: Abingdon, 1936.

MacArthur, K. W. *The Bible and Human Rights.* Revised Edition. New York: The Woman's Press, 1949.

Machen, J. Gresham. *Christianity and Liberalism.* Grand Rapids: Eerdmans, 1923.

Macmurray, John. *Creative Society*. London, 1935.

Maness, William H. *Brainwashing and the National Council of Churches of Christ in the USA*. Jacksonville, Fla: Crawford, 1964.

Maness, William H. *How to Investigate the National Council of Churches of Christ in the USA*. Jacksonville, Fla.: Convention Press, 1964.

Manwaring, David R. *Render Unto Caesar*. Chicago: University of Chicago Press, 1962.

Marty, Martin. *The New Shape of American Religion*. New York: Harper, 1959.

Mast, Russell L. *Christianity and Communism*. Newton, Kansas: Faith and Life, 1962.

Mathews, Shailer. *The Social Gospel*. Philadelphia: Griffith & Rowland, 1910.

Maury, P. *Politics and Evangelism*. New York: Doubleday, 1959.

McIntire, Carl. *Servants of Apostasy*. Collingswood, New Jersey: Christian Beacon Press, 1955.

McNeill, J. T. *Christian Hope for World Society*. Chicago: Willett & Clark, 1937.

Mead, Sidney E. *The Lively Experiment, The Shaping of Christianity in America*. New York: Harper & Row, 1963.

Mecklin, John M. *The Story of American Dissent*. New York, 1934.

Meyer, Frank (ed.). *What Is Conservatism?* New York: Holt, Rinehart and Winston, 1964.

Miller, Perry, et al. *Religion and Freedom of Thought*. Garden City, New York: Doubleday, 1954.

Miller, Perry. *The New England Mind: From Colony to Province*. Boston: Beacon, 1953.

Miller, William Lee. *The Protestant and Politics*. Philadelphia: Westminster, 1958.

Moon, Robert. *What's Wrong With the Far Right?* Fresno, California: First Methodist Church, 1965.

Morrison, Clinton D. *The Powers That Be*. Naperville, Ill.: Allenson, 1960 (Studies in Biblical Theology, Number 29).

Muehl, William. *Mixing Religion and Politics*. New York: Association, 1958.

Muller, Herbert J. *Religion and Freedom in the Modern World*. Chicago: University of Chicago Press, 1963.

Munday, D. L. *The Idea of a Secular Society*. London: Oxford University Press, 1963.

Murray, John Courtney. *Morality and Modern War*. New York: The Church Peace Union, 1959.

Murray, John Courtney. *We Hold These Truths*. New York: Sheed and Ward, 1960.

Myers, G. *History of Bigotry in the United States*. New York: Random House, 1943.

Nelson, Claude D. *Church and State, A Guide for Study Discussion*. New York: National Council of Churches, 1953.

Nichols, James Hastings. *Democracy and the Churches*. Philadelphia: Westminster, 1951.

Nichols, Roy F. *Religion and American Democracy*. Baton Rouge: Louisiana State University Press, 1965.

Niebuhr, H. Richard. *Christ and Culture*. New York: Harper and Row, 1956.

Niebuhr, H. Richard. *The Kingdom of God in America*. New York: Harper and Brothers, 1937.

Niebuhr, H. Richard. *The Social Sources of Denominationalism*. New York: Holt, 1929.

Niebuhr, Reinhold. "A Note on Pluralism," in *Religion in America*, Harper and Brothers, 1935.

Niebuhr, Reinhold. *The Children of Light and the Children of Darkness*. New York: Scribners, 1944.

Niebuhr, Reinhold. *The Irony of American History*. New York: Scribners, 1952.

Niebuhr, Reinhold. "A Note On Pluralism," in *Religion In America, Original Essays on Religion in a Free Society,* John Cogley (ed.). Cleveland: Meridian Books, 1962.

Niebuhr, Reinhold. *Pious and Secular America*. New York: Scribners, 1958.

Niebuhr, Reinhold. *The World Crisis and American Responsibility,* E. W. Lefever (ed.). New York: Association, 1958.

Nixon, Justin W. *Responsible Christianity*. New York: Harper & Brothers, 1950.

Northcott, Cecil. *Religious Liberty*. New York: Macmillan, 1948.

Oaks, Dallin H. (ed.). *The Wall Between Church and State*. Chicago: University of Chicago Press, 1963.

Odegard, Peter M. (ed.). *Religion and Politics*. New York: Oceana, 1960.

Olmstead, Clifton E. *Religion in America, Past and Present*. Englewood Cliffs: Prentice-Hall, 1961.

Overdyke, W. Darrell. *The Know Nothing Party in the South*. Baton Rouge: Louisiana State University Press, 1950.

Overstreet, Harry, and Bonaro Overstreet. *The Strange Tactics of Extremism*. New York: Norton, 1964.

Packer, J. I. *"Fundamentalism" and the Word of God*. Grand Rapids: Eerdmans, 1958.

Padover, Saul K. (ed.). *Jefferson On Democracy*. New York: Penguin, 1946 (1939).

Parrington, Vernon L. *Main Currents in American Thought,* 3 vols. New York: Harcourt, Brace, 1927-1930.

Peachey, Paul (ed.). *Biblical Realism Confronts the Nation.* Scottdale, Pa.: Herald, 1963.

Pemberton, Prentiss L. *Christians Face The Total Menace of Communism.* Chicago: Hudson, 1962.

Penner, Archie. *The New Testament, The Christians, and the State.* Altona, Manitoba: D. W. Friesen and Sons, 1958.

Perkins, Dexter. *The American Way.* Ithaca: Cornell University Press, 1957.

Perry, Ralph B. *Puritanism and Democracy.* New York: Vanguard, 1944.

Pfeffer, Leo. *Church, State and Freedom.* Boston: Beacon, 1953.

Philbrick, Herbert. *I Led 3 Lives.* New York: Grosset and Dunlap, 1952.

The Power of the Democratic Idea. Rockefeller Brothers Fund Report, Special Studies Project, Report VI. Garden City, New York: Doubleday, 1960.

Pressley, Thomas J. *Americans Interpret Their Civil War.* Princeton: Princeton University Press, 1954.

Probst, George E. *The Happy Republic.* New York: Harper & Brothers, 1962.

Quick, O. C. *Christianity and Justice.* London: Sheldon, 1940.

Rasmussen, Albert Terrill. *Christian Social Ethics.* Englewood Cliffs: Prentice-Hall, 1956.

Ratkovich, Manojlo. *The World Mission of the United States.* New York: Greenwich, 1959.

Rauschenbusch, Walter. *A Theology for the Social Gospel.* New York: Abingdon, 1917.

Rauschenbusch, Walter. *Christianity and the Social Crisis.* New York: Macmillan, 1907.

Rauschenbusch, Walter. *Christianizing the Social Order.* New York: Macmillan, 1912.

Riesman, David, and Nathan Glazer. "Intellectuals and Discontented Classes," in *The Radical Right,* Daniel Bell (ed.). Garden City, New York: Doubleday, 1964.

Robertson, D. B. *The Religious Foundation of Leveller Democracy.* New York: Columbia University Press, 1951.

Roche, John P. *The Quest for the Dream — The Development of Civil Rights and Human Relations in Modern America.* New York: Macmillan, 1963.

Rogers, Edward. *A Christian Commentary on Communism.* New York: Praeger, 1952.

Rogger, Hans, and Eugen Weber (eds.). *The European Right.* Berkeley: University of California Press, 1965.

Rokeach, Milton. *The Open and Closed Mind.* New York: Basic Books, 1960.

Rosenberg, Bernard. "The 'New American Right,'" in *Voices of Dissent.* New York: Grove, 1958, pp. 131-137.

Rovere, Richard H. *Senator Joe McCarthy.* New York: Harcourt, Brace, 1959.

Rowe, Henry K. *History of Religion in the United States.* New York: Macmillan, 1924.

Roy, Ralph Lord. *Apostles of Discord.* Boston: Beacon, 1953.

Ryan, J. A., and F. J. Boland. *Catholic Principles of Politics.* New York: Macmillan, n.d.

Sanders, Thomas G. *Protestant Concepts of Church and State.* New York: Holt, Rinehart & Winston, 1964.

Schapiro, J. Salwyn. *Liberalism: Its Meaning and History.* New York: Van Nostrand, 1958.

Schneidler, Herbert W. *Religion in 20th Century America.* New York: Atheneum, 1964.

Schrey, H., H. Waltz, and W. Whitehouse. *The Biblical Doctrines of Justice and Law.* London: SCM, 1955.

Seifert, H. *Ethical Resources for International Relations.* Philadelphia: Westminster, 1964.

Seifert, H. *The Church in Community Action.* New York: Abingdon-Cokesbury, 1952.

Sharpe, D. R. *Call to Christian Action.* New York: Harper, 1949.

Shaull, M. Richard. *Encounter With Revolution.* New York: Association, 1955.

Sherwin, Mark. *The Extremists.* New York: St. Martin's, 1963.

Shipley, Frederick A. *Protestantism in Suburban Life.* New York: Columbia University Press, 1963.

Slater, Robert Lawson. *World Religions and World Community.* New York: Columbia University Press, 1963.

Smith, Brewster M., et al. *Opinions and Personality.* New York: Wiley, 1956.

Smith, David G. *The Convention and The Constitution, The Political Ideas of the Founding Fathers.* New York: St. Martin's, 1965.

Smith, Dean. *Conservatism: A Guide to Its Past, Present and Future in American Politics.* New York: Hearst Corporation, 1963.

Smith, J. Allen. *The Growth and Decadence of Constitutional Government.* New York: Holt, 1930.

Smith, J. Allen. *The Spirit of American Government; A Study of the Constitution, Its Origins, Influence, and Relation to Democracy.* New York: Macmillan, 1911.

Smith, James, and Leland Jamieson (eds.). *Religion in American Life,* 4 vols. Princeton: Princeton University Press, 1961.

Smith, Timothy L. *Revivalism and Social Reform*. Nashville: Abingdon, 1957.

Smith, T. V. *The Democratic Way of Life*. New York: The New American Library, 1951.

Smith, Wilbur M. *This Atomic Age and the Word of God*. Boston: Wilde, 1948.

Smylie, John Edwin. "The Christian Church and National Ethos," in *Biblical Realism Confronts the Nation*, Paul Peachey (ed.). Scottdale, Pa.: Herald, 1963.

Sperry, William L. *Religion in America*. New York: Macmillan, 1946.

Spinka, Matthew. *Christian Thought From Erasmus to Berdyaev*. Englewood Cliffs: Prentice-Hall, 1962.

Stahmer, Harold (ed.). *Religion and Contemporary Society*. New York: Macmillan, 1963.

Stedman, Murray S. *Religion and Politics in America*. New York: Harcourt, Brace and World, 1964.

Stevick, Daniel B. *Beyond Fundamentalism*. Richmond, Va.: Knox, 1964.

Stillman, Edward, and William Pfaff. *The Politics of Hysteria*. New York: Harper Colophon Books, n.d.

Stokes, Anson Phelps, and Leo Pfeffer. *Church and State in the United States*, Revised one-volume Edition. New York: Harper and Row, 1964.

Stouffer, Samuel A. *Communism, Conformity, and Civil Liberties*. New York: Doubleday, 1955.

Suall, Irwin. *The American Ultras*. New York: New American Library, 1962.

Sweet, W. W. *Story of Religion in America*, Second Revised Edition. New York: Harper & Brothers, 1950.

Thompson, Kenneth W. *Christian Ethics and the Dilemmas of Foreign Policy*. Durham: Duke University Press, 1959.

't Hooft, W. A. Visser, and J. H. Oldham. *The Church and its Function in Society*. Chicago: Willett, Clark, 1937.

Tillich, Paul. "Freedom and the Ultimate Concern," in *Religion in America, Original Essays on Religion in a Free Society*, John Cogley (ed.). Cleveland: Meridian Books, 1962.

Tocqueville, Alexis de. *Democracy in America*, 2 vols., translated by Henry Reeve. New York: Vintage, 1945.

Toledano, Ralph de. *Lament For A Generation*. New York: Farrar, Straus, and Cudahy, 1959.

Troeltsch, Ernst D. *Protestantism and Progress*. New York: Putnam, 1912.

Troeltsch, Ernst D. *The Social Teaching of the Christian Churches*. New York: Macmillan, 1931.

Tyler, Alice Felt. *Freedom's Ferment*. New York: Harper and Brothers, 1962.

Viereck, Peter. *Conservatism*. Princeton, New Jersey: Van Nostrand, 1956.

Viereck, Peter. *Conservatism Revisited*. New York: Collier Books, 1962.

Viereck, Peter. "The Philosophical 'New Conservative,'" in *The Radical Right*, Daniel Bell (ed.). Garden City, New York: Doubleday, 1963.

Voorhis, Jerry. *The Christian In Politics*. New York: Association, 1951.

Vrooman, Lee. *The Faith that Built America*. New York: Arrowhead Books, 1955.

Walker, Brooks R. *The Christian Fright Peddlers*. Garden City, New York: Doubleday, 1964.

Waller, George M. (ed.). *Puritanism in Early America*. Boston: Heath, 1950.

Walter, James. *The Christian in Politics*. London: Oxford University Press, 1962.

Ward, Barbara. *Faith and Freedom*. Garden City: Doubleday, 1958.

Ward, Harry F. *Social Creed of the Churches*. New York: Eaton & Mains, 1912.

Ward, Harry F. *Social Evangelism*. New York: Missionary Education Movement, 1915.

Ward, Harry F. *The Soviet Spirit*. New York, 1945.

Weinberg, Albert K. *Manifest Destiny*. Chicago: Quadrangle Books, 1935 (1963).

West, Charles C. *Communism and the Churches*. New York: Macmillan, 1958.

West, Charles C. *Communism and the Theologians*. New York: Macmillan, 1958.

Whitaker, Urban (ed.). *Nationalism and National Progress*. San Francisco: Chandler, 1961.

Wild, John. *Human Freedom and Social Order: An Essay in Christian Philosophy*. Durham: Duke University Press, 1959.

Woodhouse, Arthur Summerland Pigott. *Puritanism and Liberty*. London: Dent, 1938.

Yinger, J. M. *Religion, Society, and the Individual*. New York: Macmillan, 1957.

Yinger, Milton. *Religion in the Struggle for Power*. Durham: Duke University Press, 1946.

Yoder, John Howard. *The Christian Witness to the State*. Newton, Kansas: Faith and Life, 1964.

C. *ARTICLES, PAMPHLETS, AND PERIODICALS*

Adams, John Kay. "Saving America," *Nation,* CXCIII (September 30, 1961), 191-2+.

Aims and Procedures. Christian Freedom Foundation Pamphlet, n.d.

Anderson, Paul B. "Religious Liberty Under Communism," *A Journal of Church and State,* VI (Spring, 1964), 169-77.

Baldinger, Wilbur H. "Marching Orders for the Political Right," *Progressive,* XXI (February, 1957), 16-18.

Baldinger, Wilbur H. "Reading from the Right," *Progressive,* XX (June, 1956), 5-8.

Barnhouse, Donald Grey. "Communism and the National Council of Churches; An Impartial Investigation of Charges made by the Controversial Air Force Manual," *Eternity,* XI (September, 1960), 6-9+.

Barron, Bryton. *This Is What Conservatives Stand For.* Christian Crusade Pamphlet, n.d.

Barth, Alan. "Report on the Rampageous Right," *New York Times Magazine* (November 29, 1961), 25+.

Billy James Hargis, His Christian Crusade, His Christian Echoes National Ministry, and Connections with Other Groups. Washington: Group Research, Inc., 1962.

Brant, Irving. "The Anti-Communist Hoax," *New Republic,* CXLVI (June 4, 1962), 15-18.

Brant, Irving. "Why Do They Get Away With It?," *New Republic,* CXLVI (June 4, 1962), 17-20.

Brauer, J. C. "The Rule of Saints in American Politics," *Church History,* XXVII (September, 1958), 240-256.

Cassels, Louis. "The Rightist Crisis in Our Churches," *Look,* XXVI (April 24, 1962), 40+.

Church, Frank. "The Future of the Radical Right," *Harper's,* CCXXX (February, 1965), 6.

Congressional Record. 89th Congress, First Session, United States Senate, III (January 12, 1965).

Cook, Fred J. "The Ultras: Aims, Affiliations, and Finances of the Radical Right," *Nation,* CXCIV (June 30, 1962), 565-96+.

Crowe, Charles M. *Christian Economics,* XV (March 19, 1963).

Danzig, David. "The Radical Right and the Rise of the Fundamentalist Minority," *Commentary,* XXXIII (April, 1962), 291-8.

Ebersole, Luke. "Religion and Politics," *The Annals,* CCCXXXII (November, 1960), 101-111.

The Fall 1962 Guide to Current American Government. Washington: Congressional Quarterly Service, 1962.

Farber, Maurice L. "The Armageddon Complex: Dynamics of Opinion," *Public Opinion Quarterly*, XV (Summer, 1951), 217-224.

Ferkiss, Victor C. "Ezra Pound and American Fascism," *Journal of Politics*, XVIII (May, 1955), 173-198.

Ferkiss, Victor C. "Political and Intellectual Origins of American Radicalism, Right and Left," *Annals of the American Academy of Political and Social Sciences*, CCCXLIV (November, 1962), 1-12.

Forrell, G. W. "Law and Gospel as a Problem of Politics," *Religion in Life* (Summer, 1962).

Gargan, Edward T. "Radical Catholics of the Right," *Social Order*, XI (November, 1961), 409-19.

Glazer, Nathan, "New Light on 'The Authoritarian Personality,'" *Commentary*, XVII (March, 1954), 289-297.

"Goldwater? No!," *Christian Century*, LXXXI (July 1, 1964), 851.

Green, Barbara, et al. "Responsible and Irresponsible Right-Wing Groups; A Problem in Analysis," *The Journal of Social Issues*, XIX (April, 1963), 3-17.

Grimes, Alan P. "Contemporary American Liberalism," *Annals of the American Academy of Political and Social Sciences*, CCCXLIV (November, 1962), 25-34.

Group Research Report, III. Washington, D.C.: Research, Inc., October 29, 1964.

Hillerbrand, Hans J. "The Anabaptist View of the State," *Mennonite Quarterly Review*, XXXII (April, 1958), 83-110.

Hofstadter, Richard. "The Paranoid Style in American Politics," *Harper's*, CCIX (November, 1964), 77-82.

Horton, P. "Revivalism on the Far Right," *Reporter Magazine*, XXV (July 29, 1961), 25-9.

Hughes, H. Stuart. "Most Unstuffy Man," *Nation*, CXCVII (December 14, 1963), 408-9.

Howard, J. E. *Christian Economics*, XIII (June 27, 1961).

"Johnson? Yes!" *Christian Century*, LXXXI (September 9, 1964), 1099.

Kennan, George F. "Foreign Policy and Christian Conscience," *The Atlantic Monthly*, CCIII (May, 1959), 44-49.

Kershner, Howard E. *Socialism — Reversal of God's Design*. Christian Freedom Foundation Pamphlet, n.d.

Knebel, Fletcher. "Who's On the Far Right?," *Look*, XXVI (March 13, 1962), 21+.

Kuttner, Alfred Booth. "A Study of American Intolerance," *Dial*, LXIV (March 12, 28, 1918), 223-225; 282-285.

Landis, Benson. "Trends in Church Membership in the United States." *The Annals*, CCCXXXII (November, 1960), 1-8.

Littell, Franklin Hamlin. "The Basis of Religious Liberty in Christian Belief," *A Journal of Church and State,* VI (Autumn, 1964), 314-32.

Lytle, Andrew. "The Quality of the South," *National Review,* V (March 8, 1958), 236-7.

Martin, H. H. "Doomsday Merchant on the Far, Far Right," *Saturday Evening Post,* CCXXXV (April 28, 1962), 19-24.

Martin, Pete. "I Call on Billy James Hargis," *The Christian Herald,* XC (February, 1967). The second installment appears in the March issue.

McCloskey, Herbert. "Conservatism and Personality," *American Political Science Review,* LII (March, 1958).

Miller, Raymond C. "The Background of Populism in Kansas," *Mississippi Valley Historical Review,* XI (March, 1925), 469-489.

Miller, William Lee. "The Principles of Religious Liberty," *A Journal of Church and State,* VI (Winter, 1964), 85-89.

Murphy, Charles J. V. "The Education of a Defense Secretary," *Fortune,* LXV (May, 1962), 102-5+.

National Council of Churches of Christ in America. *The Churches and the Public Schools* (brochure), June 7, 1963.

National Council of Churches of Christ in America. *News Release of Office of Information* (April 29, 1964).

Neufeld, Elmer. "Christian Responsibility in the Political Situation," *Mennonite Quarterly Review,* XXXII (April, 1958), 141-162.

Nichols, James Hastings. "Separation of Church and State," *Christian Century,* LXV (March 3, 1948), 265-8.

Peel, Roy V. "The Wackacobi: Extremists of Our Own Times," *Western Political Quarterly,* VI (September, 1963), 569-97.

Peffer, W. A. "The Mission of the Populist Party," *North American Review,* CLVII (1893), 665-678.

Pfeffer, Leo. "The Becker Amendment," *A Journal of Church and State,* VI (Autumn, 1964), 344-9.

Proshansky, Harold M., and Richard I. Evans (eds.). "American Political Extremism in the 1960's," *The Journal of Social Issues,* XIX (April, 1963).

Proshansky, Harold M., and Richard I. Evans. "The Radical Right; A Threat to the Behavioral Sciences," *Journal of Social Issues,* XIX (April, 1963), 86-105.

Randall, J. H., Jr. "The Churches and the Liberal Tradition," *Annals of the American Academy of Political and Social Sciences,* CCLVI (March, 1948), 148-64.

"Religion in American Society," *The Annals of the American Acad-*

emy of Political and Social Sciences, CCCXXXII (November, 1960).

Rokeach, M. "Political and Religious Dogmatism: An Alternative to the Authoritarian Personality," *Psychological Monographs,* LXX (1956).

Ross, Roy G. *What About the National Council of Churches?* National Council of Churches Pamphlet, 1960.

Rovere, Richard. "Letter from Washington," *New Yorker* (February 24, 1962).

Saturday Evening Post. Editorial (September 19, 1964).

Schecter, Harvey B. "The Liberals Have Helped the Radical Right," *New York Times Magazine* (April 29, 1962), 13, 93-6.

Schick, F. B. "Americanism Seminars and the Communist Challenge," *Western Political Quarterly,* XV (March, 1962).

Schlesinger, Arthur, Jr. "The Threat of the Radical Right," *New York Times Magazine* (June 17, 1962), 10+.

Schmuck, Richard, and Mark Chesler. "On Super Patriotism," *Journal of Social Issues,* XIX (April, 1963), 31-46.

Shenton, James P. "The Coughlin Movement and the New Deal," *Political Science Quarterly,* LXXIII (September, 1958), 352-374.

Shannon, Jasper. "Conservatism," *Annals of the American Academy of Political and Social Sciences,* CCCXLIV (November, 1962), 13-24.

Smedes, Lewis B. "The Gospel According to Carl McIntire," *Reformed Journal,* XV (January, 1965).

Sowing Dissention in the Churches. New York: Episcopal Church Center, n.d.

Van Den Haag, Ernest. "Communism, Democracy and Religion," *National Review,* V (March 22, 1958).

Washington Report. American Security Council (April 15, 1963).

Westin, Alan Furman. "The Deadly Parallels: Radical Right and Radical Left," *Harper's,* CCXXIV (April, 1962), 25-32.

Wilcox, Walter. "The Press of the Radical Right: An Exploratory Analysis," *Journalism Quarterly,* XXXIX (Spring, 1962), 152-60.

Williams, Bernard. "Democracy and Ideology," *Political Science Quarterly,* XXXII (October-December, 1961).

Williamson, Rene de Visme. "Conservatism and Liberalism in American Protestantism," *Annals of the American Academy of Political and Social Sciences,* CCCXLIV (November, 1962), 76-84.

Wood, James E., Jr. "The Christian State," *Journal of Church and State,* VI (Autumn, 1964), 277-287.

Woodward, C. Vann. "The Populist Heritage and the Intellectual," *American Scholar,* XXIX (Winter, 1959-1960), 55-72.

Wright, Esmond. "Radicals of the Right," *Political Quarterly,*
XXVII (October-December, 1958), 336-378.

Index of Subjects

227

INDEX OF PERSONS